THE BOY FROM A TOWN That Isn't Even a Town

A Memoir

by
Gordon Braun

Paperback ISBN: 9798218279042
ebook ISBN: 9798218279059
Library of Congress Number: 2023917172

Copy Editor: Lauren Alexander
Cover and Layout Design: Jill Flores

Printed by Village Books Publishing

First printed edition 2023

Village Books
1200 11th Street
Bellingham, WA 98225

To Laura and Traice.

Author's Notes

THIS STORY TAKES place over fifty years ago. It is written in first-person, present tense from the perspective of an adolescent boy. Back then, I knew things that I couldn't put into words, and I carried these unlabeled memories around until I learned the words over the course of a lifetime. This memoir puts grown-up words to the things I knew, felt, and remember—the exact words I would have used at the time if only I had access to them.

I also knew things then that you might not expect a twelve-year-old to know because I watched *Jeopardy!* on TV and read the *Funk and Wagnalls* encyclopedia that my mother bought from the local supermarket as volumes were released in alphabetical order. School was easy for me. Things stuck. For example, the story of Sisyphus repeatedly pushing the same boulder up the same hill for all of eternity resonated with my soul the first time I heard it as a young boy.

And it still does.

Most of this story is absolutely true. The rest of it is mostly true. I've done my best to connect the dots where memory fails, and I've taken artistic license as necessary to keep the story moving. If I couldn't remember the name of a minor character from a half-century ago, then I made it up. Some names and identifying characteristics have been changed to protect the privacy of real people. Dialogue is representative of actual conversations.

Language is true to the times and, regrettably, the times were cruel and crude when it came to matters of race, gender, sexual orientation, and people with disabilities. Boys of my generation were often steeped in terms and expressions that are understandably unacceptable today. The inclusion of this language is true to my experience of the 1960s and is not meant to condone its use today.

Contents

Paper Route and Vicinity - 1968

Shoreline
High School
7-11
Paper Shack
185th St.
Enco
Cromwell
Park
1st Ave. NE
2nd Ave. NE
3rd Ave. NE
St. Mark
Church
180th St.
179th St.
178th St.
I-5
175th St.
Cordell Hull
Jr. High
Aurora Ave. N.
Meridian Ave. N.
5th Ave. NE
10th Ave. NE
15th Ave. NE

★ Denotes location of my house

Introduction

by Linda K. Thomas

I'VE NEVER MET Gordon Braun, but we grew up in the same town (which wasn't even a town back then) and graduated from the same high school, Shoreline, north of Seattle.

A couple of years ago, I made contact with him on a Facebook page for Shoreline where he'd posted an excerpt from a draft of *The Boy from a Town That Isn't Even a Town*. His writing style pleased me—he wrote the way pros tell us to write—and his content made me grin. He was writing about a place I knew well, our high school neighborhood.

This coming-of-age memoir lets us know and enjoy this tender twelve-year-old finding his way through pubescent wonderings and imaginings and conversations with friends. We get acquainted with a plucky kid just beginning a big job as a paperboy delivering the *Seattle Times*, a job he carried out with a keen sense of responsibility and integrity—there was no slacking for Gordon—as well as a sense of fun and adventure.

The Boy from a Town That Isn't Even a Town is rich in local historical details, late-1960s Seattle TV and radio personalities, star athletes, and popular songs, all of them thoroughly enjoyable for this reader. Sometimes Gordon's accounts made me laugh aloud and other times made me ache. I couldn't help but admire this downy-cheeked kid with a sharp mind, perceptive heart, and a rich and expansive inner life.

He brings readers along on his escapades with Art and John, with Crazy Ken, and with Anthony, an excitable Italian kid who didn't have the slightest grasp of cause and effect. We tag along with Gordon while, delivering the *Seattle Times*, he deals with a deranged German shepherd and a psychopathic rooster.

Throughout this poignant memoir, we get acquainted with a youngster who watched a lot of television, bickered with his sisters and parents, and spent a lot of time with his buddies, a sensitive young man who kept trying to make his way in a less-than-perfect world, an innocent and self-conscious junior high boy who, sweaty and nervous and tongue-tied, once danced with a cheerleader, and it was a slow dance at that.

I still haven't met Gordon, but in reading his book and exchanging emails with him, I came to know him. And like him. And admire him. Joshua Graham's words could have been written about Gordon: "I survived because the fire inside me burned brighter than the fire around me." He kept pounding one foot in front of the other, singing of dreams and destinies. Lessons he learned along the way, several hard-fought, inspired young Gordon to cling to determination and personal strength and to grow into a kind, well-educated, successful man.

When I finished reading the last page of *The Boy from a Town That Isn't Even a Town*, I sent Gordon an email: "I'm sitting here with tears in my eyes as I type. I can't believe I'm at the end of your memoir. It was so good." His message, his mind, his fortitude, his wit changed me, made me a better person.

And isn't that the value of story? As a memoir teacher, I believe in the power of story. Stories can change us. Frederick Buechner writes, "My story is important not because it is mine, God knows, but because if I tell it anything like right, the chances are you will recognize that in many ways it is also yours." (*Telling Secrets*)

So, I thank Gordon for sharing his story, and other readers will thank him, too, for we'll all recognize that his story reflects ours in many ways, and that he gives us clues about how to live despite the difficulties and disappointments we each face: with grit and grace; with an inquiring and fine-tuned mind; with an intact heart that helps discern the difference between right and wrong; with love and forgiveness and tenacity and hope and humor; and with success won through hard work and humility.

— Linda K. Thomas
Memoir teacher, blogger, and author of two memoirs, *Please, God, Don't Make Me Go: A Foot-Dragger's Memoir and Grandma's Letters from Africa.*

Chapter 1

Not Even a Town

MY HOMETOWN ISN'T on any maps because it isn't even a town. Wedged between the northern limits of Washington State's biggest city at 145th Street and the Snohomish County line at 205th Street, Shoreline is an afterthought—an aptly named sixty-block strip of unincorporated King County stretching from the banks of Lake Washington on the east to the bluffs overlooking Puget Sound on the west.

Outsiders might be vaguely aware of Shoreline as a school district or as a modest suburb, but the simple truth is that no one gives it much thought at all. It was thrown up on the fly out of necessity and in the rush to make up for lost time and get things done, no one filled out the paperwork to turn twelve square miles of suburban sprawl into an official place. With two high schools, four junior highs, and twenty elementary schools, the sole purpose of my hometown is to accommodate GIs who survived World War II and Korea and their urgent need to warehouse and educate the mindless inevitability of pent-up, post-war, pre-pill passion: an onslaught of children like me.

Fittingly, our main drag looks nothing like Main Street, USA, as depicted in Norman Rockwell paintings. Aurora Avenue is a gritty, gravel-shouldered, four-lane segment of US Highway 99 that, more or less, runs the length of the West Coast from Canada to Mexico—notable for stoplights, filling stations, greasy spoon cafés, drab motels, used car lots, and the occasional wrecking yard, drive-in movie theater, and prohibition-era roadhouse. Discount retailers like Valu-Mart, supermarkets like QFC, and fast-food chains have been moving in lately along with requisite paved parking and inescapable traffic congestion.

Movers and shakers live in fancy houses with water and mountain views along the eastern and western edges of the town that isn't even a town. At its core though, where I live, Shoreline is strictly working class: Boeing employees gearing up to start production of the 747 Jumbo Jet in Everett next year or working on the Supersonic Transport at the East Marginal Way plant; commercial fishermen and cannery workers migrating back and forth to Alaska according to season; loggers and mill workers, tradesmen, small business owners, civil servants, and hordes of housewives. None of us regular people are rich, and some families, like mine, are barely getting by.

Dad was a fireman for the City of Seattle until they let him go last year.

"Fired from the fire department … How ironic," Mom said flatly when she heard the news, fully understanding that sporadic child-support payments from her ex-husband were about to become nonexistent.

My family and the other folks living in the heart of Shoreline make do in nondescript little houses on a grid of unimpressive little streets. Three-bedroom ramblers are the norm, with one bathroom, a one-car garage, and three or four kids. Living room windows face the road to reveal views of our driveways and the living rooms of our neighbors, who can be seen looking back at us from across the street. With so little indoor space, kids and dogs spill into the great outdoors where we run free.

I've got the smallest of three bedrooms at our house to myself since I'm the only boy. Maureen and I shared a room until I turned six and she was almost five. I wasn't privy to what went into Mom and Dad's decision to split the two of us up. All I knew was that one night I was all alone in the dark, convinced there was a monster under my bed while the swingin' theme song from *Surfside Six*, starring Troy Donahue, Van Williams, and Lee Patterson, could be heard playing on the TV in the living room.

Surfside 6. (What's that?)
Surfside 6. (An address?)
Surfside 6. (Where is it?)
In Miami Beach.
Cha Cha Cha
Cha

Monsters aside, I soon grow to appreciate having a place where I can escape and be alone. Maureen takes to saying, "You get everything because you're a boy." As time passes, the refrain becomes shriller as her resentment deepens. She's right when she says that there are advantages to being a boy. And I know it's not fair that I get my own room while she shares hers with Leslie and Roberta.

But I don't care.

Actually … maybe I do care.

I care and I don't care at the same time, but the emotions cancel each other out so that, truth be told, I feel nothing at all. When we pass in the hallway going to or from the bathroom, we glare at each other, and someone usually gets an elbow to the ribs or a sock in the arm.

I don't make the rules around here, but when you think about it, there aren't that many rules, and Mom is usually too tired to enforce them anyway. We're on the honor system, which is just another way of saying we're on our own. Mom is up at 4:30 a.m. and out the door hours before the alarms go off for the rest of us. Dad is no help when it comes to financial support, so she is working three jobs to make ends meet.

Every minute matters for the head of the household, every weekday carefully choreographed. At four forty-five I often hear the garage door slam and know she's behind the wheel of her Plymouth Valiant on her way to job one—a small Lake City accounting firm where she moonlights in solitude from five to seven. Then it's back in the car for the uphill drive to Allstate Insurance on Meridian Avenue. Depending on traffic, she tells us, that leaves her about thirty minutes of quiet time in the company cafeteria to drink coffee, smoke cigarettes, and read novels from the paperback book exchange. At seven forty-five she's at her desk processing timecards and preparing the weekly payroll for five hundred employees until her shift ends at four fifteen.

Saturday is no day off our mother. While we sleep, she takes a purse full of discount coupons to Safeway to buy food for the week. While we loll, bicker and watch cartoons, she's doing laundry, dusting, and annoying us with her vacuuming. By mid-afternoon while we're trying to figure out what to do with our free time, she's busy keeping the books for a building contractor at the dining room table. A ten-key adding machine sits at her fingertips as she makes ledger entries in her perfect penmanship.

Being on the honor system means that we kids feed ourselves a bowl of cereal or peanut butter on toast in the morning before school, get dressed, get to class on time, and pay enough attention so that teachers won't send home notes requiring parental action. We've been doing this for years already, and only Roberta has a problem with any of these rules—particularly the one about paying attention.

"Use a dish," Mom says when she's around and when she sees me heading toward the kitchen on the hunt for food. It's one of her few rules and a not-so-subtle way of saying she is tired of vacuuming up cookie crumbs and scrubbing stains out of an already sad excuse for a carpet.

"Soak your dish," she says when I'm done eating. This is a lame, but logical extension of the *use a dish* rule. It's her way of reminding me that she is sick of handwashing dishes with food particles cemented onto them.

"Put it in the sink," she says, in keeping with the same irritating theme, when I put the soaked dish on the drainboard as a logical alternative. This rule is arbitrary and capricious as far as I'm concerned, so I generally ignore it and give her lip when I get caught. She used to smack my rear-end with a wooden spoon when I was younger, but I'm too quick for her now, and all she can do is give me a look that says, "What did I do to deserve this?" She doesn't deserve it, but I don't care about that either.

As the only male in the family, I'm responsible for putting down the toilet seat, mowing the lawn, taking out the trash, and making sure the lid stays on the garbage can so that raccoons and dogs running free won't get into it and dump trash all over the driveway, yard, and street. We generate so much waste that by Thursday or Friday before the weekly pickup on Monday, I'm climbing into the garbage can every day and jumping up and down in an effort to compress the contents enough to get the lid back on the can.

I wouldn't tell just anyone this, but it's a simple pleasure to feel boxes, cans, and miscellaneous voids collapse under my weight as I jump on the garbage. It amuses me to think about Mom's clever observation that it might look preposterous to somebody passing by, "Look, someone's throwing away a perfectly good kid."

I won't have to worry about cutting the grass again for a couple more months since it's dormant this time of year. For the most part, lawn maintenance is on a seasonal hiatus throughout the neighborhood. Kids running free have learned the hard way to watch their step when playing in their yards given all the dogs running free and the likelihood that none of the soggy lawns have been scooped since October.

Putting down the toilet seat is by far the single highest daily priority, given the gender mix of the house. I'm so good at it that I've overheard Mom telling her friend Jan Wanezek that all the training seems to be paying off. She might call it training, but I look at it as capitulation to four nagging females. I suspect that her idea of *training* also includes repeatedly telling me how much she wants me to be as different as possible from my father—especially when it comes to booze and keeping my word.

"When you're grown-up," she tells me, "get a steady job, come straight home at the end of the day, and don't drink away your paycheck."

I mostly tune her out because it's tiresome and because I already see her point. Dad's a bad guy, and I have no intention of growing up to be like him. If I've learned anything from my father though, it's that good intentions aren't always enough. For now, Mom will have to be content with a little toilet seat etiquette.

Jan Wanezek is one of Mom's best friends. She used to live next door but still comes by for frequent visits. A short, stout woman, Jan is a devout Catholic with a generous heart and an infectious laugh. As the two of them sit at the dining room table drinking Folgers coffee and smoking cigarettes, Jan entertains us all as she tells stories about being marooned in France by the stock market crash while visiting her wicked aunt in 1929. Or about salmon fishing with her husband, Burt, off the Washington coast near Westport. Or her bowling league at the Polynesian-themed Leilani Lanes. Or her children and their piece-of-work Boston terrier named Barney. Or about Rusty and Lori, the two women who own the dry-cleaning business where Jan runs a steam press and who live together under suspicious circumstances.

She smokes unfiltered Pall Malls out of a red pack while Mom smokes filtered Tareytons as they share their time together.

There is something appealing about the way Jan tamps down the tobacco by repeatedly tapping the cigarette against her left wrist before she lights up. Every now and then she'll stop talking and tilt her head back to delicately remove a bit of tobacco from the tip of her tongue. In these brief instances she looks wistful to me. But I'm twelve, so what do I know? The interlude is momentary and easy to miss because she is promptly on to another story.

Jan is laughing and so is Mom. It's a pleasure to see Mom behave like this—laughing as if her world, and the world around us, isn't going straight to "Hell in a handbasket" as we've all heard Jan say on more than one occasion. And when she says it, Mom, Leslie, Roberta, Maureen, and I all nod our heads in agreement.

My middle sister, Roberta, is fifteen and recently fell in love with an Adonis. Jack Adamos is a six-foot three-inch, jug-eared, blond, blue-eyed senior at Shoreline High School where Robbie is a sophomore.

There is a framed picture of them from the Tolo Dance sitting on Mom's spinet piano. Robbie looks beautiful in her high heels and miniskirt, and Jack is smiling broadly, a man-child with a pretty girl on his arm and the world by the tail. People are saying there is a good chance he'll wind up in Vietnam by this time next year.

I walk into the house after school and find them making out on the living room sofa with Jefferson Airplane's *Surrealistic Pillow* playing on our Sears-brand turntable. Slamming the front door doesn't make them stop, and the music is so loud that clearing my throat to get their attention isn't an option.

This is stomach turning.

Grumbling to myself because the lovebirds are interfering with my TV-watching plans, I head to my bedroom to change out of my school clothes into my goofing-around clothes.

Maybe Art is home, I think to myself.

Adamos is okay, his lust for my sister notwithstanding. He was nice enough to give me the five-speed bicycle that I use to get around, telling me that he found it abandoned in the woods up at Hamlin Park. I was so grateful that I didn't question his story. There was the time he came by the house while test-driving a Sunbeam Alpine two-seater, and the two of us went tearing through the neighborhood with the top down. And just after the first of the year, Adamos walked in and threw a couple of *Playboy* magazines on my lap as I sat watching television on the living room couch.

"Here. You might enjoy these," he said with a wink.

They were the November and December 1967 issues, and I could see from the mailing label that he must have stolen them from the Carlsons next door—probably when Robbie was babysitting their three-year-old son. I browsed through the pages that day, slack-jawed, paying special attention to centerfolds Kaya Christian and Lynn Winchell.

This is much better than the lingerie section of the Sears catalog, I thought before realizing this was about the stupidest understatement that had ever crossed my mind.

Robbie warned me, "Don't play with yourself. Only queers play with themselves."

I'm still not sure what a queer is, but I'm pretty sure it has something to do with being a homo, even though I don't exactly know what that is either. It's obviously a bad thing, though, and I worry constantly that I might be a queer because after seeing those magazines, it seems I'm either fighting the urge to do what Robbie warned me about or I'm feeling worried about the implications of having just done it. For all I know this frowned-upon activity might qualify as a mortal sin, so the most concerning implication is that I could wind up in Hell if I keep it up.

When I finish changing my clothes, I pass through the living room on the way to the kitchen only to see that Robbie and

Adamos are still at it. The music has stopped, but they're too focused on smooching and pawing each other to turn the record over. I don't say anything, and they ignore me while I prepare a peanut butter sandwich that I plan to eat over the kitchen sink.

Why dirty a dish that I would just leave on the counter to the dismay of my mother?

I purposely make more noise than necessary in the hope of disrupting what's going on in the other room, all the while muttering "Jesus Christ" under my breath and shaking my head in disgust.

A short time ago, Robbie was a tomboy bringing home frogs and stray dogs. And it was about a year ago that I finally beat her in a wrestling match after having been systematically and routinely destroyed by her my entire life up to that point. She leaves me alone now, but Jesus Christ, that guy has his tongue in her mouth! Just because he's been nice to me doesn't mean I wouldn't like to beat the crap out of him and throw him out onto the unscooped, dogshit covered front lawn if I could. She should be ashamed of herself, and if I ruled the world, I would send her to her room so she could sulk on the bottom bunk of her bed like Maureen is doing in the top bunk.

If Kaya Christian and Lynn Winchell have brothers, they would probably feel the same way about me as I feel about Jack Adamos, but I don't care. Or maybe I do. How is it possible that two such contradictory feelings can exist at the same time?

My oldest sister, Leslie, isn't home yet and won't be for a while. Between the drive to First Hill for freshman classes at Seattle University and her part-time job, she is around only slightly more than Mom. Mostly she leaves me alone like everyone else leaves me alone, but when she is home, she is generally kind to me.

My affection for Leslie goes beyond appreciating all the babysitting and care she provided when I was too young to look out for myself. She taught me some good stuff. Take for example the time she coaxed me into a game of *heads I win and tails you lose* when I was seven. Leslie kept her patience and a straight face and won fifty coin-flips in a row before I figured out the trick. She burst into laughter when the flash bulb finally went off in my head.

Lesson learned.

Good fortune is as fickle as sunshine in the Pacific Northwest, but luck is more or less a fifty-fifty proposition. Too much bad luck can only mean one of two things: either you're being cheated or your luck is about to change. By playing that game with my sister that day, I learned to be vigilant about the former and to have faith in the latter.

As for having too much good luck?

I don't know.

I'm still working on it.

I suppose it's possible to have too much good luck. If so, what is the flip side of being cheated in a game like *heads I win and tails you lose*? What should I be looking out for and how do I keep it going? If the opposite of being cheated is to be treated fairly, that doesn't seem like a fair tradeoff because being cheated is more bad than being treated fairly is good. If luck is more or less a fifty-fifty proposition, how is it possible not to feel depressed about knowing your run of good luck is about to change?

Anyway, Leslie and I laughed quite a bit together on the day of the coin-flipping game. On the one hand, I felt like an idiot by falling for Leslie's trick. On the other hand, I didn't care. And that's not the way I feel around most people.

Leslie shows up in time for dinner every night and tries to study in the living room while I'm glued to the TV and Mom sits in her gold-colored rocking chair, smoking and nervously flicking ashes into her beanbag ashtray.

Television is my window to the world, and the hand-me-down Philco set we got from Grandma Wertz is on pretty much all the time. Network news with Walter Cronkite is on in the background as we eat dinner. I don't know what to make of hippies and race riots, but I'm thrilled by the space program as I try to imagine how a rocket, nearly as tall as the thirty-eight-story Smith Tower in downtown Seattle, can fly faster than a bullet. It's clear to me that we're winning the war in Vietnam, though. According to the body-count graphic at the bottom of the screen, only 416 of our men were killed last week, but the Communists lost 15,515. This obviously can't go on for much longer, so Robbie's boyfriend doesn't really have anything to worry about.

Once dinner is over, I'm in front of the TV straight through until bedtime. Even I know that it's mostly a waste of time, but at least it's something to do. I'm not much of a reader, and doing homework is unnecessary since I'm right where I want to be grade-wise anyway: slightly above average, not being noticed as remarkably bright or particularly dim. Besides, it's not like Mom has an opinion one way or another about how I spend my free time.

Some of my earliest TV-viewing memories go back to shows like *The Adventures of Ozzie and Harriet*, *The Donna Reed Show*, and *Leave It to Beaver*. If these shows are to be believed, then my family isn't normal. There aren't any broken homes like mine on television. No children are pretending that it's okay for their parents to be divorced or for the father to drink too much.

I wish we were normal like everybody else.

Boys like Wally and Beaver normally dress like me except when they break out their blue suits for church and special occasions. I don't have a suit, and Mom doesn't wear pearls in the middle of the day like Donna Stone and June Cleaver.

Television moms and kids often wait patiently for the father to get home from work so he can be presented with the dilemma of the day and calmly dispense wisdom. Ozzie Nelson is the exception to the work rule. As far as I can tell, he just sits around all day in his cardigan sweater eating ice cream.

I've never seen Ozzie Nelson or Ward Cleaver with a stubby bottle of Olympia Beer or smoke anything other than a pipe—they don't even utter foul words stronger than "golly" or "gee." In contrast, my cardigan-less father smokes like a chimney, drinks like a fish, and cusses like a sailor. He doesn't eat much ice cream, and I don't feel any the wiser after one of his lectures.

More recently I've found myself drawn to action shows like *The Man from UNCLE*, starring Robert Vaughn, and *It Takes a Thief*, with Robert Wagner, as I try to picture myself growing up to be cool, living dangerously, and prevailing against the odds like Napoleon Solo and Alexander Mundy. A good deal of my attraction to men like these is that gorgeous women seem to be attracted to the same type. It seems like mission impossible that a kid from a town that's not even a town might one day crisscross the globe in the pursuit of adventure, but that doesn't mean a boy can't find hours of pleasure dreaming about life in an exciting alternative universe.

Get Smart is a parody of James Bond and all the other spy shows and movies. I love the clever thirty-minute television comedy with its catchy theme song. Maxwell Smart, played by Don Adams, drives a Sunbeam Alpine like the one Jack Adamos and I took for a spin. He is a bumbling, wisecracking good-guy working diligently to ensure that CONTROL triumphs over the evil of KAOS. I don't fantasize about growing up to be like Agent 86, but if I was smart, I would think up something witty to say about how he and I have a few things in common. Like, I'm a wisecracker too, in a secret one-man battle to control real-life chaos any way I can.

Chapter 2

Just Another Kid

I'M REALLY NERVOUS as I dial the telephone and then hear it ringing on the other end of the line.

"Hello. This is the *Seattle Times*. How may I direct your call?"

"My name … my name is Gor … Gordon Braun," I stammer into the receiver.

"Yes. How may I direct your call?"

"I was wondering if you had … if the *Seattle Times* had … any paper routes that I could … I could have?" I ask.

It's embarrassing to get tongue-tied like I do when I talk to grown-ups like this.

"I'll put you through to the circulation department. Please hold."

The phone is ringing.

In my mind I'm plenty grown up, and I know lots of big words, but even the easy words don't always come out of my mouth right when I talk to old people.

"Circulation. This is Dick Jones. How can I help you?"

"My name is Gor … Gordon Braun. I was wondering if you had any paper routes that I could have?"

That's better. Almost like I rehearsed it.

"Where do you live, son?"

"Well, I have … I have a Seattle address, but I don't … don't live in Seattle."

"What's that?"

"I live in Shoreline, but it's not even … isn't even a town, so I have a Seattle address."

"So, you live in North King County? Is that right?"

"Yes."

"I'll transfer you to the district adviser out there. His name is Arnie Pederson. Hold on."

There is a click and a brief pause. And then the phone starts ringing again.

I don't just know big words, I know a lot of highfalutin terms and expressions because I keep my ears open, watch *Jeopardy!* on TV, and read the *Funk and Wagnalls* encyclopedia. But for some reason only simple, run-of-the-mill vocabulary comes out of my mouth when I converse with grown-ups. It bothers me to stumble over plain language in these situations. But try as I might, I can't get it right. I'm beginning to think this is why adults treat me like I'm just another kid.

"Hello. This is Arnie Pederson. How can I help you?"

"My name is Gordon Braun. I was wondering if you had any paper routes I could have?"

Perfect. Third time's a charm.

"Well, Gordon, routes come up periodically. How old are you?"

"Hello?" A new voice interrupts the conversation. "Is someone there?"

This is embarrassing.

"Yes! Get off the line," I yell into the mouthpiece.

"Oops. Sorry," the voice says.

Click.

"Who was that?" Mr. Pederson asks.

"We have a … have a party line," I respond calmly.

"Oh. I see. Now, where was I? Uh, right. How old are you?"

"Almost twelve and a half."

"What grade are you in?"

"Seventh."

"And whereabouts do you live?"

"Near … not far from … from Shoreline High School."

"Do you know if you live east or west of the freeway?"

That's a dumb question. Of course I know which side of I-5 I live on.

"On the … on the east … I mean … the west side," I say.

"Are you sure?"

"Yes … west. I live west … west of the freeway, but the freeway … the freeway is east of me."

"Can you give me your phone number and address so I can contact you when something opens up?"

Of course I can give him my phone number and address. So that's what I do.

"Just to make sure I've got it right, your first name is Gordon, spelled G-o-r-d-o-n. And your last name is Brown, spelled B-r-o-w-n. Is that right?"

"No. It's pronounced *brown*, but it's spelled B-r-a-u-n."

"What's that?"

"It's German for brown and it's pronounced *brown*, but it's spelled … it's spelled B-r-a-u-n."

"Like Werner Von Braun, the famous rocket guy at NASA?"

"Yes. But it's pronounced … pronounced *brown* not *brawn*."

"Got it … I think. Anyway, I'll call if something comes available. Thank you for calling. Goodbye."

"Bye."

Paper Route Headlines

New Pueblo Talk with Reds Unsatisfactory, Says Johnson

Reds Used Deceit, Surprise to Attack Holidaying Saigon

Allies Battle Escaping Reds; Artillery Opens Up in North

Reds Set to Hold Hue

President Asks Restraint on Wages, Prices

Khrushchev Breaks into Moscow TV

31 Hurt in Train Wreck

Chapter 3

Thinking About It

FOREST GREEN, WINDOWLESS, plywood shacks can be found all over town. Situated as they are on neglected vacant parcels and in the far reaches of potholed retail parking lots, you might think the eyesores are homes for hobos and other down-on-their-luck characters. But if you do, you'd be wrong. It's at places like these that boys like me rendezvous every day to pick up fifty or sixty copies of the *Seattle Times* for delivery to suburban doorsteps.

Today, at 6:00 a.m., it's still dark as I make my way to the shack on Tenth Avenue Northeast to retrieve the load of newspapers for Route #0073. There is no traffic to worry about at this time of day, so there is no need to glance over my shoulder for fear of getting hit by a car as I cover the last block in a slow, nonchalant, diagonal path across Northeast 185th Street. The not-looking gives me a devil-may-care sensation, which only partially offsets my growing anxiety about the task ahead.

I've been on my own for three days now after tagging along with Scott Hansen earlier in the week to learn the ropes of the newspaper delivery business. Among other things, he told me that on most weekdays after school and on Saturday afternoons, the load of papers should be light enough to strap to the handlebars of my Schwinn five-speed.

"Wednesdays and Thursdays can go either way," he warned. "Sometimes they're normal size and sometimes they're huge. It's safest to use a cart on Wednesday and Thursday. Ride your bike if you want to risk it, but you don't want to get all the way down to the shack and find out the load is a little too big that day. It's a waste of time to ride home and walk all the way back with the cart."

"Where do I get a cart?" I asked.

"I'll sell you mine for fifteen dollars."

"How about Sundays?"

Scott cocked his head and eyeballed me from head to toe.

"Good luck on Sunday," he said with a condescending smirk.

I live two blocks west of the interstate on Second Avenue, and it's all downhill heading east on 185th from the freeway overpass to the newspaper shack on Tenth. This means that on at least four afternoons a week, I should be able to stop pedaling my bike once I get to the bridge above I-5 and blissfully coast the last six blocks on the way to getting my newspapers. The location of the shack in relation to the overpass also means that a heavy load of newspapers has to be muscled up the grade seven days a week on the return trip.

It wasn't easy, but I made it in good shape on Thursday when I pushed my newly acquired newspaper cart up the hill by myself for the first time. And by standing up on the pedals of my bike, I managed to wobble the load slowly up the grade on Friday and Saturday.

But today is Sunday.

Today the *Seattle Times* will be a mammoth morning paper jammed with advertising circulars; classified ads for autos, jobs, and real estate; funny papers; *Parade* magazine; and the *TV Times*. So, I'm not coasting down the grade on my Schwinn five-speed as I make my way to the shack this morning. I'm on foot, pulling a yellow two-wheeled cart capable of handling the day's burden.

I'm alone in my thoughts while the restlessness of the sky suggests it's thinking about drizzling. In the Pacific Northwest, except perhaps between July 5 and the first Sunday in September, it's usually either raining, drizzling, or it's thinking about it.

When you're twelve and a half like me and you're from this place, water falling out of the sky is perfectly normal. I've been playing in it my entire life, and I've been walking to and from school under a brooding sky or in some kind of precipitation every day for the better part of eight years. Parents and teachers rave about the moderate climate, the lush landscape, and the majesty of the towering evergreen trees, but I don't get it.

"Thank God we don't live in the Midwest or on the East Coast," adults will say. "Why would anyone put up with those winters? Can you imagine? And the humidity! We're so fortunate to live where we do!"

But in the days leading up to the Fourth of July and Labor Day, they change their tune because good fortune is fickle. Self-assurance morphs into self-deception.

"Maybe we'll get lucky with the weather this year," the adults will say rather than cancel plans and let go of any hope that anyone will be anything but miserable at a holiday picnic in the Pacific Northwest.

"The weather forecast isn't good, but those guys are never right."

I don't know anything about Midwest winters and East Coast humidity, but I know this: eating hot dogs huddled under a plastic tarp on the Fourth of July and Labor Day is an annual occurrence for boys like me. When you're shivering and shrugging your shoulders to keep the rain from running down your neck, you don't notice or give one whit about the lush landscape and the majestic evergreen trees. In the Pacific

Northwest, sunny optimism is for fools and people who aren't from around these parts.

A Plymouth Valiant heading the other direction on 185th slows down, and the driver offers up a short toot on the car horn. I can barely see the old man behind the wheel, but he is giving me a friendly enough wave. I reflexively wave back. He looks vaguely familiar, but I can't say for sure how I know him.

The wheels make a crunching sound, and I feel a tug on my right arm as the empty cart rolls off the asphalt and settles into the gravel of the pie-shaped lot with only a shabby green shack standing in the middle.

Just across the way to the north is the sparkling new 7-Eleven mini-mart that opens two-and-a-half hours before the Safeway on Fifteenth Avenue, and that stays open late into the night for the convenience of people in no rush to get to bed. There is no need to plan ahead anymore now that they've relaxed the old Blue Laws, and you can get what you want anytime you need it at 7-Eleven: a dozen eggs, a gallon of milk, a loaf of bread. Metal tins of Band-Aids, female products, toilet paper, beer, and cigarettes are available like never before in the event of after-hour emergencies.

Regular gasoline is selling for 24.9 cents a gallon according to the well-lit sign at the Enco station across the street to the south. A guy named Vic owns the place. He once sold Mom a '52 Olds 88 with touchy power brakes that sent us flying and an electric eye that magically dimmed the high-beam headlights when oncoming traffic was detected.

The jet-black Oldsmobile with the snow-white roof was eventually scrapped for leaking oil. Vic then gave Mom a good deal on what turned out to be an even-leakier fire-engine red Corvair. A couple months later, he forgot to tighten the lug nuts after rotating the tires, causing the right rear wheel to wobble and nearly fall off on the drive home.

I overhear a couple of boys from the Catholic school talking as I pass by behind them with my empty paper cart. They're taking the advertising, comics, and magazine sections from one big stack of papers and inserting them into the hard news sections taken from another stack. The process of making one large pile of newspapers out of two smaller piles is called *stuffing* the paper in paperboy lingo.

"… and so Animato says, 'Look at the boobs on that chick. I'd like to give those a blow job!'"

"No way! He said that? What an idiot! Animato doesn't even know what a blow job is!"

I pretend not to be listening in, but my mind goes into overdrive sensing that this could be important information.

What did he say?

What kind of a job?

I must have heard wrong.

What rhymes with blow?

Snow-mow-joe.

Snow job? Mow job? Joe job?

That doesn't make sense.

The way the second guy says "What an idiot" with a combination of both delight and disdain, and the way the two roared with laughter, makes me grateful not to be part of the conversation. I have no idea what they're talking about, but if I *had* been involved in the exchange, I would have faked it by laughing uproariously with them at Anthony Animato's expense.

I don't know the two boys from St. Mark School except for the fact that they show up every day at the shack to get their newspapers and always seem to be in on the same private joke. But I know Anthony Animato from homeroom and a couple of classes we share at the public school. Bridging the two worlds is unusual, and particularly so in this case, because Animato attends Mass at St. Luke's instead of St. Mark's and doesn't have a paper route. After mulling over the situation, I can only conclude that one detail trumps all others: Animato has the personality of a fellow who gets around.

Known almost exclusively by his last name, Animato is an excitable Italian kid who, in addition to getting around as much as he does, has a knack for being in the wrong place at the wrong time. If there is ever a commotion going on in the halls of Cordell Hull Junior High, you can bet that he will be in the middle of it and that, guilty or not, he will be rounded up with the others and made to pay a price.

The guy is seemingly incapable of embarrassment or self-consciousness and has not, as yet, demonstrated the slightest grasp of cause and effect. It never seems to cross Animato's mind that people make fun of him because he is always blurting out stupid stuff. On the other hand, he possesses something our seventh-grade social studies teacher, Mr. Carr, calls moxie, and I can't help but admire it.

Unlike Animato, I don't have much moxie. I care what others think of me, and I'm plenty capable of embarrassment. The idea of being found the fool is much worse than keeping to myself the sad fact that I wouldn't know a b*low-snow-mow-joe job* if it came up and bit me. There is no perfect solution to my problem. Keeping my ignorance a secret means I'll have to stay on my toes in case the subject ever comes up in conversation, but asking about it directly would immediately expose me as an idiot. Maybe someday I will feel comfortable asking dumb questions and risking ridicule, but for now keeping my eyes and ears open and my mouth shut seems a lot less dangerous.

Wait and see. Observe and file away scraps of data to be made sense of later; that's what I do. Lately, I've noticed that seemingly unrelated tidbits of information stored in my head often come together inexplicably to reveal a coherent truth, if only I pay attention and stay patient. Animato's assertion that a *whatever-it-was-they-said* has something to do with a girl's boobs doesn't seem totally unreasonable to me. But ridicule is a fact that has to be taken into account. So, I make a mental note then and there to stay on the lookout for anything that might clarify the matter.

Blow … I'm pretty sure they said blow job.

Blow like the wind or like blowing up a balloon?

Job like a paper route or working in a gas station or taking out the garbage?

That doesn't make any sense.

And come to think of it, it doesn't make any goddamn sense that anyone would blow or snow on boobs or get paid for it like it was a goddamn job either!

Oh man …

I don't swear out loud very often, but I sure seem to be having more and more conversations with myself that feature more and more four-letter words and, all too often, involve using the Lord's name in vain. Dad is a reflexive serial curser, so maybe that's where I'm getting it from. What is the expression? Like father like son? I don't want to be like him. How can a grown man, and a Catholic at that, be so casual about the real possibility of going to Hell by peppering his observations, complaints, and general conversations with such frequent uses of "goddammit!" and "Jesus Christ!"?

"Goddammit!" Dad would yell at the grainy black-and-white TV screen while watching the NBC Saturday game between the New York Yankees and that afternoon's underdog. Or when Mom overcooked the meat for dinner. Or if any of us four kids made too much noise.

"Jesus Christ!" he would exclaim when making a point, telling a joke, or when confronted with the adversity of a home project that wasn't going right. Home projects like taking the back off a misbehaving television set, pulling vacuum tubes at random, and then driving back and forth to the tube-testing machine at Valu-Mart as many times as it takes to find the faulty part.

Cursing the way my father does is a mortal sin. At least that's what the nuns teach us during the one hour available to them on Wednesday afternoons in catechism class, I mean CCD class, whatever that's supposed to mean. The job of these humorless women from the convent at St. Mark's, dressed in their imposing black-and-white habits with giant crucifixes dangling from their necks, is to scare the fear of Hell into boys like me. And they are very good at what they do! An hour a week is plenty of time for them to get the job done.

Dealing with the big black mark that swearing leaves on your soul is a tricky situation. There is always a chance that you might get to confession before you die and be able to wipe the slate clean of your mortal sins, but that's a risky bet. I rationalized that if I didn't curse *out loud* and kept the worst words *inside my head*, I would be committing a mere venial sin, and the damage to my post-life-on-earth future would be limited, seeing as how venial sins are punishable by just a few years in Purgatory.

Sure, the torture in Purgatory is as bad as Hell, literally, but it doesn't last forever like it would if I actually said the words out loud and was condemned to spending eternity with Satan. God doesn't seem totally unreasonable when it comes to venial sins, and the nuns tell us that, even though souls in Purgatory are in agony, they're still happy because as venial sinners, they are assured of one day getting to Heaven. For them the hard part is over because they're already dead. You can only commit a mortal sin and wind up in Hell when you're still alive.

Two other boys are in line in front of me waiting for the shack manager to count out their papers. I don't know them very well either and not because they go to Catholic school, but because they go to Kellogg Junior High instead of Cordell Hull Junior High like me. I-5 is the boundary between the two public schools. If you live on the west side you go to Cordell Hull, otherwise you go to Kellogg.

I'm just standing around in line with nothing to do, looking at my feet and kicking at the gravel. For a second, I think about lifting my head and striking up a conversation with these two strangers, but I'm not the kind of fellow that gets around like Anthony Animato, so I keep my mouth shut and head down.

Too bad.

I'd be curious to know if the Kellogg guys know some grade-school classmates of mine from back before the freeway was built. Susan, Gary, Bobby, Robin, Mary, David, Bill, and Carol seemed to have vanished between the time fourth grade let out for the summer and fifth grade started in the fall. In actuality, and unbeknownst to me at the time, they had been trapped on the other side of our local version of the Berlin Wall, transferred to North City Elementary, and eventually wound up at Kellogg.

Finally, it's my turn to get my papers from Mike, the shack manager, a fifteen-year-old sophomore at Shoreline High School with a paper route of his own, a key to the padlock of the shack door, and the additional responsibility of carefully counting out and recording the number of papers given to each boy. Mike is a red-headed, gap-toothed, cheerful type who reminds me of a cross between Howdy Doody and a sincere version of wisecracking Alfred E. Neuman from *Mad Magazine.*

"Hi Gordon, how many today?" he asks. I like that he knows my name. In fact, he seems to know everyone's name, and everyone seems to like that about him.

I need fifty-three newspapers and tell him so. The count is important since I'm paying the *Times* for every one of the papers I take from Mike and the cost is netted against the fixed subscription price charged to customers—an amount I'm responsible for collecting at the end of each month.

A daily and Sunday subscription is two dollars and seventy-five cents. Sunday papers cost me ten point six cents and the dailies cost me five point three cents. The math works out so that I should make about fifty dollars a month. A bit more with tips, less in five-Sunday months or in months with thirty-one days. Or if I get my counts wrong. Or if a customer skips without paying. On top of everything else, paperboys get docked fifty cents for every customer complaint called into the *Seattle Times*' office.

Barring any irate customers, this month should be reasonably profitable seeing as how there are only four Sundays and because February only has twenty-nine days, 1968 being a leap year.

It takes me four trips to lug the entire load over to a bench where I begin stuffing my papers. When you pick up and glance at the same front-page headlines fifty-three times, you can't help but get a feel for what's going on in the world, even though what's going on doesn't really make sense and you can't bring yourself to care all that much anyway.

Reds are set to hold Hue at all costs as the Tet holiday offensive enters day six? North Korea captures the USS Pueblo and wants an apology before they'll give it back? Rapid transit is needed because Seattle's population will double by 1985? Nikita Khrushchev is mentioned on Moscow TV for the first time since he became an "unperson" in 1964?

Unperson?

I allow room in my head to let the ridiculousness of the word rattle around, but I generally stay focused on the task at hand, and after a short while I'm done stacking the assembled newspapers onto my cart. My hands are covered with the black ink that's rubbed off the newsprint as the enormity of the job ahead really begins to sink in. The papers weigh more than I do, the handle of the cart hits me at mid-chest and the wheels are almost up to the axle in gravel.

I look around to see if anybody is curious to see if the short, skinny kid can do the impossible and get a cart filled with the *Sunday Times* to budge. I don't really expect any help and would have initially refused assistance as a matter of pride if any had been offered. Secretly though, I'm hoping someone will press the issue in such a way that I'll have no choice but to cave in and graciously allow them to bail me out of my jam.

For better or worse, no one seems to notice or care about me or my predicament, so I'm left to solve the problem on my own as I fight off the urge to cry. I haven't shed tears since I was ten. Ever since my sister Roberta told me that "boys don't cry" and I believed her.

I put downward pressure on the handle of the cart, tip it rearward onto the wheels, and begin to pull. Nothing happens. I increase the effort, cuss, and wiggle the cart back and forth until the wheels move a few inches. Exasperated, I let go all at once, and the whole kit and caboodle crashes back to the ground.

"One more time," I whisper to myself.

"You can do it," I mutter without the slightest bit of conviction.

This is it.

The moment of truth.

Regripping with both hands, I pull with every ounce of strength I can muster while wiggling the cart from side to side and letting go with a string of swear words that would make my father proud. After a few seconds, I let the cart down and examine the outcome. It's heartening to see that my all-out effort has provided promising results. The wheel tracks in the loose gravel must be at least a foot-and-a-half long.

It takes a series of hard-earned eighteen-inch victories over the next four or five minutes before I finally reach the asphalt of the street. All the while I've been checking to see who might be watching and maybe even laughing at me. It's a relief that no one finds humor in my situation, but it's kind of sad that something causing me so much personal grief doesn't register in the slightest with anyone else.

Wait a minute ...

The two loud-mouths from the Catholic school and the two guys from Kellogg are gone. With so much on my mind, I didn't see them leave. Is it possible they struggled just as much as I did?

I doubt it.

Still, you can't laugh at someone or help out unless you hang around long enough to notice him in the first place.

I stand at the edge of the road, taking a break and postponing the inevitable. After a tentative glance back to the shack and a deep breath, I grip the handle of the cart with both hands and manhandle the intimidating load back onto the two wheels until I find the balancing point. With my pride reasonably intact, I manage to get the newspaper cart rolling over the pavement and begin the long, tortuous push up the grade to the freeway overpass.

The sun must be up there somewhere because the clouds have turned a slightly lighter shade of charcoal gray. Traffic is still thin, but beginning to pick up. After less than a block, I look over my shoulder to see the headlights of a fast-moving Buick Skylark approaching from behind with no obvious intent of moving over, so I'm forced off the road onto the gravel shoulder where the wheels get buried again. I struggle to get the cart back onto the asphalt, pulling and wiggling and fighting off tears.

Two blocks later, here comes a Ford Galaxie 500 station wagon, and I'm forced off the road again.

"Next time, screw 'em. I'm not moving," I mumble as I work to get the cart back onto the pavement. I almost thought about letting go with the f-word, but even thinking it would be a mortal sin, so I don't even let it cross my mind.

I'm panting and perspiring and my legs ache as I push the cart of papers the rest of the way up the hill to the overpass. A couple of times I don't think I'm going to make it.

"Are you a man or a mouse?" I ask myself.

"I'm a man, goddammit," I growl between gritted teeth while shaking my head at the absurdity of the statement. And in that very same moment, I'm overtaken by an unexpected surge of determination.

On I labor, swearing and exhorting myself to be a man until, at long last, I crest the hill with my load of newspapers and a dozen or more mortal sins on my soul—one for every blasphemous cuss word spewed. For a moment though, I'm the king of the hill, the proud overcomer of a Sisyphean challenge. For the time being I'm not worried about rushing to confession or going to Hell.

Stopping to catch my breath, I'm hot and cold at the same time—warmed by the physical effort and chilled as the dampness of the morning air sneaks under my jacket to mix with the sweat on my skin. I step up onto the curb and look over the railing of the bridge to see cars rushing by on the freeway below. The natural thing to do is to spit, so I do, and then watch the loogie fall through the air, just missing the windshield of what looked to be a hardworking Studebaker doing about seventy miles an hour.

I back away from the railing and turn toward the suddenly not-so-daunting yellow cart full of heavy newspapers. Streetlights reveal water droplets forming on my sleeve, and I feel moisture hit my face when I direct my gaze upward. The restless Northwest sky has finished mulling things over and has decided that it's time to drizzle.

Paper Route Headlines

B-52s Saturate Red Positions at Khe Sanh

Record 543 G.I.s Killed in a Week

Yanks Rout Red Guerrillas Threatening Big Air Bases

Laws, Aid Urged to Avert Race War

Jetliner Hijacked, Flown to Havana

21 Workers Trapped in Louisiana Salt Mine

Bobo the Gorilla Dies in His Sleep

Drug Use Rising, Say Teenagers

Johnson Visits Dallas After 4 Years

Chapter 4

Ripping Off the Band-Aid

I'VE BECOME A MASTER of the sideways glance. It comes in handy when I'm curious about something, but not curious enough to stare or to risk getting caught looking. Getting caught with your eyes lingering over the wrong things is akin to being found the fool—something to be avoided at all costs. The key to the effective sideways glance is to not turn your head. Keep facing forward at all times and let your eyes do all the work. The technique is particularly handy in the locker room and in the halls between classes where I can't help but notice that girls I never noticed before are suddenly worth checking out.

On the first day of school this year, it was chaos in the locker room before seventh period PE, and it only took a few seconds after walking in the door to realize that it might matter if the other boys knew exactly what I was looking at. Ninth graders were still toweling off outside the showers after their just-ended class, and I got the uneasy feeling that I was a boy among men. It was just an impression, a possibly incorrect impression, the uncertainty of which almost caused me to take a long, ill-advised, all-out gander. This was where I employed the sideways glance for the first time. And this was how I confirmed that there was a huge difference between the body of a fourteen-year-old freshman and the body of a just-turned twelve-year-old seventh grader like me.

I had just used six of the ten minutes allotted between classes to push my way from my math class held in a portable near the gym, through the crowded corridors to my street locker in the main building by the Student Activity Center, and then back up to the gym. All this effort to retrieve a brown paper bag with my school-mandated gym gear: white cotton shorts, white cotton t-shirt, a pair of white tube socks, white low-top sneakers, and an off-white, size small, BIKE-brand jockstrap that was still in the box.

Except for the jockstrap, all the gym gear came from Sears and Roebuck where Mom got a 10 percent employee discount. She worked at Allstate Insurance, but Sears was their parent company and pretty much everything we owned came from the telephone book-sized catalog.

I had four minutes left to get changed and only the vaguest idea of how to put on the jockstrap. Getting it wrong and possibly putting it on backward would be a disaster. Do you really *strap it down* with the elastic bands that seem to run in every direction? If so, what was the purpose of the pouch where all the stretchy straps came together?

Using only my eyes and without moving my head a fraction of an inch to either side, I noticed a couple of other confused-looking boys sitting on a bench nearby. Jockstraps in hand, they were nervously studying the bizarre contraptions while giving each other panicky sideways glances in the hope the other guy would show the way.

This was perfect! Time was running out and one of them was going to have to commit. I would just pace myself as I undressed and take advantage of them figuring out the solution to our mutual dilemma. By the time I had my undershirt off, I could see, courtesy of my sideways glance, that the pouch of the jockstrap went in front. And once I had a general lay of the land, figuring out how to untangle the elastic bands wasn't that tough.

I heard laughter from a row of lockers behind me, and I poked my head around the corner to see what was going on. Mark Madsen, who looked like Sherman from the *Mr. Peabody and Sherman* cartoon with his scrawny body and Roy Orbison glasses, had a jockstrap on his head and an expression of mock confusion on his face while the guys around him were rolling on the floor.

Just then, Mr. Zimmermann walked in and blew the black referee's whistle attached to a lanyard around his neck. "Everyone out!" he yelled. "Now! Everyone out!"

Suddenly the place went from mildly chaotic to a complete mad house! Jokers and dawdlers were hopping around on one foot, threading skinny limbs through tangled jockstraps before tugging up shorts, pulling on t-shirts, and scrambling to tie their shoes. It wasn't clear to anyone at first what the teacher meant by the word *out*, but herd instinct quickly took over, and we followed the alpha-male through the double doors and marched down the hall to the main gym.

On the near wall of the gym was a red and black mural of the Cordell Hull Hawk mascot. On the far wall were the words to the school fight song, which I later learned was sung to the tune of "When the Saints Go Marching In":

Now when the Hawks come flying in
Now when the Hawks come flying in
Sound your cry and squawk for vic'try
For the Hawks will win and win
Stand up and shout (yea team)
Stand up and shout (yea team)
Now when the Hawks come flying in.

Sound your cry and squawk for vic'try
For the Hawks will win and win

"Everyone stand over by the bleachers. Sound off and get up here when I call your name," Mr. Zimmermann yelled again. "Animato."

"Here," one of the boys said without moving.

"Get up here!" Mr. Zimmermann bellowed, sounding much more irritated than you'd expect in light of the situation. "Everybody pay attention! Animato, grab your shirt on either side at chest level and pull it tight."

The excited kid fumbled around for a second or two before finally figuring out what he was being told to do. Mr. Zimmermann then used a fat-tipped felt pen to write "ANIMATO" in bold, black letters on the flat surface created by stretching the front of the t-shirt.

"Sit down over there," Mr. Zimmermann barked while pointing to a spot near the foul line.

And so it went alphabetically … AUSTIN, BECKER, BECKETT, BRAUN … MADSEN … YERKOVICH, until six neat rows of five clearly labeled seventh graders were formed in the middle of the basketball court.

The teacher said my name wrong when my time came. "It's *brown* not *brawn*," I corrected him in a voice so low that I could barely hear myself. Dad was a stickler for how our last name is pronounced. It sounds the same in both German and English. It's just spelled differently. I'm tired of correcting people when they say it wrong. Or when they say it right and then spell it wrong.

I wish I had a simpler name.

"You've got a name you can be proud of," Dad always says.

I wish it was true.

"This is Bob, my teaching assistant," Mr. Zimmermann announced while nodding at the ninth grader standing at his elbow with "HOWARD" printed on his front. He was wearing red shorts while the rest of us wore the standard white shorts.

What's that about? I wondered.

"This is where you should be sitting when the bell rings every day for class. Anyone that is late will do ten push-ups. We've got a few minutes before we hit the showers today, so everybody outside!"

I could see on the clock next to the basketball scoreboard that it was only 3:06 p.m. We'd been there for thirty-six minutes and class was over at 3:20 p.m. "Fourteen minutes? What can we possibly do in fourteen minutes?" I muttered to myself as I followed the crowd outside. Soon enough I found myself milling around with everyone else under the rim of the outdoor basketball court.

"We're going to do a little cross-country run. Everybody follow Bob. Let's go! Hustle!" the teacher yelled while clapping his hands emphatically.

And just like that we're off, all thirty of us decked out in white, running after Bob the TA in his red shorts as he trotted toward the baseball diamond on a warm September day. He then veered off into foul territory and led us up a trail behind where a left field foul pole would be if we had one. The athletic fields at Cordell Hull consisted of a large boggy expanse of grass and mud surrounded on three sides by steep hills. The school's cross-country course was a rocky trail a little more than a half-mile long that roughly followed a contour line along the perimeter.

By the time we made the first turn behind the baseball backstop, I was right in the middle of the surprisingly strung-out pack. I could see guys laughing and joking in front of me, and I could hear other guys panting and complaining behind me. One unidentified hot dog was about twenty-five yards ahead of Bob the TA, and I could tell he was already in trouble. I was feeling okay and expecting to feel much worse as I inched by four or five classmates, one of whom had BEATY on his t-shirt. He looked at me with sweat dripping down his forehead and said, "This is fucked up, man."

We got to the halfway point at the far end of the field, and Mr. Zimmermann looked like an ant in the distance as I heard him screaming at the top of his lungs for the stragglers to "Stop walking!" and to "Shut up and get moving!"

Glancing over my shoulder, I saw someone labeled FAVELL, another labeled FLYNN, and several more boys working hard but not getting anywhere very fast. Behind them were a bunch of other guys that couldn't care less and weren't even trying. Next thing I knew I was passing the hot dog clearly recognizable as ANIMATO, who was now walking and, from the looks of it, about to throw up.

A steep hill was coming up, and I could count the bodies ahead of me as they climbed to the top. I was in eighth place. Not bad. I high-kneed it up the hill, turned left, and ran alongside a cyclone fence for fifty yards. Then it was down the hill, across the flats to the basketball court, and we were done.

Some guy labeled MAYER finished first by outsprinting Bob the TA and was getting a congratulatory pat on the back from Mr. Zimmermann. Everyone else was bent over at the waist trying to catch their breath, so I did too—not because I felt particularly tired, but because it seemed like the thing to do.

"Good job, BRAUN," Mr. Zimmermann said to me while patting me on the back. I didn't feel like I deserved any special praise, but I was surprised at how good it felt even though he mispronounced my name again.

"Hit the showers!" Mr. Zimmermann yelled, almost before I could finish my thought.

Hit the showers? Oh man … I don't know about this. Showering with other people … I don't even like being naked when I'm alone! This is really—I don't know—weird.

I did a slow walk back to the locker room, trying to decide if I'd do as I was told or just get dressed and go home all sweaty. It was the last class of the day so who cared?

As I stepped through the door, it was too late for a sideways glance as I saw a naked, glasses-less Mark Madsen parade in front of me on the way to the showers. I averted my eyes immediately, but I was left with only three words to describe what I was sure will be forever etched on my brain: *pink and hairless*. Mark Madsen was ridiculous looking and apparently not the least bit self-conscious about it.

I was pretty sure I knew how this was all going to play out. Eventually I'd have to shower with these guys and be seen in all my hairless pinkness. If I got it over with then, I wouldn't be noticeably the first and I wouldn't be noticeably the last, which was where I liked to be anyway. I figured not being a chicken was pretty close to being manly. Besides, if Mark could do it, I could do it. So, I talked myself into doing the manly thing rather than the mousely thing and stripped off my clothes like I was ripping off a Band-Aid.

Off I padded toward the sight of steam and the sound of running water, passing rows of street lockers and wire baskets full of smelly gym gear. I kept my head down and eyes pointed straight ahead. In my peripheral vision, I could tell that guys were giving me the sideways glance and feeling better about themselves.

Paper Route Headlines

Pope Pleads for Mideast Peace

U. District Store Manager
Pistol-Whipped by Robbers

Cary Grant Leaves Hospital

Senate Approves 10% Income Tax Surcharge

President Plans Plea to Congress as
Violence Follows King Slaying

Slayer Suspect 'Wore Silly Smile'

Fresh Looting, Arson Fires Flare in Nation's Capital

Vietcong Blow Up U.S. Army Barracks

Easter '68—Love Among the Turmoil

Columbia River to Be Trickle as Dam Fills

Chapter 5

Oh, Jesus

I WALK IN THE front door after school to see Robbie and Maureen sitting together on the living room floor. Robbie looks up with a smile and says, "I have something to tell you," in a way that feels ominous. Maybe it's because the last time anyone started a conversation with the words "I have something to tell you" was when Mom was about to break the news that she and Dad were getting divorced. It was the same day nine-year-old me promised my mother that I would get a paper route when I was old enough to help support the family.

"What?" I respond curtly since I'm anxious to get down to the shack to pick up my newspapers and get them delivered. It's drizzling outside, and I'm thinking ahead to how stressful it is trying to keep newspapers dry when the weather conspires against it. Nobody likes a waterlogged newspaper.

"I'm pregnant," Robbie says. And with those words, all the gears in my head disengage at once and begin to whir and to spin independently of each other as I try to make sense of what I've just heard. She doesn't look pregnant. Pregnant means being fat like Mrs. Betts up the street was last year. It means being grown up and being married.

She's fifteen.

Oh, Jesus.

"What!" I say again, only this time it's an exclamation not a question. This time I hear a tone of disbelief and despair coming out of my mouth. In abstract I know how these things happen, and I get a flash of how it means that Jack Adamos must have screwed my sister. And then the shame of how she must have let him do this to her begins to set in. Answering the inevitable questions about Robbie will be just as excruciating as answering questions about my father. I can see it now: I'll look at the floor, speak softly, and be as elusive as possible until the questioner gives up.

"Jack and me are getting married a week from Sunday."

Married? That makes sense, I guess. It's what I think is referred to as the "honorable thing." Jack Adamos is going to do the honorable thing. Maybe he's not such a bad guy after all. But aren't there places that pregnant girls go to have their babies in secret? Where they put them up for adoption and come home as if nothing has happened? Robbie was adopted. Isn't that what her real mother did? Why wouldn't she do that instead of putting me in the position of having to explain all of this to people?

"Does Dad know?"

"Not yet."

It was a dumb question. Of course Dad doesn't know that Robbie is pregnant, otherwise he'd be calling at all hours to berate Mom for being a bad mother—something he does on a regular basis anyway. It's a sure thing that I would have picked up one of those calls, and it's not like he gives up easily when he is determined to get through.

You never know when Dad might call, but if the phone rings within five minutes of ending a call with him, you can be certain he is calling back to elaborate on the lecture he just gave you. So we just don't pick up the second call. The phone will ring twenty times, stop for a minute, and then start ringing again. It's a stalemate. But we can't give in because we know he's just getting drunker and angrier with every pause in the ringing.

If Dad already knew that Robbie was going to have a baby and if I had answered any of his calls, I suspect he would have tried to pawn off some of the blame to me. And maybe I had it coming.

Just last year, in a father-son moment, he advised me that "Dating a gal is like trying on a pair of pants. If you shit in 'em, you own 'em." It was my responsibility to pass the word on to guys like Jack Adamos, and I had clearly failed in my role as understudy for the man of the house.

A man is needed in these kinds of situations, and only a mouse is in the house.

"Are you going to call Dad, or is Mom going to call?" I ask Robbie.

"I'll do it," she replies.

It seems out of character for her not to let Mom do the dirty work. But this time is different. This time I believe her. I can see by the look in her eyes that she loves everything about the situation. She loves the drama. She loves the idea of marrying Jack Adamos and playing grown-up. She loves the idea of having a baby to love.

I think of how different she is from the rest of us. She was always the tenderhearted one, the pied piper for neighborhood kids and stray animals for as long as I could remember.

On summer nights around dinner time, Robbie was usually nowhere to be found.

"Call Robbie," Mom would say.

I would go out on the front porch, scream her name at the top of my lungs, and listen for a response. No response? No problem. I would repeat the process until I heard her calling back from off in the distance, "I'm coming!"

I feel like screaming her name now too.

"Well, at least you won't have to share a room with her anymore," I say to Maureen. I can see she has already thought of the silver lining in this dark cloud, and that part of her can hardly wait. It's just a matter of time before Leslie moves out too, and Maureen can finally have a room to herself.

"Is there anything I can do?" I ask Robbie. I've heard adults ask this question before, but it's the first time for me.

"Go on and do your paper route," she says, giving me the answer I was hoping for.

• • •

IT'S ALMOST HIGH noon on an unusually fine spring day. Normal for April is wet, gray, and blustery, but today the air is calm, the sun is shining, and the sky is a brilliant blue. The fluffy white clouds look like something out of a picture I've seen hanging in the lobby of the school at St. Mark's when I'm there for CCD classes on Wednesdays—the one with angels playing harps as they float around on their clouds unaffected by the turmoil below. You would think the favorable weather portends good things, but it's hard to be optimistic about the shotgun marriage of a fifteen-year-old girl and a just-turned eighteen-year-old high school dropout.

I'm standing on the front porch of the Adamos family home watching guests mingle on the front lawn, and I can smell the fragrance of lilacs. I know the scent because I posed for my first communion picture in front of a lilac tree just like the one growing next to me now.

A stinky old dog with a white muzzle is stretched out on the walkway leading between the street and the front door. He is still free, but his days of *running* free are long past. Wedding guests step over and around him. A few reach down to scratch his ears or rub his belly, making his hind leg shimmy.

The bride is nowhere to be seen. I'm told that it is bad luck for the groom to set eyes on the bride before the ceremony, so she is holed up in a back bedroom working on her hair and makeup with help from Leslie, Maureen, and Jack's sister, Julianne. Mom is in the kitchen trying to be useful, but the boisterous Greek women ignore her. She is a tiny person anyway and looks even smaller today.

Jack Adamos is circulating dutifully in his dark suit with a white carnation tucked into the lapel. His freshly cut hair makes his ears stand out more than usual. In his left hand is a Dixie cup half-filled with Jack Daniels from the bar set up inside on a card table, and there is blue smoke wafting from the unfiltered Camel cigarette held nervously between the fingers of his right hand. He is still just a teenager, but it seems that if you're old enough to marry, you're too old to be scolded about the perils of nasty adult habits like smoking and drinking.

These Greeks are a demonstrative bunch what with all the hugging and crying and back slapping going on. Their behavior is shocking given the strict no-touching policy in my immediate family. I try to remember the last time Mom offered me a hug or a kiss, and I'm stumped. Meanwhile, Jack is peppered with questions and each time there is a tear in the eye, a hand on the shoulder, or a smack on the back.

"Do you have a place to live?"

"Yeah, we found a one-bedroom apartment up on 178th near the Gateway QFC."

"Have you found a job yet?"

"Yeah, I've got work as an apprentice drywall taper starting Monday."

"I guess you don't need any advice about what to expect on your wedding night, do you?"

Ha ha ha.

"No, I guess not."

"How about the draft?"

"I'm pretty sure I'll be re-classed from one-A to three-A and won't have to worry about it."

"That's good. You're a lover not a fighter anyway, right?"

Ha ha ha.

"Yeah, for sure."

It's slightly after twelve o'clock and the best man, Jack's fifteen-year-old brother, Greg, encourages everyone to move inside. I'd been inside already, and it's packed in there—that's why I'm on the front porch to begin with. But I go inside anyway and squeeze my way to a place against the east wall near an open window facing the street.

A large woman crowds in front of me so that my nose is even with her shoulder blades and her giant ass is inches from my chest. I stand at attention to avoid contact with her blubbery bottom—hands by my side, shoulders back, chin in. I notice that all the other windows are open too, but the spring breeze can't keep up with all the body heat. I feel dampness in my armpits, so I give them a discrete sniff. So far so good.

Jack's sister takes her place at the family's piano and after a false start settles into a commendable version of the wedding march. Robbie, dressed in white, emerges from the bedroom on the arm of Mr. Adamos.

I thought Dad was supposed to give her away.

"Where is he?" I ask myself.

The crowd makes room for them to pass. Much to my chagrin and embarrassment, I find myself momentarily nestled into the large woman's backside so that I know she is wearing an oversize version of the girdle Mom hangs from the shower rod at home.

The music ends. The room quiets down, and guests look expectantly to the justice of the peace. I can just make out Mom's profile in the front row with Grandma Wertz standing next to her. Leslie and Maureen are somewhere in the crowd. Otherwise, it's pretty much an all-Greek affair.

"Dearly beloved," the justice of the peace begins. But before he can finish the sentence, a familiar voice from out front booms through the open windows and echoes across the room in reaction to a stinky old dog blocking the walkway.

"Get outa the way, ya goddamn flea factory!"

My father made it after all.

Paper Route Headlines

Telephone Industry Hit by Strike

Barnard Planning Third Transplant of Heart in 6 Weeks

123 Reported Dead in Crash of South American Airways 707

Las Vegas Shaken in H-Bomb Test

Montlake Terrace Woman Cab Driver Shot, Throat Cut

Yanks Rout Red Unit Halt Invasion of Hue

Clay's Appeal Is Denied by Circuit Court

Derby Winner Disqualified for Drugs

Chapter 6

Martians Living Among Us

IT'S FRIDAY MORNING, and I'm jumping on the garbage when Art Betts stops by on his way to school. He is wearing a yellow Little League cap with a capital *C* for Casey's Drive-In above the brim. The team sponsor is up on Aurora Avenue and is known for a wide variety of milkshake flavors and decent burgers. Root beer shakes are my favorite.

It's rare for a seventh grader like Art to still be playing Little League. He's young for our grade because the birthday cutoff date for kindergarten is different in Canada where he was born and lived until his father got a job working in the press room of the *Seattle Times*.

I probably spend more time with Art than anybody else. He's a head taller than me and athletic. I've grown accustomed to having him clobber me in every sport we play, and he never seems to get tired of winning.

He'll pretend to be Oscar Robertson, and I'll be Elgin Baylor, the ex-Seattle University great, when we play one-on-one or HORSE or PIG in my driveway.

Bounce, bounce, swish is the sound of Art making his shot.

Bounce, bounce, clunk is the sound of my miss hitting the back of the iron.

I'll be Willie Mays, and he'll be switch-hitting Mickey Mantle when we play Wiffle ball in his backyard. I still don't have a chance when he bats off-handed, but it's less likely to be a massacre.

"What are you doing?" Art asks in reference to me jumping on the garbage. There was a time he would have added the obligatory Canadian "eh" to the end of his question, but we've teased that habit out of him, and he says "huh" like an American now.

"What's it look like I'm doing?"

"I don't know. That's why I asked. But whatever it is, it looks weird."

"Don't you ever jump on your garbage?"

"Huh? That's weird. I never even thought about it," he says with a grin as he begins to see the absurdity of both the conversation and the fact that I'm standing in a garbage can like it's a normal thing to do.

I'm finished with the job anyway, so I climb out of the can and put the lid on securely while puzzling over the revelation that Art doesn't have to jump on his garbage multiple times each week. And then I have an epiphany:

"You have two garbage cans, right?"

"Sure."

"Okay. That explains it." We both laugh and I join him on the walk to Cordell Hull.

It's a beautiful May morning. The sky isn't even thinking about drizzling, and the end of the school year is just a couple weeks away. We're both in good spirits.

"What's going on?"

"Not much."

"Wanna play some Ping-Pong after school tonight?" Art asks as we make the turn off 180th and onto 1st Avenue.

"Sure. After dinner as usual?"

There are no famous Ping-Pong players that we know of, so we can't pretend to be anyone but ourselves at the table next to the washer-dryer in the middle of his wide-open, unfinished basement. I get better every time we play, but Art seems to get better faster.

"Did you know there's a nigger family living in that house?" Art asks matter-of-factly as we pass by a normal-looking house just a few off the corner.

I'm not offended by Art's choice of words even though I know it's not polite. He doesn't seem to mean any offense, and even though the word isn't used often in these parts, it isn't uncommon either.

"Really?" I say, not quite believing him since news like this, if true, would have undoubtedly been picked up by the neighborhood grapevine by now.

"That's what my dad says," Art replies confidently.

Negroes in Shoreline doesn't compute. He might just as well have said there are Martians living among us. I can think of only three kids that stand out in the crowd at school, and they're all Oriental. David Goldstein is Jewish, so I guess he counts as being unusual, but not particularly different looking. Catholics are a minority in the public schools, but we're largely indistinguishable from all the Norwegians, who are a dime a dozen. Nelson, Olson, Hansen, Carlson, Peterson, Anderson, Erickson, and Knutson are all names of classmates, but negroes? I'll have to file this away and maybe make sense out of it later.

A black Labrador retriever is lying in wait on his front porch halfway up 178th Street when he spots us and starts his charge, barking viciously. He does this every day. Art and I break into a jog without giving it a second thought, confident that the dog will give up once he gets to the property line and realizes he's made his point. More kids will be coming down the street shortly anyway, so the dog is wise to pace himself.

"Got a game tonight?" I ask, nodding at his cap after we slow back down to a walk.

"No."

"When is it?"

"When is what?"

"Your next game."

"Oh. The season is over, but I made the All-Star team."

"Cool."

"We play next week."

"Who does?"

"The All-Star team.

"Oh, when?"

"Don't know."

And so it goes as we make the turn onto Meridian Avenue, cross with the light at 175th Street, and part ways by the flag pole in front of the school.

"Have a good one."

"You too."

I look up at the flag, half expecting it to be at half-staff, but instead I see it fluttering gently in the breeze right next to the gold ball on the top of the pole. It seems like somebody important dies on a regular basis, and when they do, the flag gets lowered. I remember President Kennedy getting shot. Then General MacArthur and Winston Churchill died of old age. And then the Apollo 1 astronauts burned to death last year.

For a brief second, I speculate about what I would have to do to get them to lower the flag when I died someday and if I would be assassinated or if I would live to be an old man in, say, the year 2035 when I'd be eighty. The year 2035 seems like a long way off, and I picture a world with flying cars like on the *Jetsons* cartoon.

Last month Martin Luther King was shot, and the flag was flown at half-staff for a while. I delivered the known details of the shooting to all of my customers the next day. The main headline wasn't so much about the shooting itself as the aftermath: "President Plans Plea to Congress as Violence Follows King Slaying." Below to the left was a picture of Lyndon Johnson and a bunch of serious faces sitting around a table to "discuss the implications of the slaying." In bold print further down the page were the words: "Slayer Suspect Wore a Silly Smile."

A silly smile?

We talked about Dr. King in social studies over the next few days and about the riots, the marches, and the eulogy. No one took to the streets of Shoreline. But in the hallway between classes, a schoolmate said, to no one in particular, that his dad told him, "James Earl Ray should get a sharpshooting medal."

Those within earshot laughed at the joke, including me. My reaction felt similar to what happens when I watch a bad situation comedy on TV. It's not funny, but the laugh track makes me laugh anyway. I'm mildly ashamed that I laughed and slightly disappointed that anyone else would either. But I keep these thoughts to myself, along with the secret that it feels sinful not to have stronger feelings about the murder.

I care, but I don't care enough.

In my mind's eye I can see the same headline on all fifty-three of the newspapers I delivered the day after Martin Luther King died. The same sad story repeated over and over again as my canvas newspaper bag with the *Seattle Times* logo got thinner and lighter. On the one hand, my teacher is saying Dr. King was a great man of peace and nonviolence. On the other hand, he died violently, parents use the N-word and kids parrot cruel jokes. His death made headlines, but life in Shoreline goes on pretty much as usual because, Art's revelation notwithstanding, Black people aren't a problem around here.

Back before Mom and Dad got divorced, I was down at Grandma Braun's house in White Center one Sunday watching a show about World War II. Just the two of us were home at the time, which was unusual since the place was always packed with family. The narrator was talking about something called concentration camps and how they were somehow related to something else called the Holocaust. There on the screen in front of me were grizzly shots of starving people in dirty, striped pajamas. Dad and at least five of my uncles fought in the war, and I'd listened in on many stories told over many Sunday dinners, but I'd never heard anything about this.

Grandma came through on her way from the kitchen to the bathroom and stopped for a moment to digest what was on the TV screen before glancing over at me. Then she looked at the TV again and then back in my direction. Our eyes met. After a long pause, she finally said, "Don't feel sorry for the Jews."

And just like that, she continued on her way.

I was eight years old at the time, and I took what she said at face value. But there was something unsettling about it then.

And there still is.

I love my grandmother because that is what grandsons do. It embarrasses me when she hugs me to her ample bosom, but I appreciate that she never gets tired of playing Crazy Eights or Old Maid with me and Maureen. She makes a delicious sheet cake she calls *zuckerkuchen*, and she trusts us not to burn ourselves when we fish feather-light homemade donuts from a pot of boiling oil on her stove.

It's 7:58 a.m. when I get to my locker, and I have two minutes to ditch my sack lunch, pick up my social studies book, and get to homeroom with Miss Kristianson before the bell rings. I hurriedly enter the combination: right 17, left 36, right 6 and give the locker handle a yank. Nothing happens except an obnoxious clunk—a sound that brings to mind an errant basketball shot hitting the back of the rim.

Wait … that's my gym locker combination.

Right 22, left 33, right 9, and I'm ready to start the school day.

Paper Route Headlines

Reds Drive Closer to Saigon's Heart

Paris Peace Talks to Begin Monday

12-Year-Old Sought in Hippiedom

Police Plan Crackdown on Youth-Gang Toughs

79 Die as Tornadoes Sweep 9 States

562 Yanks Killed High Total of War

Oil Slick in Atlantic May Be Clue
to Missing Nuclear Sub

Three More Heart-Transplant Patients Die

Robert Kennedy's Condition
Remains Extremely Critical

Kennedy to Be Buried in Arlington Saturday

Chapter 7

That's a Big Woman

I FIGURE I'VE eaten at least one Hostess pie or one package of Hostess Cupcakes, Twinkies, Ding Dongs, Ho Hos, Snoballs, Suzy Q's, or Tiger Tails every day for the last four months, and I'm sure I'll never get tired of them. At fifteen cents apiece at the 7-Eleven next to the newspaper shack, you can't go wrong. Cherry pies are my favorite, but I'm nuts for anything with a marshmallow center. Throw in a Slurpee and the occasional Big Hunk or Mountain Bar or a package of Pixy Stix or box of Boston Baked Beans, and I've got all the fuel I need to climb to the top of the overpass with my load of papers.

• • •

IT'S HARD TO concentrate because there are just a few more days before school lets out for the summer. Mr. Carr is going on about something that I couldn't care less about. Nothing he can say or do at this point will change my grade in social studies anyway, so I don't feel like I'm under any particular obligation to be here—other than playing my role in the age-old cat and mouse game between teacher and student.

I get the sense that Mr. Carr is counting the hours too. He's been talking more and more lately about the scenic ferry trip from Mukilteo to his cabin on Whidbey Island and about how he plans to catch up on his reading while lying in a hammock tied between two trees near the beach. We also know that he hasn't seen his younger brother since their mother's funeral in Cleveland five years ago and that the two of them are going to fly in a De Havilland Beaver floatplane on their salmon fishing trip to Bella Bella, British Columbia, sometime in July.

We were seated alphabetically by last name at the beginning of the school year, and the letter *b* puts me right in the middle of the first row by the window. I love sitting by the window. Sitting where I do makes it easy to keep up with what's going on at the blackboard and still be able to take in the view without too much risk of being caught. Room 408 looks out onto the athletic fields, which is far better than classrooms with views of the teachers' parking lot or the side of another building. I've sat in this exact spot for first period class every morning for nine months and have watched the seasons change from sunny to drizzly to sunny again.

No stray dogs are humping out on the fields today, so Mr. Carr hasn't had to scramble to draw the blinds, and I haven't had the pleasure of watching Mr. Zimmermann, with his bum knee, charging awkwardly after the copulating canines to break it up. But the ninth-grade girls dressed in light blue, one-piece gym outfits playing field hockey are pretty interesting. I can see a boys' PE class playing soccer, and there are a couple of lonely-looking guys out on the cross-country course, undoubtedly being made to run as punishment for screwing around or cussing or fighting.

My gym class has probably run the cross-country course twice a month since the beginning of the school year, and I'm always in the top eight or ten even though I can't say that I've really given it a full effort—at least not yet. A lot of the guys think of it as torture and grouse about having to run, but I keep quiet. I've been daydreaming about being a track star lately, inspired by seeing Jim Ryun from Kansas set a world record in the mile run on *Wide World of Sports* last summer.

And maybe I have some natural talent. I almost won the fifty-yard dash at the annual Fireman's Picnic held at Norm's Resort on Cottage Lake when I was six years old. After being told to "stand here," somebody fired a gun and I found myself running across a field with a hundred other boys, not quite sure what the point was.

I wandered off afterward, looking for my parents when a race official spotted me and gave me my second-place prize: a dart gun with knockdown animal targets. Dad took the tiger, lion, hippo, and elephant off the original stand, and they now hang on a cabinet door at the far end of the garage. When pulling into the garage at night, the car headlights illuminate the beasts, and I fantasize about taking an African safari someday and shooting them for real.

While Mr. Carr drones on in the background, I insert a few more bullets into the stream of fire coming from the hand-drawn jet plane on my Pee-Chee folder. Then I add a machine gun and gunner to the turret of the Sherman tank I started yesterday at about this time.

I put down my pencil, close my eyes, and fight the urge to rest my head on the desktop. My mind wanders to the *Playboy* magazines that I've stowed under my mattress at home, and fighting off boredom, I fall deeper into a stimulating daydream about Lynn and Kaya, the centerfold models that I'm on a first-name basis with now. I feel a stirring sensation that makes me squirm in my chair. *This can't be normal*, I think to myself, and I worry again that I might be a queer, whatever that means.

The words *stiff as a cock* come to mind, and I think back to when I first heard them. It was just after Robbie and Jack

Adamos started dating last fall, and our old neighbors, Dode and Lorraine Leach, stopped by for a visit with Mom.

I was named after Dode. His given name is Gordon like me, but as a kid he mispronounced it as "Doden" and the nickname stuck. He is a very funny guy with a dry wit, and I'm proud to be his namesake, even though Gordon is an old man's name. I would have preferred to be named Doug, like the actor Doug McClure who plays the amiable Trampas character on *The Virginian*.

Adamos had something wrong with his car, so he, Dode, and I had the hood up in our driveway trying to figure out the problem. What did I know? I was barely twelve, and I was there to learn. It was a hot, dirty, sinister-looking place under the hood, and I tried to look more interested and less scared than I really was.

Adamos and Dode poked around, wiggled wires, tested belts, wiped off dipsticks, and gave each other quizzical looks.

"What do you think of this?" Adamos asked after wiggling something deep in the bowels of the engine compartment.

Dode reached in, gave the mystery object a wiggle, shook his head, and said with a straight face, "Yep, stiff as a cock," making Adamos laugh out loud. I didn't get it, but I laughed anyway.

After a few more minutes of friendly banter and fruitless results, Dode shrugged his shoulders to indicate he'd done all he could. Adamos said, "Thanks anyway," slammed the hood shut, and we went back inside, the problem left unresolved.

Momentarily coming back to real life, I can see outside on the playfields that somebody must have scored a goal in the soccer game because guys on the skins team are patting each other on their sweaty backs and then wiping their hands on their shorts. Meanwhile the shirts team is heading back to midfield with dry hands at their sides and their heads down.

And then I'm back to thinking. *Wait a minute ... if Dode knows about cocks getting stiff, then maybe everyone else does too.*

How could I have missed this? If I'm piecing things together correctly, maybe this phenomenon that is causing me so much distress is somehow normal.

The first time I paid attention to Mrs. Dahl, who lives on 185th Street, was when I saw her bent over gardening in a pair of floral-print shorts while I was delivering newspapers. I start thinking about the pleasing sight of those flowery shorts as Mr. Carr continues making white noise in the background.

It's a treat to run into her, and you never know when it might happen. I'm always optimistic and walk a little taller on the way in from the street with her newspaper, and I try not to feel too disappointed when our paths don't cross.

"Oh, hi," she said that first day as she stood upright and turned around to face me. "I didn't hear you."

I made an audible gulping sound.

She laughed.

What a beautiful giggle.

"Hello, uh, hello, Mrs. Dahl," I stammered. "Here's your paper."

"Thank you. Call me Patty."

It was all I could do not to avert my eyes from her enchanting gaze, but I held on as best I could.

"Okay … Bye," I said, trying desperately to conjure up what Alexander Mundy from *It Takes a Thief* or Napoleon Solo from *The Man from UNCLE* would have said under the circumstances.

"What's your name?" she called to me as I headed back to my bike, feeling disgusted with myself for being such an ignoramus.

I think I said "Gordon," but I can't be sure, seeing as how I was distracted by all the things I couldn't think to say.

Patty … What a beautiful name …

I accidentally make eye contact with Mr. Carr and break it off immediately. I get the feeling he doesn't think I'm paying attention.

I look at the clock over the door. Twelve long minutes to go.

Then there was that time, I must have been four because I was just up from my nap, still feeling a little sleepy, holding Mom's hand while we stood on the front porch of our house. This time it was Dad and his friend from the fire department, Bob Albin, with the hood up on a car in the driveway. They must have been talking about doing something major with Dad's Ford because Dad said in a somber tone, "We'll need a half-ton wench."

Bob Albin replied without missing a beat, "That's a big woman."

Mom started laughing.

I was four, and I didn't understand Mom's response, Bob Albin's wry grin, or Dad's look of puzzlement. So, I filed it away.

Until just now!

Mystery solved!

He meant half-ton *winch* not half-ton *wench*!

I try not to laugh out loud while sitting there at my desk by the window, but I can't help but smile a toothy smile. If anybody were to look at me, they would take me for a fool because there is absolutely nothing funny about Mr. Carr's lecture. So I cover my mouth with my hand to hide evidence of the fact that I'm having a pretty good time when everyone else is bored out of their minds.

The school bell rings, and I'm off to French class. I begin to anticipate that within a few minutes, I'll be sitting across from cute chicks in their jumpers and knee socks or, better yet, short skirts and nylon stockings. The sideways glance doesn't work very well in the French class seating arrangement, but I've learned to make do.

Bonjour, Mademoiselle, I muse to myself and grin again, like a fool again, at another private joke. I make my way through the crowded halls, alone in my own little world, knowing full well I don't have the nerve to say something like this out loud to an attractive girl.

My path takes me within sight of the flagpole in front of the school, and I see that it's at half-staff again.

Did I miss it this morning or has something happened?

And then I remember. Yesterday I tossed copies of the *Seattle Times* onto fifty-three doorsteps with the front-page headline of "Robert Kennedy's Condition Remains Extremely Critical." Based on the position of the flag, I can only guess that I'll be delivering worse news to the same fifty-three customers after school tonight.

Paper Route Headlines

James Earl Ray Arrested in London by Scotland Yard

Military Victory in 'Classical Sense' Impossible, Says Gen. Westmoreland

Market Hits Record Mark

Allied Troops Wage 'Scorched Earth' War

**Lobby Weakened
3 Gun Makers Back Controls**

Man Slain, Detective Wounded in Shooting

Truck Spills Liquid Wax, Jams Freeway

Chief Justice Warren Reportedly Resigns

Chapter 8

That's Never Happened Before

I'M LYING IN BED with my hands behind my head, looking at the ceiling through half-open eyes and listening to the rain outside. It's the first day of summer vacation, and I know it's raining and not merely drizzling because the sky is talking to me in a language that only a well-trained ear like mine can understand. Drizzle speaks in a gentle voice. If it was drizzling, I would be hearing a soft whisper encouraging me to go back to sleep. But this is rain talking, and rain couldn't care less about what I do.

"Get up if you want," the rain is saying, "but you'd be crazy to leave your warm bed for what I've got in store for you."

So I lie there on my back, entertaining myself with nonsense, not quite sure how soon a full bladder will triumph over sloth.

I scan the room in the half-light after having exhausted everything of interest on the ceiling. My jacket hangs from the back of a chair that matches the small, wooden desk well enough, but most of my clothes are in a pile on the floor where I left them last night.

World record holder Jim Ryun is running right at me in the photo I cut out of *Sports Illustrated* magazine and tacked on the wall at the foot of the bed. Next to him is a picture of the great Willie Mays following through with one of his powerful swings. It appears that the blur of the homerun ball he's just connected with will miss Ryun's head by mere inches. The champion miler is so focused that he doesn't seem to notice.

Willie Mays and the San Francisco Giants are my favorites. I was sick enough to stay home from school and watch them play in the 1962 World Series against the Yankees. Dad was working nights that week at Fire Department Station 21 on Phinney Ridge, so we watched a couple of day games together. He ate pickled pigs' feet straight out of a jar, and I sipped ginger ale through a straw trying to settle my stomach.

Next summer we'll have the Seattle Pilots playing at Sick's Stadium. I'll have a new favorite team, but nobody could ever surpass Willie as my favorite player. Too bad the Pilots will be in the American League so I won't be able to see Mays, Willie McCovey, Juan Marichal, and Gaylord Perry in person.

That's assuming I can find a ride to the ballpark down south on Rainier Avenue. *Mom won't be interested. I can't count on Dad. Oh, man … What am I going to do?*

My eyes move on to a poster of the Seattle SuperSonics. Thumbtacks are too obvious in each of the four corners.

I probably should have used Scotch tape.

The team has just finished their first season in the NBA thirty-three games behind the Division Champion St. Louis Hawks, but I don't care. I love my team and take pride in the fact that, as bad as they are, they're still better than the hapless San Diego Rockets.

I hit the sack early on game nights to catch Bob Blackburn's play-by-play of the second half. The clock radio has better sound, but usually I hunker down under the blankets and listen to the action through the earpiece on my nine-volt transistor radio, eyes closed, imagining the action on the court. Rookie center Bob Rule is my favorite player. Guard Walt Hazzard is a close second.

Two School Safety Patrol Certificates signed by Governor Dan Evans, one for fifth grade and one for sixth, hang next to the bedroom door from my days of stopping traffic at Cromwell Park. I didn't mind getting up a little early so that I could get to my assigned crosswalk in time for the rush of students walking to school in the morning. Besides, I also got the benefit of getting out of class early when I had the afternoon shift. And I was proud to carry the red STOP flag and wear the badge and the uniform of the Safety Patrol—white hard hat and red vest or yellow slicker, depending on the weather. But I'm in junior high now. This is kids' stuff, and I make up my mind that the certificates have to come down.

It's 9:15 a.m. and I don't feel any urgent need, biological or otherwise, to be up before *The Dick Van Dyke Show* reruns come on at ten thirty on Channel 5, followed by *Jeopardy!* with Art Fleming at eleven, so I make a plan then and there to doze to music for the next hour. I switch on the clock radio in time to catch the tail end of a song:

What's that you say, Mrs. Robinson
Joltin' Joe has left and gone away
Hey, hey, hey … hey, hey, hey

"Joltin' Joe," I say out loud in a low voice.

What a great nickname!

I try to imagine an action word like *joltin'* that goes with Gordon, but come up empty. Then *Flash Gordon* comes to mind, and I get excited for a second before remembering that name has already been taken.

The music fades and disc jockey Lan Roberts abruptly cuts

in to tell me something I already know. "That's this week's Fab-50 chart topper, 'Mrs. Robinson,' by Simon and Garfunkel. It's 9:17."

And then he cheerfully announces that it's time for a word from "our" sponsors.

I grouse to myself about the bad luck of tuning in just in time for a block of commercials—Phillips 66, followed by Olympia Beer, followed by Hamm's Beer. Hamm's has a catchy jingle played to the beat of Indian tom-toms:

From the land of sky-blue water
Comes the beer refreshing
Comes the beer refreshing
Hamm's

I wonder if Phillips 66 will ever change their name—after all it's 1968 already. And it seems a little early in the day to be doing beer ads, especially back-to-back by competing brands. I won't be twenty-one for another eight years and two months, but I'm already leaning toward buying Olympia when I'm old enough because the tom-toms on the Hamm's ad are catchy, but hokey. Besides, Dad drinks Oly and I like the stubby bottles that it comes in.

Then comes the KJR station identification with the distinctive chorus:

Kaay JAAY arr
Seeattlle
Chann-Nell ninetee-FIIVE

"We're back and it's time to check the stupid question hotline," Lan Roberts deadpans. "Today's question: How come we never see bald Indians?"

And before I can finish the thought, *come to think of it, I don't think I've ever seen a bald Indian*, the DJ is spinning his next forty-five, "Do you know the way to San Jose" by Dionne Warwick, and I'm tapping my foot under the covers:

Do you know the way to San Jose?
I've been away so long
I may go wrong and lose my way

I sleepily reminisce about one of the only real summer vacations I've ever been on. It was in 1961 and one of the stops was in San Jose to visit my Aunt Eleanor. Or was it Aunt Agnes? Or Aunt Agatha? Or Aunt Helen? Or Aunt Dorothy? Dad was the tenth of thirteen children, and I couldn't keep them all straight. Add in all the spouses, and there are twenty-four aunts and uncles to keep track of, excluding four more on Mom's side of the family.

No one seems to know the exact count of grandchildren on the Braun side, but the best guess is close to forty. I have first cousins older than my youngest aunt, and kids I used to play with at Grandma's house were more often than not first cousins once removed, whatever that means. I don't see that side of the family much anymore anyway except for maybe Uncle Walt or Aunt Margie and their kids on the rare occasions I happen to be visiting Dad in the South End. Uncle Albert, Aunt Rose, and their three children live just a few miles away over in Kenmore, but I haven't set eyes on any of them since my parents "tore up the sheets," as Dad would say.

Dionne Warwick's song fades out and Lan Roberts starts in, but I ignore him. I've still got San Jose on the brain.

The 1961 road trip to California on Highway 99 was a watershed event for the Shoreline branch of the Braun family. It represented a dividing line between the good times and the bad, between the time Mom thought there was a chance to save the marriage and the time after which Dad was gone. The two-week vacation became a reference point around which other memories were indexed. Ask Mom about something from the past, and she'll undoubtedly start by saying, "Well let's see, it was before the trip to California …" or "It must have been after the trip to California …"

I was five years old at the time, and the memories I have of the trip to California are real. I know the memories are real because Mom and Dad didn't take any photographs. Sometimes photos can confuse your memory: Do I really remember what I think I remember, or do I only think I remember because I've seen pictures?

The mental images I have of the trip aren't in any particular order in the pages of my mind. I can still see and smell the two-toned 1954 Ford sedan with a light-green body and a dark-green roof, four doors, bench seats, a three-on-the-tree, and a chrome jet plane hood ornament with two canvas water bags hanging from it. Luggage was securely strapped to top carriers on the roof of the car while we kids were left to rattle around in the backseat.

"Dad, how'd they make this?" I asked as we drove the car slowly and deliberately through the heart of a giant redwood tree.

"With a chainsaw," Dad said.

I remember being bothered by swarms of flies as we picnicked on a grassy hill in San Jose and how the adults, including Aunt Eleanor—or was it Aunt Agnes or Aunt Agatha or Aunt Helen or Aunt Dorothy?—held their drinks in one hand and fly swatters in the other. I remember that the night before our day at Disneyland was as exciting as the night before Christmas. And I remember going on the Dumbo ride with Dad in Fantasy Land. And how Mom got nauseous and spent time with her head in a bucket on the Submarine Voyage in Tomorrowland. And I remember that my Uncle George—or was it Uncle Jim or Uncle Fred or Uncle Harold?—wore an orange cap with the cartoon character Goofy printed above the supersized bill and how delighted I was when he gave it to me at the end of the day as a souvenir.

"Dad, why does the water way up the road always dry up before we get there?" I asked while speeding across the Mojave

Desert on a two-lane highway to see Uncle Ed—or was it Uncle Jake?—in Las Vegas.

"It's a mirage," Dad answered.

"He's touching me," Maureen whined.

"Cut it out," Dad said.

"She started it."

"And I'm going to finish it," Dad threatened.

"Dad, I've got to go to the bathroom."

"You're going to have to hold it."

"Dad, I want some ice cream."

"Later."

"Dad …"

"Shut up and go to sleep! All of you!"

My attention is diverted back to the present by the radio disc jockey as I lie there in bed. "Next up, it's the Ohio Express with 'Yummy, Yummy, Yummy!'"

Yummy, yummy, yummy
I got love in my tummy …

"Boy, that's a dumb song," I mutter under my breath. I then briefly consider tuning the dial to 1300 Kolorful KOL, only to conclude that changing stations takes more effort than it's worth.

Where was I? Oh yeah, the trip to California.

Mom's side of the family was easier to track. Grandma Wertz's parents, Mammo and Grandy, lived in Redwood City; Mom's dad's sister Pat in Berkley and Mom's sister Brownie in Merced. Brownie had already given me seven cousins as of 1961 and three more since. Add in Aunt Jeri's three kids in Guam—Uncle Ken was in the coast guard—and I had somewhere around fifty first cousins on both sides of the family combined.

I remember how disappointed I was when Dad and Grandy left me at the house in Redwood City one afternoon while they went to see Willie Mays play centerfield for the Giants at Candlestick Park. I remember playing "Sunny Side of the Street" over and over again by sticking a holey roll of paper in Aunt Pat's player piano and pumping the pedals maniacally until it drove Mom crazy. I remember asking Dad how the Chinese waiter would be able to understand us at a restaurant in San Francisco's Chinatown. "Watch and learn," Dad said just before ordering our meals in plain English.

Lan Roberts interrupts my thoughts again, this time to say, "This score just in: Us 31, them 7," followed by an Air West commercial: "We fly to small towns too" and an ad for Ball Park Franks: "They plump when you cook 'em."

I look at the clock and see that it's almost a quarter after ten. Not long now until I'll be getting up, so I run over the last hour in my head and rate the experience. "Mrs. Robinson" and "Do You Know the way to San Jose," great. "This Guy's in Love With You" by Herb Alpert, okay. "Yummy, Yummy, Yummy" by the Ohio Express, ick. "Angel of the Morning" by Merrilee Rush and the Turnabouts, not my cup of tea, but the song gets bonus points because she grew up in Shoreline like me. "The Look of Love" by Sergio Mendes and Brasil '66, nice. But they misspelled *Brasil* on the record jacket I saw at Woolworths, and they should update their name to Brazil '68.

And how about the new one by the Rolling Stones? "Jumpin' Jack Flash" is on its way to the top of the charts!

It's a gas! Gas! Ga-aa-aas!

Lan Roberts again: "We're back! It's ten after ten and here's the Rascals with 'A Beautiful Morning' on this fine, wet morning."

It's a beautiful mornin', ah
I think I'll go outside a while
And just smile

The Rolling Stones really woke me up, but the Rascals actually make me get up. I climb out of bed and open the curtains to see that the song belies the gray sky, but I don't care. School is out for the summer, which by definition makes it a beautiful morning. I wait until the song ends before shutting off the radio, strapping on my Timex, and pulling on a pair of Sears and Roebuck jeans from the pile on the floor.

It's quiet in the house as I make my way barefooted up the short hallway. Mom and Leslie are off to work already, and I assume Maureen is either in her room sleeping or reading. I'm figuring I'll see her sometime around noon when it occurs to me that, even though I've been listening to the radio for almost an hour, I didn't hear even one Beatles' song.

Not one Beatles' song in an hour?

I don't think that's ever happened before.

Paper Route Headlines

Fires Ravage Forest Lands in California

DC Police Evict 'Poor Marchers'

Stadium Site Choice Delayed

5 Copters Crash in Saigon Drive

Sirhan Postpones Plea

Johnson Calls for End of Nuclear Race

Airliner with 18 Aboard Hijacked to Cuba

Chapter 9

And So It Goes

I HAPPEN TO BE STANDING by the front window when I see Grandma Wertz pull up in her MG Magnette sedan. It's a temperamental British four-door that she got stuck with in the divorce from her strange second husband—a bald-headed Cosmo Spacely look-alike named Wilbur Wertz. "He had creepy eyes," I overheard Grandma say once. "I never should have married him in the first place."

"Grandma's here," I announce to the audience in my best Don Pardo imitation.

"Get your shoes on and get ready to go," Mom says as she walks in from the kitchen, drying her hands with a dish towel. "Leslie, do you want to come with us?"

"Sure," Leslie says. "I could use a break."

"Go where?" I ask.

"I told you we're going to have a picnic on Camano Island."

Oh, yeah. I forgot.

"It looks like it's going to rain," I say.

"Don't be such a pessimist," Mom replies. "The weathermen are never right."

"How far is it?"

"A couple of hours."

"A couple of hours up and back, or a couple hours up and a couple hours back?"

"We're in no hurry. We'll be gone maybe five or six hours."

Six hours!

"I call dibs on one of the doors," I shout in the nick of time.

"I want a door this time," Maureen whines.

"Gordon, you're sitting in the middle," Mom says in a way that isn't exactly a command, but is clearly nonnegotiable.

"I don't want to sit on the hump. Why do I have to sit on the hump?"

"Because it's the gentlemanly thing to do," Mom says as Maureen snickers.

Now I get it. "Gentlemanly" is akin to "ladies first." There's no way to win once the ladies first card has been played.

Grandma puts a picnic basket in the trunk of Mom's Valiant and gets in the passenger seat with a bag full of knitting. Leslie sits in the rear behind the driver, and I climb in on the other side.

"Move over," Maureen says to me.

"I am over."

"Mom, Gordon's being a jerk again!"

"Gordon slide over," Mom says.

So I do. I move over a quarter of an inch while Maureen crowds in.

"You're such a jerk."

"I am not."

"Move over!"

I notice that Maureen hasn't locked the door, so I reach past her and push down the button.

"We wouldn't want the door to fly open and have you tumble out into a ditch," I say.

"Very funny."

Yes, very funny. I'm a funny guy. And as all self-respecting funny guys know, you should never take a joke too far. So I move over to give Maureen room to breathe.

It's as if Mom reads my mind about giving Maureen room to breathe because she promptly lights a cigarette; the car fills with smoke and now no one can breathe. My sisters turn their door cranks and crack their windows to vent the smoke and let in some cool fresh air.

Mom backs down the driveway, and we head up Second Avenue. A German shepherd is standing in the middle of the street staring straight at our car like he's challenging us to a game of chicken. He saunters off to the side of the road just as we reach the Baileys' house.

I look at my watch as we wait to turn left into traffic at 185th.

One minute down. Five hours and fifty-nine minutes to go.

We make the turn, go one block, and miss the stoplight at First Avenue. Just for grins, I start to sing "Light My Fire" by the Doors under my breath and tap my feet rhythmically as we wait.

Come on, baby, light my fire
Come on, baby, light my fire
Try to set the night on fire

"Gordon, quit kicking the seat," Mom orders.

"Sorry."

I sit there looking straight ahead as we move west on 185th, bobbing my noggin to the music in my head. Then I look to my left and give Leslie a big smile. She gives me a big smile back. I look to my right and give Maureen a grin with my eyes crossed and my tongue hanging out.

"Ha ha ha," Maureen says sarcastically. "Stop looking at me!"

Mom is a white-knuckle driver and avoids the interstate whenever possible. Since we're heading north today, we'll be turning right just past Dunn Lumber onto Aurora. The old highway peters out for a while north of Everett, and she'll be forced to merge slowly and reluctantly onto I-5. Until then, it will be forty-five miles an hour, tops, with stoplights every half mile.

We take a free right onto the four-lane road, and Grandma opines, "The speed limit might be forty-five miles an hour, but I think everyone should go a little slower just to be safe."

I can hear the *clickety-clack* of Grandma Wertz's knitting needles over the road noise. She is a human knitting and purling machine the way she cranks out row after row. The ball of yarn dances on the seat next to her as it unwinds, getting smaller with every stitch.

"What are you working on now, Grandma?"

"I'm knitting a hat for Lennie," she says in reference to my cousin Leonard.

"What will you work on after the hat is done?"

"A matching set of mittens," she replies.

Good to know. I can expect a stocking cap and mittens for Christmas now that the gift theme of the year has been revealed.

Grandma glances up from her work. "I'd rather fight than switch," she says without warning at the sight of a Tareyton cigarette billboard.

Clickety-clack. Clickety-clack.

"Road work ahead," she warns.

"I see it Mom, you can relax," my mom says.

Clickety-clack. Clickety-clack.

Grandma then begins to ramble nonstop about family news. First, it's Aunt Gladys this. Then it's Gladys Marie that. Harold just got out of the hospital. Barton is doing fine. Lennie hit a homer. Jeri got a new job. So-and-so is getting married and yakity-yak had a baby.

I think Harold is Grandma Wertz's brother, which makes him Mom's uncle—not to be confused with my Uncle Harold, who is married to my father's sister, my Aunt Eleanor. Or is it Aunt Agnes or Aunt Agatha or Aunt Helen or Aunt Dorothy?

Clickety-clack. Clickety-clack.

Grandma falls silent for a brief few seconds because she's counting stitches, but we know she's not done talking, not by a long shot. We know what's coming next. And sure enough, the one-sided conversation she's been having turns into a slow burn about her supervisor at the State Liquor Control Board warehouse on East Marginal Way where she works. For a full ten minutes, she fills us in on all the petty indignities that Gerry Garcia has subjected her to. "That GERRY makes me SOOO mad," she says, her voice quivering, when she is finally ready to let it go.

This is our cue in the back seat to silently mouth the words "That GERRY makes me SOOO mad" with raised eyebrows and upturned palms. Making fun of Grandma is a good way to help pass the miles.

Clickety-clack. Clickety-clack.

"Put a tiger in your tank."

"Only you can prevent forest fires."

Clickety-clack. Clickety-clack.

"Slug Bug!" Maureen hollers at the sight of a Volkswagen Beetle. And then without missing a beat, she punches me in the arm.

"Ow!"

"You snooze you lose," Maureen says.

As I rub my bicep, the stench of rotten eggs fills the air as we approach the pulp and paper mill in Everett.

"Who cut the cheese?" Maureen asks playfully so that everyone can hear. Punching me in the arm has obviously improved her mood.

I lean forward and stage whisper into Grandma's ear, "Grandma, did you cut the cheese?"

"That's not me," Grandma giggles. "It must be your mother."

Mom shakes her head while focusing on the road. Just as

we're about to merge onto the freeway north of Everett, I see horses grazing in a field next to the road.

"Grandma, did you ride a horse to school?"

"No, but I remember the ice man making house-to-house deliveries in a horse-drawn cart."

There is the wispy white stripe of a contrail high in the sky. "Grandma, have you ever flown in an airplane?"

"Once, in a 707 to Hawaii to visit Barton."

"How was it?"

"I had a grand time. You know, Mama used to say that if man were meant to fly, he'd have been born with wings."

"Mama?"

"Mammo was my mama."

"Oh, yeah. And Grandy is your papa."

"That's right," Grandma says. "Papa is Grandy to you, but Papa to me."

There is a mile-long freight train off in the distance. "Grandma, would you rather ride in the engine or in the caboose of a train?"

"Given the choice between the caboose and one of those newfangled diesel engines, I'll take the caboose. But if it was a steam locomotive like when I was a girl, I'd sooner be up front."

"Like that old steam locomotive at the zoo?"

"Yes, like the one at the zoo."

"Why?"

"Oh, I don't know. Just because, I guess."

"I'd rather ride in the caboose."

"Why?" Grandma asks.

"Just because," I say. Two can play the just-because game.

The honest answer to why I'd prefer to ride in the caboose is that Mom used to sing me a song when I was small called "Little Red Caboose."

Little red caboose, chug, chug, chug
Little red caboose, chug, chug, chug

Little red caboose behind the train, train, train, train

A long silence ensues once Grandma is out of A-material, and I can't think of any more penetrating questions. Mom is hunched over the steering wheel, going five under the speed limit and nervously glances in the rearview mirror.

"That jerk," Mom mumbles as cars whoosh by us on our left in the two fast lanes. I peak over my shoulder to see a tailgater flashing his high beams at us.

"Hey Mom, maybe you should step on it," I suggest.

Grandma has stopped knitting and seems to be dozing off. She looks peaceful, and I imagine a cartoon thought balloon over her head filled with *ZZZZZZ*s. Maureen and Leslie seem perfectly content to just watch the world go by from their window seats.

I look at my Timex.

One hour and eight minutes down. Four hours and fifty-two minutes to go.

I think the expression is "Desperate times call for desperate measures," so I begin to sing.

Ninety-nine bottles of beer on the wall
Ninety-nine bottles of beer,
Take one down and pass it around
Ninety-eight bottles of beer on the wall

I pause and look to Leslie and then Maureen. Grandma opens her eyes. And then, in unison, the whole family joins in.

Ninety-eight bottles of beer on the wall
Ninety-eight bottles of beer,
Take one down and pass it around
Ninety-seven bottles of beer on the wall

And so it goes until raindrops begin to pitter-patter on the windshield. Mom fumbles for the wipers and the quintet falls silent with ninety-five bottles of beer still on the wall.

"I can't believe it's going to rain on our picnic," Mom moans.

"I can," I say.

Paper Route Headlines

2 Men, 1 With Pistol, Rob Northgate Store of $5000

U.S., Russia Plan Missile-Curb Talks

Massive B-52 Raids Hit North Vietnam

Troops Wait Out Red Barrage
Then Throw Back Big Assault

Wing Failure in TFX Test Revealed

West Seattle Husband Slays Wife, Man
and Kills Himself

Man with Shotgun Robs Renton-Area
Bank of $5,432

Lumber Yard, Laundry Burn

Marines Win 8-Day Battle for Hill 689

Chapter 10

Quite a Sight

"WHAT DO YOU want to do?"

"I don't know. What do you want to do?"

"I don't know."

It's not quite nine thirty on Wednesday morning, and I'm sitting in John Ryan's living room. I started the day with peanut butter on toast and then decided to skip the *Dick Van Dyke Show* and *Jeopardy!* to hop on my bike for the uphill ride to my friend's house on Ashworth Avenue. Now we're going through the normal back and forth required to figure out what to do with the rest of the day.

"I've got until four, five at the latest, before I have to get down to the shack."

"We could go down to the school and climb up on the roof."

"We were just up there last week."

Climbing up a spindly cedar tree growing next to Room 3 at Cromwell Park Elementary School to access the flat tar roof is a standard got-nothing-else-to-do activity. Nothing but wide-open space to run around on, twenty feet up in the air. The view of the playfield and surrounding neighborhood is spectacular.

Plus, as of last week, there were still a bunch of brightly-colored playground balls lying around up there from when kids accidentally or purposely kicked them onto the roof during recess. Why Mr. Pollock, the school janitor, hasn't cleared off the roof now that school has been out for the better part of a month is something of a mystery.

John and I like to gather up as many of the rubber balls as we can find, chuck them off the roof all at once, and then watch them bounce and roll around randomly on the asphalt below. It's quite a sight. When we're done, we shimmy down the cedar tree, play a few games of two-man foursquare, and throw the balls at each other in a scaled down game of soak 'em before punting or dropkicking them back up onto the roof.

"How about a bike ride?"

"Where to?"

"I don't care."

"Wait a minute, I've got something to show you," John says, changing the subject. He disappears into the hallway and comes back two minutes later with some kind of electrical device that looks like a ray gun with a flared barrel.

"What is it?"

"I don't know, I found it in my mom's dresser. It's weird," John says as he plugs it in and turns it on.

The ray gun makes a humming noise.

"Watch this," John says. "It's impossible to put this thing on your nose without sneezing."

He puts the cone-shaped barrel of the ray gun on his nose, and ten seconds later, he lets go with a gigantic sneeze.

"Here, you try it."

The ray gun is vibrating like crazy in my hands as I place the flared tip of the barrel over my nose, or the old "snot locker" as Dad calls it. Ten seconds later, I let go with a monumental sneeze like John.

"Gesundheit."

"This is weird," I say, handing the thing back to John, ready to get back to the problem at hand. Time is wasting.

"So, what do you want to do?"

"I don't know."

"We could build a log raft," I say as an inside joke about last summer's disaster at Haller Lake when John nearly went down with the ship.

"Very funny," John responds. "We could always jump off the roof of your house, you know."

Our Huckleberry Finn rafting dreams had been dashed by a poorly designed watercraft featuring hunks of firewood nailed to a sheet of plywood. Building that raft took the combined genius of two guys that didn't know what they were doing. But jumping off the roof of my house was my lamebrained idea. It never occurred to me to ask a buddy to join in.

"I'll jump if you jump," I say, even though I'm bluffing. There is no way I'm ever doing that again. And based on what I had told John, I don't think he'll accept the dare.

Last summer, I was lying on the couch with nothing to do, as per usual, when I found myself thinking about *Ripcord*, a show about skydiving starring Ken Curtis as Jim Buckley and Larry Pennell as Ted McKeever. Every week these guys found themselves in predicaments requiring them to jump out of their single-engine Cessna, maybe to rescue someone or to catch a criminal. My favorite episode involved finding a box of volatile nitroglycerin vials hidden onboard the plane. They jumped with it clutched to their chests to save the plane rather than shove it out the door for fear of hurting innocents on the ground.

After careful consideration and impeccable logic, I convinced myself that the landing impact experienced by a grown man jumping ten or twelve thousand feet *with* a parachute would be about the same as an eleven-year-old boy jumping ten or twelve feet off the roof of a Shoreline rambler *without* a parachute.

So I got a ladder out of the garage, climbed up onto the roof, scrambled up over the peak, and then eased my way down the other side of the roof to a spot just above the bathroom window.

I remember taking a deep breath.

It was a beautiful day. Blue skies above. Green grass below. A dog barked off in the distance. The dull roar of the freeway in the background brought to mind the sound of ocean waves crashing on the beach at Westport.

"Don't forget to tuck and roll like the guys on *Ripcord*," I reminded myself.

Another deep breath.

"Are you a man or a mouse?"

And then …

"Geronimo!"

For the briefest of moments, I hung in the air, suspended in time and space like Wile E. Coyote in a *Road Runner* cartoon.

And then, just like Wile E. Coyote, I realized this was all a terrible mistake!

While plummeting to earth, my inner voice screamed, *Tuck and roll you fool! Tuck and roll!*

I hit the ground. A colossal shockwave traveled through my ankles, knees, hips, back, and neck. My jaw snapped shut, making my teeth rattle. I rolled once. I rolled twice. Just before completing a third full revolution, I came to a stop, resting on my left side.

My mind was like a TV set just after someone pulls the plug or clicks off the power. All was black except for a dot of light in the middle of the screen. The light brightened, and details filled in as the electricity began to flow again to the vacuum tubes in my head and the circuits to my extremities. It wouldn't be long before my body would register the consequences of my reckless and ill-considered act.

"Jesus Christ!"

I lay in the fetal position for a long time before turning over onto my back and squinting up into the midday sun. I wiggled my toes, flexed my knees, and moved my jaw from side to side.

Everything was sore, but everything seemed to be working.

I got up and felt like Amos McCoy, played by Walter Brennan on *The Real McCoys*, as I hobbled around to the front of the house. "Dag nabbit," I whispered to myself in a West Virginny accent while shaking my head, because that is exactly what the gammy old hillbilly would have said and done after just such a misadventure.

Now what?

I could only conclude that the puzzlingly painful outcome was the result of not enough tucking and too much rolling.

"Practice makes perfect," I reminded myself.

"Are you a man or a mouse?" I muttered.

If Jim Buckley and Ted McKeever can do it, then I can too.

So I climbed back up the ladder and made my way across the roof. Without hesitation, without giving myself time to chicken out, I jumped again from the exact same spot!

"Geronimo … oh … oh nooooo!"

While plummeting to earth, I realized again that this was all a big mistake.

"Tuck and roll, dag nabbit! Tuck and roll!"

The second jump was more excruciating than my initial attempt because I still hadn't completely recovered from my earlier injuries and because I blew the landing again. It turned out that finding the perfect balance between tucking and rolling was a lot tougher than I thought it would be.

Maybe I'm not cut out to be a skydiver. Or maybe the landing impact of an eleven-year-old boy jumping ten or twelve feet off the roof of a Shoreline rambler *without* a parachute is different from the landing impact experienced by a grown man jumping ten or twelve thousand feet *with* a parachute.

I pick up the pillow sitting next to me on John's living room couch and throw it in his face.

"So, do you want to go on a bike ride?" I ask.

"Where to?" he says as I duck and use my forearm to block his return shot.

"Aurora Village?"

"We do that all the time."

"Northgate?"

"Maybe, but the hill on Meridian going up to 145th is a killer."

"Green Lake?"

"That's further than Northgate."

"Yeah, but we've never done it."

"All right. Green Lake."

• • •

IT'S A TOUGH six-and-a-half-mile bike ride to Green Lake from John's house, but the worst part is almost over. It has to be close to eighty degrees, and I'm sweating like a pig as I approach the top of the Meridian Avenue hill at 145th Street. Only a quitter would dismount and push their bike on foot, and I'm no quitter. The trick is to pretend it doesn't hurt as much as it does.

I'm standing up on the pedals of the Schwinn, giving it all I've got, astonished that a bicycle can stay upright when the wheels are turning so slowly.

"Stick with it, man. You can't let John beat you to the top," I say to myself between puffs of breath.

You've got a green light!

You can make it.

Almost there.

"Goddammit!"

I squeeze both the front and back brakes simultaneously, dismount hurriedly, and wait impatiently for the light to change. Traffic rushes by in both directions on 145th while John—walking and pushing his bike like a quitter—eats into my lead.

I can't believe it.

My friend times the green light perfectly, mounts his bike before I can get rolling and lucks into being the first to cross the city limits into Seattle proper. Art would have given me the finger at this point, but John isn't that kind of guy. He just keeps facing straight ahead, pumping the pedals methodically on his Raleigh three-speed.

I catch up in no time and pull alongside.

"How you doing?"

"Okay."

A horn blows behind us. *Wait a second … that's not a car horn, it's a city transit bus!* I hit both brakes again and try to tuck in behind John to get out of the way, but his reflex is to slow down too. My front tire strikes his rear wheel, and we both find ourselves in the gravel shoulder trying to stay upright.

The bus roars by, leaving behind a lingering cloud of diesel exhaust.

Time slows down.

I begin my descent into the ditch. Blackberry brambles and broken beer bottles lie dead ahead. "This is going to hurt," an objective and remarkably calm inner voice whispers in my ear.

The front tire bumps and bucks down the lumpy bank, and I'm like a rodeo cowboy hanging onto a Brahman bull. Through the low spot in the bottom of the dry ditch I careen, stopping instantly when the wheel rams the steep slope on the other side. With the jolt, my body pitches forward over the handle bars, but my grip holds, and I crash back into the saddle.

I'm sitting upright in the bicycle seat and get a feeling similar to what happens in that first split second after leaping from the roof of a Shoreline rambler. Here I am again, suspended in time and space. In less than a heartbeat, I'll find out if my fate is to fall over sideways into the busted glass and sticker bushes, or if I'll stay upright long enough to see if my feet will reach the low spot in the ditch before my balls get crushed by the center bar of the bike.

My legs aren't long enough!

I'd have screamed except I can't breathe, and I'd have puked except my testicles are wedged into my esophagus. I somehow manage to swing my right leg over the seat, drop the bike, and crawl up the bank to lie in a fetal position in the gravel. My right ear is pressed against the ground, and based on the rumbling energy being transmitted through the earth, I know another major vehicle is coming. I hear the roar and smell the distinct odor of diesel exhaust as a fully laden dump truck passes by.

"Are you okay?" John asks, bending over me.

I open one eye and notice he is trying not to smirk.

I don't hold the smirk against him. I would smirk too if the roles were reversed. There is something inherently funny about a guy getting it in the nuts.

The pain is beginning to subside, and I have the presence of mind to say "Yes, I'm just dandy" in a high-pitched Mickey Mouse voice, which gives John permission to fully express himself. He lets go with a belly laugh before climbing down into the ditch to retrieve my bicycle.

I stand up and dust myself off as he hands over the Schwinn. No obvious damage has been done to the bike. I take a few tentative steps and then a few more before gingerly swinging my leg over the seat. It only hurts when I push down on the pedal with my right leg.

Now it's a little better.

Better still.

I'm going to be okay.

• • •

WE CONTINUE DOWN Meridian Avenue on the way to Green Lake, past Ingraham High School and Haller Lake—scene of last summer's rafting debacle. We see traffic signs pointing in the direction of Northwest Hospital and then pedal along the backside of the expansive Evergreen Washelli Cemetery on our right.

I can't resist inflicting one of Dad's dumb jokes on my friend:

"Hey John," I yell up ahead.

"What?" he yells back over his shoulder as we coast down the grade.

"Do you know how many dead people are buried here?"

"Huh? No."

"All of them," I shout over the rush of the wind and the whoosh of a passing car.

Once we get across Northgate Way, it's a short ride to the modern, low-slung Allstate Insurance building coming up on the left. Mom is in there somewhere working away. The road then takes us uphill by the future site of what is supposed to be North Seattle Community College, now under construction, where we stop to catch our breath while watching earth movers and cement trucks for a few minutes. Finally, the arterial jogs over to Wallingford Avenue at Ninety-Second Street, and it's an easy downhill stretch to the corner grocery across the street from Green Lake.

John and I dismount, put down our kickstands, and step inside the store to pick out two bottles of Coke from the refrigerated case in the back. Standing next to our bikes parked on the sidewalk, we see the sights and hear the sounds of a summer day at the lake. The sun glistens off the rippling water, and children scream and splash in the wading pool just across the way. After hanging around long enough to finish our pop, the two of us go back inside to get our three-cent bottle deposits back.

I look at my friend and belch. John doesn't miss a beat and belches right back. The cashier just stands there, shaking her head in disgust.

"Now what?"

"I don't know, what do you want to do?"

"I don't know."

"Let's head over to the Westside bathing beach."

It's a short ride on a gravel trail along the lake. Once there, we put down our kickstands again and buy grape-flavored snow cones at the concession stand for fifteen cents apiece. Grandma Wertz would call the price highway robbery, and it seems steep to me too for what is essentially Kool-Aid and crushed ice, but at least it's a decent size for the money. John and I sit on a park bench outside the brick bathhouse watching kids jump from the high dive on the raft straight in front of us. We discretely ogle the high school girls sunbathing in their bikinis.

"Boy, she's cute."

"I'll say."

"Want to take a dip?"

"I don't know."

"Well, what then?"

"I don't know. What do you want to do?"

"Let's take a dip."

We peel off our shirts and shoes, leaving us in just our cutoff jeans. John is a bit taller than me, but just as skinny and just as pasty white. We walk down to the water's edge, past the girls in bikinis, hoping to catch their eye. No luck. Of course it is wishful thinking that sun-bronzed, teenage goddesses would be interested in pale faces like us, but that doesn't make it any less disappointing.

My friend takes two steps into the water, dives in, and stays under until he emerges on the other side of the ropes. Coming up for air, John heads out to the raft using a nice overhand crawl. He is almost an Eagle Scout and has already earned his merit badge in swimming.

I took a couple of swimming lessons at the Kenmore pool and feel reasonably confident that I could save my life in an emergency, but that's about it. While John jumps off the high dive, I stand in chest-deep water, fart around, and keep an eye on our bikes and the girls in bikinis.

John's dad died a few years back, before he moved up from Shelton for the start of fifth grade. He's lucky. Unlike me, he has a good reason for why his father isn't around. There is no shame, and there aren't any secrets to keep behind his front door. Having a dead dad is easier to explain than having a drunk dad. Coming from a broken home is something you don't want the world to know about.

Why can't I just have a normal father and a normal family like on TV?

Mrs. Ryan is a single mom with four kids like my mom. Unlike my mom though, John's mother works full time and still manages to get out in the world. According to John, she goes to PTA meetings, is involved with a monthly book club, joined a worthwhile sounding group called Parents Without Partners, got her three boys involved in Scouts, and signed them up with the Big Brothers program so that they would have positive adult male role models.

"Hey Mom, why don't you give Parents Without Partners a try?" I had asked her once with visions of having a good-looking, rich guy take us away from all this.

"I'm never doing that again. Ever," she replied coolly.

Nothing ever came of my suggestions that Cub Scouts and Little League might be fun either, so I don't even bother to ask about stuff like that anymore.

What's the point?

My mother's life philosophy is something I've learned to live with even though I'm beginning to think it's crazy: "I don't want to belong to any club that will accept people like me as a member." She says this often enough that you'd think she made it up, but I learned on *Jeopardy!* that it's a Groucho Marx line.

John is back from his swim.

"Ready to head for home?"

"We just got here."

"Well what do you want to do?"

"What do *you* want to do?"

"Not this again."

"How about the Aqua Theater?"

Back on our bikes, we drip dry as we peddle south along the lakeshore trail. More pretty girls. Moms with kids in strollers. Canoes and paddleboats cruise by on our left. Aurora Avenue comes up behind us on our right and runs parallel to our path for a block or two before veering off. Traffic noise momentarily assaults our ears.

On the other side of the highway across from us is the aptly named Twin Teepees Restaurant. I've never been in there, but I've been by it a million times on the way to Grandma Braun's house. As little kids, we'd whoop like Indians and duck from imaginary arrows being shot at us by savages hiding inside.

"Hey John, where the Hekawi?" I ask.

My friend smiles and nods his head as a way of acknowledging my reference to the directionally-challenged, lost tribe of Indians on the show *F Troop*.

"You're full of them today," John says.

"Where the Hekawi?" is a running joke good for a laugh pretty much anytime.

Right up there with "Sorry about that, Chief" from *Get Smart*. And Artie Johnson's line, "Want a Walnetto?" from *Laugh-In*.

No surprise, there is nothing happening at the Aqua Theater this time of day. It's locked up tighter than a drum and, strangely, not at all how I remember it. It's a sorry sight to see, what with the graffiti, the rusty cyclone fence, and broken pavement. Quite a contrast from when I saw the Aqua Follies here during the 1962 World's Fair. A memorable night under the stars—Esther Williams-style synchronized swimming. Clowns doing pratfalls from the tower into the lake. Cornball comedians. A few songs. A little soft shoe.

"Now what?"

"I don't know."

"Don't you ever have any ideas?"

"What do you want to do?"

"Want a Walnetto?"

"Ha ha ha."

"Let's go to the zoo."

Lower Woodland Park ball fields and tennis courts are across Green Lake Way. From there it's uphill through the trees to three arched pedestrian bridges over Aurora Avenue. The bridges connect Lower Woodland Park with Upper Woodland Park where the zoo is located. The need to distinguish between the upper and lower portions of the park and the need for foot bridges has to do with the fact that city fathers built a six-lane highway through the otherwise pristine place during the early years of the Depression. As they say, you can't stop progress.

We pause to take a rest on the northern-most bridge, shoot the bull and spit on cars passing by below. Then it's through the open gate to the zoo where admission is free. Giraffes on the left, buffalo on the right. Snowy owls, bald eagles, ostriches, and peacocks. Lions. Tigers. Bears of all kinds. Elephants from Asia and Africa.

Cotton candy for twenty-five cents is high, but we spring for some of the pink fluffy stuff anyway. After spending so much on food and beverages, we elect not to go on any of the rides in the small amusement park adjacent to the zoo. Besides, I've been on rides with John before, and I have to say, it's not that much fun. He is a wild man when it comes to maximizing the spin on rides designed to make you throw up.

So today we just hang around for a while watching other kids having a good time getting sick. And then we wander over to look at the rusty steam locomotive and coal car frozen in time on a few feet of track to nowhere: Engine #1246 with the Great Northern Railway mountain goat logo painted on the cab. Standing there with my cotton candy, I picture Grandma Wertz as a girl riding up front in the cab.

There is nothing but a car tire dangling from a rope in one of the glassed-in cells at the primate house. This is where Bobo the Gorilla lived for fifteen years before he died last winter. People talk in hushed, reverent tones all around us out of respect for the dead ape. If you're from around these parts, you know the story of Bobo: taken from his mother in Africa and brought to America when he was two weeks old, raised just like any ordinary child by a couple in Anacortes until his natural wildness and superhuman strength couldn't be contained. Then it was off to the zoo in Seattle where he entertained young and old and where he frustrated the same folks by failing to mate with Fifi, a female brought in specially for him.

For me, the idea of Bobo was always better than the reality of Bobo. He might have been animated and fun to watch when I wasn't around, but the most I ever saw him do was suck on an orange and stare blankly at the crowd watching him from the other side of the glass. He mostly looked bored and lonely. I'd always enter the primate house excited and hopeful whenever I came for a visit, thinking that this would be the time that Bobo finally put on a show for me. Every time I would leave feeling let down and a little depressed.

Today is no different.

Just an empty cell and a tire swing.

Poor old Bobo.

• • •

JOHN AND I ARE walking our bicycles down the grassy hill heading back toward the ball fields at Lower Woodland Park when we hear the sound of a *clink* on the other side of a cluster of maple trees.

Then another *clink*.

And a few seconds later, yet another.

The noise is coming from the general direction of where we're headed anyway, so we don't have to go very far out of our way to take a peek at what is causing the noise. It turns out to be just a couple of old men playing horseshoes at one of the park's courts.

"What do you think?"

"Kinda looks like fun."

"Yeah, I think so too."

We watch one of the men take careful aim and then let it fly.

Clink.

"That's a leaner," he says to his partner.

"Let's see what I can do about that," the other old guy says as he gets ready to throw, holding the horseshoe at chest level and closing one eye while taking careful aim.

I get an idea …

"Maybe my great-grandfather is lawn bowling today."

"What do you mean?" John replies.

"I've told you about Grandy. My Grandma Wertz's father lawn bowls here."

"Huh? Where?"

"I don't know, but it's around here somewhere. I think it's on the other side of that picnic shelter," I say, nodding toward a rustic-looking log structure with no side walls and a moss-covered roof.

Before long, we squeeze through a gap in a laurel hedge to find ourselves standing on the wrong side of a chain-link fence looking in on the immaculately maintained bowling greens. Small groups of men, dressed in white like cricket players I've seen on the *Wide World of Sports*, take turns rolling something resembling croquet balls that are squished in slightly on both sides. In the hands of an expert, the unusually shaped balls can be made to follow a curved line toward the target.

I know a little bit about croquet and croquet balls since I'm the second-best player in my family. The best player is Grandy, and he shows us no mercy when we set up wickets and stakes in the front yard. Going back to when we were just little kids, he would take glee in whacking our balls into the flower beds at the far end of the yard. In fact, Grandy was kind of a jerk about it. I'm hoping to get even with him someday. I'm still getting better, and he is just getting older, so I figure time is on my side.

When we visit him at Grandma's, where he shares her rented house on Queen Anne Hill, Grandy looks feeble, generally ignores us, focuses on his crossword puzzle, and acts as if he is going deaf. His long silences only provoke Grandma into talking louder and shriller to get his attention until he begrudgingly acknowledges her. She speculates that his hearing problem has to do with absentmindedly poking the eraser end of a pencil in his ear when he is cogitating over a particularly vexing crossword clue.

Croquet is about the only time I ever see Grandy get excited about anything, especially since Mammo died a couple years back. Ernest and Lotta Brown—that's Brown pronounced *brown*, not Braun pronounced *brown*, because they're on Mom's side of the family—celebrated their sixty-third wedding anniversary not long before her death, and they got their pictures in the *Seattle Times* that day.

"Wed in Paris and honeymooned in Rome back around the turn of the century," they used to say.

"That's Paris, Kentucky, and Rome, Indiana."

Ha ha ha.

I scan the lawns and groups of men through the fence, and sure enough, there is my great-grandfather. He looks very British in his lawn bowling attire, more alert than I had grown to expect from an eighty-seven-year-old man, and obviously comfortable and relaxed in his surroundings. I'm pleasantly surprised to see him roll back his head to laugh out loud, cuss, and slap a buddy on the back after a bad shot.

"Yeah, yeah. It's your turn Ernie. Let's see if you can do any better."

Grandy takes his shot and shrugs his shoulders afterward. No one gives him any grief or praise, so it's apparently a decent, if not particularly remarkable, effort.

He finally sees John and me watching from the sidelines, and his face lights up. I've never seen him smile like this before. He waves and comes over to chat.

"It's good to see you! What brings you by today?"

"We're just out for a ride."

"You're a long way from home. What have you got there? A Schwinn?"

"Yep."

"How about you? What's that you have there?" he asks John.

"It's a Raleigh."

"Raleigh? Never heard of it, but it looks like a fine machine."

Grandy's friends wander over and he introduces them one by one, but the names go in one ear and out the other without registering.

"I'd shake your hand, but I'm not about to climb that fence," one of the men jokes so that everyone laughs.

"They're a couple of fine-looking boys," another man says, and everyone nods in agreement.

"Good thing neither one of them takes after you, Ernie," another one of the old guys wisecracks.

Ha ha ha.

It's heartening to see that even old guys can be regular guys. Up to that moment, I had never even thought to think it was possible.

I can't help but notice that Grandy hasn't asked anyone to repeat themselves even once. He seems to be tracking the conversation just fine. I begin thinking that maybe his alleged hearing problem might be a ruse—a convenient excuse to ignore his daughter, granddaughter, and great-grandchildren.

For a brief second, my feelings are hurt.

Why would he want to tune us out?

Just as quickly, I let it go and give him the benefit of the doubt. I can't condone it, but I think I get it. Sometimes regular guys just need to be left alone in their thoughts.

Paper Route Headlines

U.S. Marines Attack Red Stronghold

Nigerians, Biafrans Seek End to Civil War

Home Mail Deliveries May Go to 4 a Week

Four Cut Ceiling and Flee County Jail

Braman Not Alarmed by Report on Police

House OKs 'Loophole' in Gun Controls

B-52s Pound Vietcong Supply Line

Paroled Felon Was Issued King County Gun Permit

Reds Ambush Marine Tank Column

Czech Revolt Near, Say Russ

Chapter 11

I am I

ROBBIE TOOK HER record collection with her when she moved out, so the pickings are slim. As much as I like my three albums, *Meet the Beatles!*, *The Doors*, and *The Monkees*, I've listened to them so often that I've resorted to playing Leslie's girly stuff like Elvis's soundtrack from the movie *Blue Hawaii* and "Honey" by Bobby Goldsboro. Beyond that, all that is left are the soundtracks from a few Broadway musicals that we kids have given Mom over the last several Christmases.

It's clearly time for me to break down and buy some new music. My only hesitance is that I like having money in the bank more than I like spending it. Laying out $2.99 plus tax for an LP at Valu-Mart on Aurora Avenue or at Woolworths in Aurora Village is not a decision to be taken lightly, even though I have $206.27 from my paper route on deposit at Greenwood Savings and Loan.

Sergeant Pepper's Lonely Hearts Club Band is a year old, but still worth picking up. I love the drum solo from "In-A-Gadda-Da-Vida" by Iron Butterfly, so that is a for-sure buy. Creedence Clearwater Revival and Steppenwolf play some great stuff too. Maybe I'll just buy the forty-fives of "Suzie Q."

and "Born to Be Wild" instead of whole albums to save a couple of bucks.

When no one is around I like to sing along to whatever is playing, and I know every track from all five go-to albums by heart—even the skips and the pops. I don't generally need props, but it's not out of the question to use a wooden spoon or pancake turner from the kitchen as a fake mike or a broom as my pretend guitar. The tunes range from cheerful and upbeat to dark and edgy to just plain sappy, so I emote as appropriate: come hither smiles, frowns of heartbreak, arched eyebrows, mock tears, hip wiggling, toe tapping, and finger snapping. My vocal range is limited and off-key more often than not, and my voice cracks if I really try to belt out the high notes, but I don't care about any of my shortcomings as a singer. I belt it out pretty much any time I've got the house to myself.

There are a few minutes to kill before heading down to the newspaper shack, so I decide to put the soundtrack from the Broadway cast of *Man of La Mancha* on the turntable for the first time to broaden my horizons. I usually go to my room whenever Mom or Leslie play show tunes like *Man of La Mancha*, *Camelot*, *The Sound of Music*, and *West Side Story*, but I'm curious since it came up on *Jeopardy!* the other day:

> Category: BROADWAY MUSICALS FOR $30
> Answer: HE DREAMED THE IMPOSSIBLE DREAM
> Question: WHO IS THE MAN OF LA MANCHA OR DON QUIXOTE?

The front door and the dining room window are open, and I can feel the cross breeze as I remove the vinyl disc from its jacket. Holding the LP by the edges, I blow off the dust like I'm putting out candles on a birthday cake. The record spins when I hit the power switch, and I luck out by placing the needle perfectly into the leading-edge groove on my first try. The speakers crackle for a short second and the overture for *Man of La Mancha* begins.

I stretch out on our old couch with the stuffing sticking out in places, examining the all-yellow record jacket with caricatures of a knight, a monk, and a wench printed on it.

"That's wench not winch," I chuckle while thinking about Dad and Bob Albin fiddling around under the hood of Dad's car that day when I was four.

Man of La Mancha: A new musical; Richard Kiley, Irving Jacobson, Ray Middleton, Robert Rounseville, Joan Diener. Lyrics by Joe Darion. Music by Mitch Leigh.

Resting the record jacket on my chest, I close my eyes like I do when I'm listening to basketball on my transistor radio during the winter. With the Sonics, Bob Blackburn's play-by-play paints a picture of the action on the basketball floor. Since I've seen NBA and college games on TV, it's easy to imagine Walt Hazzard, Bob Rule, Bill Russell, and Wilt Chamberlain running up and down the court hitting jumpers and hauling in rebounds. But there are no lyrics in the overture to *Man of La Mancha*, and the setting for the story is somewhere I've never been. So it's a surprise to be transported to a different time and place by just the music.

The overture fades out, the record snaps and pops for a moment, and the hero of the story steps onto the grand stage in my head as I hear Richard Kiley's baritone voice sing these magical words:

I am I, Don Quixote
The Lord of La Mancha
My destiny calls and I go

Don Quixote? Destiny calls?

This is fantastic!

By the third refrain, I've changed the words slightly, and I'm singing them to myself as a rehearsal for when I really belt it out while holding a fake wooden spoon microphone sometime soon.

I am I, Gordon R. Braun
A boy here in Shoreline

My destiny calls and I go

This song, track two on Side A, is called "Man of La Mancha (I, Don Quixote)," but I don't get it. That name is way too complicated. Plus, it doesn't work with my new lyrics. And technically it should be "Lord of La Mancha" not "Man of La Mancha."

The misnamed song ends before I'm ready for it to be over, and I'm less enthusiastic about the numbers that follow. They're nice enough and clever enough, but they don't capture me like the overture and the song I now call, "I am I."

My eyes remain closed, and I melt into a daydream about more chivalrous times, which reminds me of lying on my belly near a worn spot in the living room carpet, chin in hands, watching *Jeopardy!* with Mom when I was seven years old.

Category: POETRY FOR $50
Answer: SIR WALTER SCOTT IMMORTALIZED THIS YOUNG KNIGHT

Without hesitating, I blurted out, "Lochinvar." A few seconds later, the buzzer went off as time expired for the three baffled TV contestants. Art Fleming shook his head in an apologetic gesture and announced, "The right answer is, 'Who is Lochinvar?'"

Mom was so astonished that a second grader would know anything about a Walter Scott poem that she forgot to point out that my answer wasn't in the form of a question. I was quite proud of myself and grinned up at her over my shoulder. It was a million to one shot. A student teacher had come to class a month earlier and taught us the poem, so it was still fresh in my mind.

O, young Lochinvar is come out of the west,
Through all the wide Border his steed was the best;
And save his good broadsword he weapons had none,
He rode all unarm'd, and he rode all alone.
So faithful in love, and so dauntless in war,
There never was knight like the young Lochinvar.

I get off my ass, as Dad would say, walk over to the stereo, and recite the poem to myself while turning over the record album—swapping out the name Lochinvar for Gordon when I reach the end of the stanza. The revised poem strikes my fancy as much as the Gordon R. Braun version of the song "I am I." The fact that Gordon doesn't rhyme with war in the last lines of the altered poem doesn't faze me in the least.

So faithful in love, and so dauntless in war,
There never was knight like the young Gordon.

Flat on my back again on the couch, I decide that the first song on Side B is nothing to get excited about. It's getting late—probably time to get up and get going on my paper route. And then Richard Kiley starts a new song called "The Impossible Dream."

To dream the impossible dream
To fight the unbeatable foe
To bear with unbearable sorrow
To run where the brave dare not go

Hmmm … Maybe I've got a few more minutes to spare before heading out.

To right the unrightable wrong
To love pure and chaste from afar
To try when your arms are too weary
To reach the unreachable star

Oh, man … This is great too!

When the song ends, I roll off the couch and shuffle over to the record player where I carefully lift the tonearm to play the track again. And then again—just hanging out on a lovely summer day, captivated by an idealistic man's dedication to his glorious quest—listening to a song about unbeatable foes, unrightable wrongs, unbearable sorrow, and unreachable stars.

What does it mean to "march into hell" and to "run where the brave dare not go"?

Wait ... isn't this what Congressional Medal of Honor winner Audie Murphy did in the movie "To Hell and Back"?

And when the Lord of La Mancha sings that "my heart will lie peaceful and calm when I'm laid to my rest," does he mean dying and going to Heaven?

I think so.

Maybe I need a glorious quest like this guy, Don Quixote.

When the song ends, I switch off the turntable and flip the album back to Side A to play "I am I" again. Still standing next to our Sears-brand stereo while taking in this beautiful music, I can't help but wonder what destiny has in store for me or if I'll ever even get the call.

I'm aware of the clock, and there are newspapers that need delivering. When the song finishes this time, I turn off the record player and head through the empty house to the garage where the Schwinn is parked, humming my new favorite tunes as I go.

You'd think the light switch to the bare bulb in the ceiling fixture of the garage would be right next to the utility room door, but if you did, you'd be wrong. When a house is a no-frills proposition like my house, the light switch is on the far wall behind boxes and paint cans stacked on the work bench.

I'm just as likely to get hurt stumbling blindly through the dark in search of the switch as I am by feeling my way through the pitch blackness to the car-sized door on the east wall, so I creep cautiously toward the exit, hands extended out in front of me like a sleepwalker.

Safely reaching the opposite end of the garage, I feel for the handle of the overhead door and yank it up to let brilliant sunshine flood the space. I find the canvas *Seattle Times* delivery bag lying near an oil-stain on the concrete floor and pull it over my head before walking my bike out of the narrow one-car garage and onto the sunlit driveway.

With a gentle shove, the Schwinn rolls down the driveway, and I swing my leg over the top of the bicycle seat, imagining it's the saddle of a horse and I'm a knight in shining armor. I begin peddling slowly and deliberately up Second Avenue, past the Crosbys' house, then the Schmidts', the Ryders', the Bettses', and the Crosses', all the while singing "The Impossible Dream" under my breath.

When I get to the monkey tree behind the cyclone fence at the Baileys' house, I stand up on the pedals to get some speed going as I approach the Isaacson home coming up on the left. There is potential danger ahead if their German shepherd is on the loose.

Sure enough, King is out and here he comes!

He's frothing at the mouth and snarling like a jackal I once saw on *Mutual of Omaha's Wild Kingdom with Marlin Perkins*. The hair goes up on the back of my neck, and I sing faster and pump harder before feeling the heat of his breath on my leg, expecting his fangs to puncture my unarmored calf at any moment. He lunges and I kick him in the chops so that he falls back a bit. He catches up. I kick at him again and miss, but he stops in his tracks anyway, giving me one last snarl.

Until next time, King, I think while continuing on my way and singing.

I am I, Gordon R. Braun
I'm faster than King dogs
My paper route calls and I go

Paper Route Headlines

Vietcong Attack 7 Saigon Outposts

Hydros to Rockets, It's Seafair's Greatest Day

Eisenhower Has a Major Heart Attack

Britain Proposes Ban on Germ Warfare

New Spy Satellite Launched Secretly

Jet's Strafing Error Kills 8 U.S. Troops

Site of Nuclear Tests Bikini Atoll Safe for People

New Battles Break Out Near Saigon

21 Killed in L.A. Helicopter Crash

Two 15-Year-Old Boys Face Homicide Charges

Chapter 12

Sneaky Devil

THERE ARE EIGHTY-FOUR houses on my paper route. I know because I counted them: twenty houses on 185th Street, twenty-nine each on Second and Third Avenues, and six on 180th Street. Fifty-three are my customers. The rest either take just the morning *Post-Intelligencer* or no paper at all.

Starting with the first house located in the shadow of Shoreline Stadium just this side of the freeway overpass, I dodge traffic while crisscrossing 185th Street before going down Third Avenue to 180th Street and then back up Second Avenue to finish at 185th across from the high school parking lot. I hate to cover the same ground twice, but that's what I do when I hang a U-turn after the last paper has been delivered and head for home a quarter mile back down the street I just came up.

On television sitcoms like *The Adventures of Ozzie and Harriet* or *The Donna Reed Show* or *Leave It to Beaver*, paperboys peddle down the sidewalks of their idyllic small towns in the sunshine and mindlessly toss their newspapers in the general direction of the house. It looks like pure luck when they actually make it to the front porch. Occasionally an errant throw winds up in the shrubs or breaking a window or getting soaked by a spinning lawn sprinkler, much to the chagrin of the irate neighborhood grump. The laugh track reminds us how funny it is.

In real life though, there aren't any sidewalks, and there are days when the wind howls and the sun doesn't shine, so you can't just throw papers willy-nilly—especially when houses are set back off the street like in suburban Seattle. It's not worth it to be constantly getting on and off my bike, so I push it from house to house, put the kickstand down, walk up to the porch, and tuck the paper behind screen doors to keep them dry or under welcome mats to keep them from blowing away in the wind.

About half the families have Darigold or Smith Brothers milk boxes by the front door where the dairyman picks up empty quart bottles and leaves fresh milk a couple times a week. When conditions call for it, I'll put the paper inside the milk box with just the corner hanging out of the lid so that my customers can't miss it. Then I walk across the street and repeat the process before moving down the road, all the while opening screen doors, pulling up mats, and lifting lids.

Kickstand up. Kickstand down. Kickstand up. Kickstand down.

I don't have a grump on my paper route that makes me laugh or that isn't civil at least some of the time. A lot of grumps seem like nice guys when they greet me at the front door in their stocking feet as I walk up to make a delivery. They'll comment on the weather and wish me well before closing the door and going back inside. Their grumpy side shows up when I come by at the end of the month to collect what they owe me.

"I thought I already paid," they'll say in an annoyed tone.

"No sir. That was for last month."

"How much is it again?"

"Three dollars."

"I thought it was $2.75."

"No sir, the price went up in April."

"Inflation is killing me. I'm not sure it's worth it anymore."

I don't respond, at which point the grump shakes his head, shuts the door in my face and goes inside to find his wallet. Sometimes I can hear him through the door as he yells to his wife, "Where's your purse?"

Inflation is killing me too. I actually make less money since the subscription price was increased because the *Times* charges me more and because I make less in tips. When the monthly price of a subscription was $2.75, it wasn't uncommon for customers to give me three one-dollar bills and say, "Keep the change." Both of us felt good about the transaction because they felt generous and I felt richer. Now, they give me the same three dollars and keep quiet while I put less enthusiasm in my thank you. Then I walk away with my head down to make sure they know that I know why I didn't get a two-bit tip—there is a difference between throwing in a little extra because it's convenient and giving gratuity out of appreciation for a job well done.

If there is an upside to the price increase, it's that I don't have to wait around for "harried housewives," a term I learned from Mom, and "henpecked husbands," a term I learned from Dad, to check under seat cushions and in pockets of dirty laundry to scrounge up seventy-five cents in loose change. Three dollars on the nose is usually quicker, if not more profitable, than two bills and a pile of nickels, dimes, quarters, or heaven forbid, pennies.

The record for pennies was the seventy-five that Mrs. Olson counted out into my hand on a rainy evening in March. For a second, I thought she was going to give me a six-cent tip because that's how many copper coins were left in her hand after counting to seventy-five, but no dice, no six-cent tip. My pants pockets were already bulging with change and adding the extra pennies to my rain-soaked jeans made it a real challenge to keep them from falling down around my ankles. So I walked from house to house with a ballpoint pen and receipt book in one hand while struggling to hold up my pants with the other.

As inconvenient as loose change can be, the new three-dollar subscription price also means fewer chances to add to my extensive coin collection. I've got every penny minted since 1941, a pile of Mercury Head dimes going back as far as 1916, a bunch of all-silver Roosevelt dimes, Washington quarters, and Kennedy fifty-cent pieces, plus two Morgan silver dollars from the 1890s and three Peace silver dollars from the 1920s. Unlike the copper-clad coins they began minting in 1965, silver will still be worth something someday according to Mr. Carr. So I make sure to set aside the all-silver coins before going to the bank to make my deposit at the end of the month.

Most people on the paper route are nice enough when it comes time to pay up for the month, although a couple of customers make me work extra hard. There is the man whose boxer got loose one time and, in his drooling exuberance to say hello, almost broke my left arm when he jumped up and knocked me into a concrete and steel trellis. The dog's owner won't even open the door when I knock at the end of the month, and I know he is in there because the TV is going, his Chevy is in the driveway, and Benny the boxer is barking.

And then there is the guy on Second Avenue who opens the door to tell me to come back after he gets paid. It doesn't matter what day of the week it is, he is always short on cash and always waiting for payday. When I go back as requested a few days later, he'll inevitably say he gave all his money to his wife and that she's not home. So far at least, I haven't asked him to check under his seat cushions or in his dirty laundry for spare change.

I read a quote in the *Weekly Reader* back in elementary school by heavyweight boxing champion Joe Lewis. He once said his opponents "could run, but they couldn't hide." That's the way I feel about the guy with the boxer and the guy who is always waiting for payday when it comes to getting paid for what I've earned—they can run, but they can't hide.

Mr. Lincoln and Mr. Stack are the two big tippers on the route, both of them give me a five-dollar bill and tell me to keep the change. Mr. Lincoln is an older fellow who lives with his ancient mother in a house halfway down Third Avenue. He invites me in out of the weather when I come to collect, offers me cookies, and effuses about how I never miss a day and about how he appreciates that I put the paper inside the screen door to protect it from the rain and wind. All the while the ancient lady crochets in her rocker and nods in agreement.

Except for the ticking of a mantel clock, the house is eerily quiet, the blinds pulled. I've rarely seen any place so neat and tidy. No kids to interrupt the peace or dogs drooling and shedding all over the carpet. Just a kind, gentle man and his mother. There is something queer about living alone with your mother at that age, which, given his gray hair and wire-rimmed bifocals, I'm guessing is over forty. By queer, I mean queer in the sense of being somehow different, not at all in the insulting homo sense, whatever that's supposed to mean, and certainly not in the playing-with-yourself sense. Anyway, he is kinder than most and a genuinely generous tipper.

Their backyard abuts the backyard of his sister's house, which faces Second Avenue. A forested trail connects the properties. Mom used to drink coffee with the sister back in the days when she was a full-time housewife. We refer to the woman as Big Anne because the name suits her size and because it differentiates her from her fourth-grade daughter, Little Anne. Her husband is a regular-sized man but looks small standing beside his large wife. We call him Big Frank solely for the purpose of not confusing him with their fifth-grade son, Little Frank.

Big Frank saved my life once. Art's house is next door to Big Frank's and is one of a handful in the neighborhood with a basement. When it was being built, Robbie and I would play at the construction site after-hours and on weekends. It was fun to feel the spring in plywood that hadn't been nailed down and to scramble between the open two-by-four studs and to peer through glassless windows. I can still smell the freshly cut lumber and hear the echo of our stomping and laughing.

There was a square hole in the floor at the top of the stairs, probably to be used for ductwork later on. I decided to hold on to the edges and support all my weight with my hands so I could dangle my feet through the opening.

"Look at me!"

"Be careful," Robbie said.

My plan was to climb out of the hole the way I went in, but somehow, I found myself hanging by my fingernails looking back up through the hole in a panic. Between my feet I could tell that it was a long way down to the basement floor and that there were chunks of wood and nails and hazardous-looking construction debris scattered everywhere. If I let go, I was pretty sure I wouldn't die, but not so sure that I wouldn't at least break a leg or land on a nail. I'd heard that having a tetanus shot was no picnic. Without the shot I might get lockjaw, and I was terrified by the prospect of living the rest of my life without being able to chew or talk.

I started to bawl.

Robbie was telling me to shut up and encouraging me to jump, but I couldn't bring myself to let go. I was getting tired though and tried to convince myself in between sobs that it would be okay to release my grip.

"Robbie," I finally said, "I'm going to jump."

No answer.

"Robbie?"

No answer again. I'd been abandoned! I was hanging there all alone!

"Calm down," a man's voice said, and at the same time someone grabbed my legs and let me down to the concrete floor.

It was Big Frank. He must have heard me crying.

"What are you doing here?" he asked.

"Nothing," I said and ran off, hoping he wouldn't say anything to my parents.

I was surprised that he was nice enough to come to my rescue. Big Frank is a serious sort. You get the feeling that he might fly off the handle with minimal provocation. I suppose the same could be said for most of the dads in the neighborhood. By and large it's safest to keep your mouth shut and tippy-toe around your buddies' houses if their fathers are around. One false step and they will be all over you, yelling at you to be quiet and to go outside. Worse yet, they'll send you home because your friend suddenly has chores to do. I'm not sure what the hair-trigger tempers are all about. I suppose it's just the way things are and that I'll have a similarly disagreeable disposition when I'm grown-up too.

Randy Leaky's father is another good example of a grown man capable of going berserk at the drop of a hat.

Randy is a year behind me in school and lives on Third Avenue. His parents are divorced like mine. I was sitting in the backseat of his dad's Mustang with Randy up front one Saturday when the man ran back into the house to say something to his ex-wife. The engine was left idling, and Randy reached across the console with his left leg to rev the engine. I said, "Do it again." So he did.

Vroom! Vroom!

Mr. Leaky flew out of the house in a rage. "Who did that? What are you doing? You could have killed yourself!" he yelled at his son.

"He told me to do it," my now ex-friend told his dad in a panic while pointing at me.

"Did you tell him to do that? Do you want to die?" the man screamed at me, his sweaty face inches from mine.

Mr. Leaky. The name fit him perfectly because it looked like he had sprung a leak. Beads of perspiration clung to his face and damp circles had formed under his armpits.

His eyes bulged, and a vein throbbed at the corner of his forehead just below the hairline. His black hair glimmered with Brylcreem, and he smelled like cigarettes, whiskey, and Gillette aftershave like my dad. He had a tattoo on his arm a lot like the one Uncle Tom got in the Marine Corps during WWII. Come to think of it, Big Frank had a tattoo too, as did a lot of the ill-tempered dads I knew.

"No," I lied about telling Randy to rev the engine. Actually, it was only half a lie or even a third of a lie, since I obviously didn't want to die and because only the second revving of the engine was done at my request. Randy started this whole thing. I would have explained the nuance of the situation to Mr. Leaky except for the fact that I was petrified and just wanted to divert attention back onto the man's son. Randy ratted on me, so I didn't owe him a thing. It occurred to me that I didn't like him very much to begin with.

And I still don't.

Mr. Stack, the other big tipper on my paper route, buys wrecked cars and fixes them up for resale in the basement garage of his house at the foot of Second Avenue. I don't really consider his extra money as an act of pure generosity, though. I think of it as hazardous duty pay. The Stacks raise chickens and have a nasty rooster with an anger problem roaming the property. I would sooner deal with King, the German shepherd up the street, than that lunatic bird. This rooster is a sneaky devil. You never know where he is or when he'll attack.

The first time was in April. I was walking up to the front door just like always when I heard the rooster crow. Before I could say to myself, "I wonder when they got a chicken?" it was all over me! I was screaming in terror, and the rooster was squawking and flapping and pecking away. Feathers were flying, my pants and shirt were ripped, and both of my legs and one arm were bleeding. I was flailing away trying to fend him off, hoping he didn't go for my eyes. I would rather have lockjaw than be blind for the rest of my life.

Since then, he attacks regularly three or four days a week, but he no longer has the element of surprise on his side. I'm always ready. I approach the house with three rolled-up papers in hand now—one for delivery and two to use as weapons. I've thumped him pretty good a number of times, but he keeps coming back for more.

• • •

IT'S SATURDAY.

"Gordon," Mom says as I walk into the living room first thing in the morning.

I don't like her tone.

"You left the toilet seat up last night."

"What do you mean?"

"I mean that I got up in the middle of the night and fell into the water."

"Maybe you should have turned on the light."

"Maybe you should have put the seat down."

"I did put the seat down. I always put the seat down."

"C'mon, you're the only one who puts it up in the first place, and you know it."

"Maureen did it," I say, changing tactics.

"What?"

"To sabotage me."

"Gordon, stop. Why would she do that?"

"Because she hates me."

"Why would you say that?

"Because she tells me all the time that she hates me."

"Other than your father, you have more petty excuses than anybody I know."

How could she possibly know how many petty excuses I or anybody else has? And I wouldn't be in this mess if she had turned on the bathroom light like a normal person. And I really don't remember leaving the toilet seat up, so sabotage is not totally out of the question.

"I do not," I say.

"You do too!"

"I do not."

"Listen to yourself. I rest my case," Mom says.

Okay. Maybe she's got a point.

Maureen walks in and has obviously been listening in on the conversation.

"He's a liar," she says.

"I am not."

Paper Route Headlines

Fire, Explosion Knock Out Power in Downtown Seattle

Yanks, Reds Fight; Civilians Lose Again

Russ Occupy Czechoslovakia Freedom Fighters Crushed

Robbers Get $50,000 at Queen Anne Bank

Use of Guns in Murders Is Up Sharply

Chicago Notebook: Terror in the Streets

Iran's Death Toll at 20,000 as New Quakes Shake Area

Dope Raid Is Biggest in City's History

Vietcong Use Human Shields

Chapter 13

Our Record Run

IT'S THREE O'CLOCK on Saturday. Art and I are in his basement sprawled out on what his Canadian mom and dad call a *chesterfield*, but what Americans call a couch or sofa or davenport, cooling down after a game of Wiffle ball in his backyard. Cream's just-released album, *Wheels of Fire*, is cranked up loud enough to feel the beat, but not so loud that his mom will stomp on the floor as a warning to turn it down. She has more patience for rock music than her husband, but she still has her limits.

Mr. Betts prefers listening to jazz pianist Oscar Peterson on their RCA color TV/stereo console upstairs in the living room—Canadian Club whiskey on the rocks in his hand, alone in the dark except for Crusher, his drolly-named toy cockapoo, snoring at his side.

One evening, before Art and I headed to the basement for a few games of Ping-Pong, I waited on the carpeted stairs of their split entry while my friend finished drying dishes in the kitchen.

"Nobody can play like Oscar Peterson," the tipsy Mr. Betts intoned from out of the blackness. "What do you think, Gord? Is he great or what?"

Mr. Betts's first name is Gordon too, and the way he called me Gord made me feel like a member in good standing of some kind of same-name fraternity.

"He's great," I responded into the inky darkness. At first it was said merely out of respect for another Gordon's opinion. The more I listened though, the more I had to agree. Oscar Peterson was great. Not KJR Fab-50 great, but still great. I would put him right up there with Jo Ann Castle the honky-tonk piano player on the *Lawrence Welk Show*.

Mr. Betts is out and about this afternoon with Art's older brother Alex. It's Alex's Cream LP we're listening to, and it's doubtful that he would approve of us fooling around with his stuff. So in addition to the sound of rock and roll, we're on the alert for the sound of slamming doors on their Chrysler New Yorker.

"I've got to get going soon. Want to help on the paper route today?"

Art doesn't really help per se. He tags along and watches me go house to house. In exchange for the companionship, I buy him a Slurpee at 7-Eleven, and we split a package of Hostess Cupcakes.

"Sure, why not?" Art replies.

"Let me go get my stuff. I'll be back in a couple of minutes," I say as I head for the door.

The Saturday paper is by far the smallest edition of the week, so it should take a little less than an hour. As I turn the doorknob, I have a thought.

"Hey Art, how fast do you think the two of us could get all the papers delivered if we really hustled? You do Second, I do Third, and we split 185th?"

I can see that Art is intrigued by the challenge.

"If I have to deal with King, then you have to deal with the crazy chicken," Art says.

"Yeah, sure."

"I'm in!"

"Back in a minute."

I run across the street to get my bike and canvas delivery bag. I've got a tattered spare bag someone left at the newspaper shack that Art can use.

When I come back, I see Art sitting on his bike in the middle of the street, already pointed up Second Avenue. It's a black, beat-up single-speed model with balloon tires and a coaster brake.

I pull up next to him and come to a stop, handing him the spare bag that he puts on over his head.

He fakes twisting the right handle grip like it's the throttle of a motorcycle.

"Vroom, vroom!" he says.

I look at my wristwatch and see that time is ticking at three nineteen and twenty-three seconds.

"We'll take off at 3:20 straight up," I say hurriedly. "We'll split the papers roughly in half at the shack to save time. You take the north side of 185th, I'll take the south side. You take Second and I'll take Third. No papers on the lawn or in the bushes. We'll meet up wherever we meet up."

"Got it."

"Vroom, vroom," I say.

"Vroom, vroom."

The second hand hits twelve on my Timex.

"Let's go!"

We're off, peddling like mad up Second Avenue—going so fast that King just watches us go by. I take my left hand off the handlebars to look at my wristwatch as we zoom through the stop sign at the corner of Second and 185th. Momentarily losing control while steering one-handed, I swing a little too wide as I turn right onto the arterial. An old man driving a black-and-white Oldsmobile slows down, gives a quick honk, and an inexplicably friendly wave, so I wave back to thank him for his understanding and for not killing me.

One minute and seventeen seconds.

We're at the overpass in slightly over two minutes. It's all downhill from here, and we pour it on, cutting diagonally across 185th in front of oncoming traffic. Another car honks, and the driver yells through his rolled down passenger-side window, "Watch it, ya crazy kids!"

At three and a half minutes we come to a skidding stop in front of the shack door. Gravel flies. A cloud of dust and dirt hangs in the air. We're in luck. No one is in front of us in line to slow us down.

"Gimme fifty-three papers, Mike. We're in a hurry."

The shack manager senses something big is happening and doesn't ask questions. He counts out the papers like the expert he is and hands them over.

"Nice talking to you. You're welcome," Mike deadpans as we grab the papers and run back to our bikes without saying another word.

Coming up to the six-minute mark, our bags are stuffed with newspapers. There is no time to tie the bags to the handlebars so we throw them over our heads and we're heading back toward the overpass.

We're not just racing the clock now, we're racing each other. Side by side. Cars give us a wide berth. Art edges ahead, then I take the lead. I try to shift gears on the hill and get stuck momentarily in between, spinning the pedals but not getting any power.

Clackity, clackity, clackity goes the derailleur of the Schwinn five-speed.

Art opens up a two-bike length lead. He looks over his shoulder and gives me the finger and the smile of a guy who knows he's won this one.

The first houses on the route are coming up.

Seven minutes and thirty-four seconds.

I cut across the street to the south side of 185th and jump off my bike just after Art hops off his on the other side of the road.

Kickstands down.

We run to our respective porches and toss the first papers.

Back to the bikes. Kickstands stay down to save time. We push the bicycles at a trot to the next houses, giving each other menacing glares as we follow parallel paths, cars passing in either direction between us on 185th.

Six houses done on my side, all taken from the front pocket of the canvas newspaper bag. The uneven weight distribution is choking me, so I quickly spin the bag around my neck and hop on my bike before peeling off down Third Avenue. Art still has the Lucks, the Madisons, and the Bickfords to deliver on 185th before heading down Second Avenue.

Just past nine minutes.

The Leakys are first. Then the *Seattle Times* newspaper tube hanging from the wire fence next door. Then the house with Benny the boxer. Across the street to the one-room shack. Down the private road to the house on the end. The cute cottage. Mrs. Olson's, who gave me the seventy-five pennies. Up the steep driveway at Eddie Lundberg's house. Then the next house and the next and the next.

I spin the bag again around my neck.

"Hi, Gordon," Mr. Lincoln says with the look of someone wanting to chat.

"No time to talk today, sorry."

The Hansens are next. Then the Solbergs in the last house on Third Avenue.

Back on my bike, I peddle around the corner to the Simpsons on 180th, hop off and run up the driveway.

Two papers left. *Just over seventeen minutes.* Back on the bike again.

The house with the chickens is coming up, and I make a quick decision and do something I would normally never do: I ride my bike across their front lawn. Hens cackle and scatter. The rooster has only enough time to let out a halfhearted crow. I throw the paper on the porch without stopping and take a sharp right toward the street, barely missing the split-rail fence along the lot line.

I'm in no mood to slow down, so I ride my bike over the Carlsons' lawn too. Three seconds later my last paper lands with a plop on the welcome mat of their house across the street from the chickens.

I peddle around the corner and see Art four houses up Second Avenue, barreling out of the Baileys' driveway. He seems to have gotten past King unscathed. Next stop: his house. He hustles his two-wheeler across the street, cuts across his parents' front lawn, and lets go of his bike while still at a trot so that it crashes onto the grass, leaving the front wheel spinning. Tossing the newspaper onto the porch, he then heads next door to open the gate of the Ryders' picket fence. Their two dachshunds, Yippy and Skippy, chase him to the porch and back, barking and nipping at his ankles the whole way. He fumbles briefly with the gate latch and kicks at the wiener dogs to make sure they don't get loose before closing the gate behind himself.

Two to go. The Crosbys' house and then my house.

Art sprints across the street to drop off the second-to-last paper, then takes a shortcut over the lawn and through the flower beds separating the two yards. The last paper lands with a rewarding smack on Mom's front porch.

"Nineteen minutes and twenty-three seconds!"

We stand silently with smiles on our faces taking in the magnitude of our accomplishment.

"Less than twenty minutes," I say.

"Amazing," Art replies.

"It's a record that will never be broken," I observe, still grinning.

"Never," Art responds with a satisfied chuckle.

"Let me buy you a drink."

"Sounds good."

We drop our bags on the lawn, and I head over to my bike.

"Aw, shoot!" I hear Art exclaim behind me.

I turn around to see him trying to scrape dog crap off his left shoe. He must have stepped in a pile when he cut through the flower beds.

I let out a laugh. "Sorry about that, Chief."

"Real funny," Art says as he continues to rub his shoe on the grass. It's a lost cause—there is no way he'll get all of it because so much is crammed deep into the tread of his sneaker.

The two of us retrieve his bicycle from the front of his house and head toward 7-Eleven. Still reflecting on the sub-twenty-minute paper route performance, we uncharacteristically forget to plan for the potential trouble ahead.

Here comes King, barking and snarling again!

"Goddammit!"

Art is riding between me and the dog, so I'm safe. He kicks at it a couple of times and misses, but King strangely gives up anyway. Maybe he doesn't like the smell of Art's shoe. Maybe it's just our lucky day.

We get to the overpass and take our inky paws off the handlebars as we coast down the grade, blissfully flapping our arms as we go. The cooling summer breeze is especially welcome after the effort involved in our record run.

Once inside the air-conditioned store, Art selects Ding Dongs from the Hostess display, and I pick up a cherry pie. At the counter we both order medium Cola Slurpees. The bill is seventy-one cents, including tax. I give the clerk a dollar bill and a penny, and he gives me back a quarter and a nickel.

It's an all-silver quarter that I'll add to my coin collection when I get home.

Art and I step back out into the warmth of the sun and take a seat on the curb in front of the Igloo ice machine and a pallet of Pres-to-logs. I take a large sip on my Slurpee, and I get an instant brain freeze. The excruciating pain is like having an ice pick shoved in my eye. Art tears into his Ding Dongs as my agony slowly subsides.

"It's a record that will never be broken," I finally manage to say again to the only person listening.

"Never," Art agrees, the instant before stuffing the entire hockey-puck-shaped Ding Dong into his mouth.

• • •

I'VE SEEN PLENTY of violence on television and in the movies. GIs, Krauts, and Japs blown up by hand grenades or stabbed in the guts with bayonets. Cowboys and Indians shot off their horses and dragged across the prairie with their boots or moccasins caught in the stirrups. Cops and crooks knocked unconscious by a roundhouse punch to the chin, an empty whiskey bottle to the side of the head or a single karate chop to the back of the neck. Wile E. Coyote clobbered by an anvil falling out of the desert sky or riding an Acme rocket into the side of a mountain.

Screen violence is usually exciting, often bloodless, rarely disturbing, and sometimes comical. Leading men recover from their injuries before the next scene as if nothing ever happened. Supporting characters either don't matter much or deserve what they get. And the lump on the top of the coyote's head miraculously disappears so that he can resume his futile pursuit of the Road Runner.

All in all, I would say that violence on television and in the movies is pretty entertaining. It's also unrealistic, but it turns out I prefer it that way.

Tonight I'm watching real violence in the streets of Chicago outside the Democratic National Convention because nothing else is on TV. The billy clubs, tear gas, and handcuffs are real. The cracked skulls, the pain, and the black-and-white blood are real too, as is the anger, terror, and utter confusion.

The police and the soldiers beating up hippies and college students in Chicago look and act exactly like the police and soldiers I saw last year trying to persuade Black people to behave themselves in places like Newark and Detroit. It didn't bother me to see what I saw back then nearly as much as it does to see what I see tonight.

I think I know why.

And that bothers me too.

Paper Route Headlines

23 Arrested Here in Drug Crackdown

95 Killed in Crash of French Jet Liner

Racial Tension Factor in Costs

Record School-Levy Request Likely

Tighter Gun Law Sought

Mayor Warns Black Panthers

4 Killed in Fiery Freeway Collision

Vietcong Suffer Crippling Defeats

Deadlock at Snarled Paris Talks Deepens

Arson Suspected in Apartment-Building Fire

Reds Blow up Saigon Oil Complex

Battleship New Jersey Hits Red Targets in N. Vietnam

Chapter 14

Don't Call Me Pal

THE STORY OF *Little Black Sambo* is told in a series of pictures hanging over the counter of the namesake restaurant where I sit with Dad, waiting for the waitress to bring us our breakfast orders. In the leftmost frame, the East Indian boy is happily walking down the road in his finest clothing. In subsequent panels he encounters a series of fierce tigers that, one by one, steal his colorful hat, his vest, his shoes, and his umbrella. Next you witness the greed and vanity of the tigers. They each want what the other has of Little Black Sambo's outfit and jealously chase each other around a tree until they all turn into butter. In the last scene, the boy is wearing his clothes again, delighted to be eating pancakes with gobs of melted butter on them—presumably butter made from vain tigers running around in circles.

The story seems farfetched to me.

I'm not having pancakes today, though, as I sit at the counter next to my father at Sambo's Restaurant. I've ordered a strawberry waffle heaped with whipped cream just like I always do when he brings me here, which hasn't been often lately. I haven't seen or heard from him since Robbie's wedding in April. It's not unusual to go long stretches of time without a word and then he pops up out of the blue. In this case, it's not really out of the blue. He is trying to make up for missing my thirteenth birthday last month.

"So, Pal," he says while flicking his Lucky Strike into the ashtray on the counter, "what have you been up to?"

I hate it when he calls me Pal.

"Nothing," I say.

"How's school?"

"It starts next week."

"What are you taking?"

"PE and French and stuff."

"Got a girlfriend?"

"No."

He takes a drag on his cigarette and looks at his hands, trying to think of another question when the waitress puts a plate of ham and eggs in front of him with a cheerful "Here you go."

"And here *you* go too," she says to me, trying to ingratiate herself by putting a syrupy emphasis on the *you*.

The waitress is wearing a name tag over her large left breast that says *Beth*. I look up into her face to see that her mood has suddenly darkened. She is giving me a cross, tsk-tsk look. I think she thinks I was staring at her boobs. I'm innocent. I was just reading her name tag. But that gets me to thinking about Anthony Animato's contention that boobs and blow jobs are somehow related, which leads me to picture the centerfolds of Kaya Christian and Lynn Winchell, which causes a stirring sensation, which makes me squirm on my barstool.

Dad snuffs out the smoke and cuts into the ham. "I missed you, Pal," he says while chewing his food, trying to get me to make eye contact.

I stop squirming for a moment and pretend like I didn't hear him.

The waitress has turned away and is hunting for something under the counter across from us. She's got a big rear-end, probably "two axe handles wide" as Mom once described the same feature on one of Dad's sisters. Determined to ignore my father, I sit facing straight ahead, resting my eyes on Beth's generous derriere in an attempt to avoid my father's gaze.

I've also got a mouthful of berries and whipped cream, which gives me a plausible excuse for not responding immediately to my father's remorseful statement. He expects me to say "I missed you too, Dad," but I just can't do it. If I wait long enough, maybe he'll forget about the whole thing.

I don't care.

Well, maybe I care a little, but that's not for him to know.

Stop calling me Pal, I think to myself. *I'm not your Pal.*

I take a sip of hot chocolate, also with whipped cream, and Dad sips his black coffee. Between tastes, he lights another cigarette and mindlessly blows smoke in my direction. I'm getting it from both sides. The guy sitting on the stool to the left of me is smoking Winstons.

By way of a sideways glance, I can tell that Dad has noticed Beth bending over in front of us. He lingers, not too subtly, over the view and lets out an almost imperceptible sigh.

When we're done, Dad pays the bill and leaves Beth a four-bit tip next to his plate. We head out to the car parked in front of the restaurant, where he gets behind the wheel of the Ford Custom sedan. "A poor man's Galaxie 500" is how Dad describes it.

I climb into the passenger seat and use both hands to close the heavy door. When I go to put on the seatbelt, I notice it's been left dangling outside. After cracking the door enough to retrieve it, I pull the door shut and secure the seat belt around my waist with a noticeable click.

The sound of the door closing a second time and the noise of the buckle being fastened gets Dad's attention. He turns his head in my direction to give me a quizzical look.

"What are you, some kind of safety nut?" he asks, nodding at my lap belt.

It takes me a second to process the question, and I flash back to the time I ordered rice instead of a baked potato to go along with my well-done ribeye at Jim's Steak House in Lake City.

"What are you, a Chinaman?" Dad had asked that day.

"Astronauts and fighter pilots wear seat belts," I say in response to his latest remark.

"You want to be an astronaut? Good for you, Pal. You can be anything you want. Try hard and it will come easy."

Try hard and it will come easy. I hate that. And don't call me Pal.

• • •

THE AREA AROUND the Hanford Nuclear Reservation in Eastern Washington is desolate, a perfect out-of-the-way place to produce plutonium for atomic bombs like Fat Man, the one they dropped on Nagasaki. It's not exactly the kind of place where you'd expect to spend an extended holiday, but it's near to where Dad was living last summer, so that's where Maureen and I wound up for two weeks last July. Other than the trip to California in 1961, the summer of 1967 is the only other time in my life that I've been away from home for more than a weekend.

I was almost twelve years old at the time and from another place, a place where water falling out of the sky and lush landscape is normal, not the extreme heat, rocky hills, and expanse of blue sky found on the other side of the Cascade Mountains. I just couldn't get over the strangeness of the place.

Over there, the sun doesn't envelop you with a warm embrace like it does at home during the summer. East of the mountains, the sun's rays feel more like the laser beam I saw aimed at James Bond's crotch in the movie *Goldfinger*. If you weren't careful, it might just burn a hole right through you.

Why Dad was living in the Tri-Cities is a mystery. He had been forced to resign from the Seattle Fire Department, but why? I didn't know then, and I still don't know. There was something about him getting drunk and maybe pointing a gun at his wife, Lucy, a waitress he met at the Beach Broiler restaurant in West Seattle and married before the ink had dried on the divorce papers from Mom. And I might have caught bits and pieces along the way about him spending a night or two in jail. I'm not sure how I know all of this, and if I thought about it more than I do, maybe I'd have questions. But I try not to think about it very much, and I don't ask questions because I don't need something else to not care about.

What I knew for sure back then was that he was divorced again, living east of the mountains, and that Mom somehow decided to drive Maureen and me to Grandma Braun's house so we could hitch a ride across the state with my grown-up cousin, Pat. I think Pat is Aunt Agnes's daughter. Or Aunt Agatha's or Aunt Helen's or Aunt Eleanor's or Aunt Dorothy's.

We found out that Dad was "shacked up," a term I learned from him, when he picked us up at Pat's house in Pasco and drove us across the Columbia River to some lady's place in Kennewick. Verna greeted us with a big hug, clutching me and then Maureen enthusiastically to her bosom.

Who does this broad (another term I learned from my father) *think she is?* Grandma Braun could get away with this kind of behavior, but I've known her all my life. Not even my mother, who I've also known all my life, would think to try a stunt like this.

It took a few days, but Verna turned out to be a good egg. It just so happens that there are worse things than to be nestled between her breasts every now and then. She seemed to enjoy it, so why not? It helped that Dad was on his best behavior when she was around. One dirty look from her was all it took to keep him from pouring another three fingers of rotgut whiskey. And it helped that she gave us dimes so Maureen and I could walk to the filling station on the corner to buy a bottle of Fresca or Orange Fanta out of the machine in front.

We would sit on the curb and drink the pop in front of the Pennzoil display rather than pay the bottle deposit. I could get away with jumping on the rubber hose running across the pavement three or four times without irritating the gas pump jockey too much.

Ding. Ding.

Ding ... Ding.

Dad worked around town as a handyman, but took time off during our visit. While Verna cashiered during the day at Kmart, the three of us drove the state highways and county roads of Eastern Washington. We joked about murdering slow-moving bugs by ramming them with the grill of the car.

Maureen and I fished for bluegill and perch in one of the many reservoirs for a few hours on most days. Dad watched from the grassy banks while keeping an eye out for rattlesnakes. He gave us casting tips and periodically unhooked the line when it found a scrubby bush on the backswing. When we hauled in a fish, Dad whacked it in the head with a miniature baseball bat until it stopped flopping around, and then he'd put a fresh worm on the hook for us.

After fishing one morning, Maureen and I found ourselves drinking milkshakes in air-conditioned comfort at the soda fountain of the five-and-dime in Umatilla, Oregon, while Dad went off to pick up a few cartons of smokes. Cigarettes are a lot cheaper across the border because the "goddamn politicians in Oregon don't tax the hell out of cigarettes like the goddamn politicians in Washington." We topped off the tank of the car because gas was cheaper there too.

At Grand Coulee Dam on the mighty Columbia River, we were told that an engineering feat like this could only happen in the greatest country on earth. Blocking the river in front of us was enough concrete to build a two-lane highway from Seattle to Miami. Enough electricity was being generated for over a million households. Dad and Maureen oohed and aahed at the colors of rainbows that formed in mist produced by water cascading over the face of the dam.

The rainbows didn't impress me much since I'm colorblind and could only see shades of gray with hints of yellow and blue. In kindergarten, before I could read the labels on my Crayola crayons, grass was just as likely to be colored red and Santa's suit, green. Once it was determined that my color choices were probably the result of faulty vision rather than low intelligence, Mom simplified my limited wardrobe to include only blues and grays. This way I would at least have a fighting chance of dressing myself without looking ridiculously mismatched.

Over time, I learned to describe common items, like traffic lights, as being red or green because that was how people described them to each other. For the most part, I just keep quiet about the color of things. Sometimes I have no choice but to offer up a guess and hope I'm right. When I guess wrong, people that don't know me cock their heads and look at me like I'm an idiot.

It was over a hundred degrees outside on these day trips in Eastern Washington with my father. Hot wind rushed in through open windows as the sagebrush rushed by. Dad smoked the Lucky Strikes he bought in Oregon while Maureen and I drank Shasta-brand colas that Verna brought home from Kmart. We found room in his Coleman ice chest to chill the soda pop next to bottles of Olympia Beer. Dad cracked open an Oly whenever we stopped, which was quite often, and poured it down his gullet in one big gulp. As the beer supply in the trunk disappeared, he changed from attentive to sullen to being a "royal prick," a term I learned from Mom.

"Talk to me, Pal. Whaddya haffta shay … fer yerselv?" he slurred as we sped down the highway.

"Nothing," I responded curtly. There was no good answer to that question when he'd had a few, and it was impossible to sound civil.

That did it though. I should have known better, tried harder. Out came the wrath. "Don't talk to me that way. I'm your father, goddammit! I deserve respect. If I talked to my father that way, he'd have hauled me out back behind the woodshed. My father. That was a man who demanded respect. You should show me respect, goddammit!"

Rage always improves Dad's enunciation. It doesn't matter how much he's had to drink. When he's angry, the words are always crystal clear.

At twilight, winding our way south along the river, this part of Eastern Washington got to be pretty goddamn lonely. Eddy Arnold's "The Cattle Call" coming out of the radio made it even lonelier, and being trapped in a car with my father when he was giving us the silent treatment made the scene sadder and lonelier still.

Dad hadn't said a word in half an hour before opening his mouth to opine, "Nobody can yodel like Eddy Arnold." He wasn't talking to me or Maureen though. Dad was off in another world.

The cattle are prowlin'
The coyotes are howlin'
Way out where the doggies bawl
Where spurs are a-jinglin'
A cowboy is singin'
His lonesome cattle call
Whoo-ooh-ooh-doo-di-di
Whoo-ooh-ooh-oop-doo-doo
Whoo-ooh-ooh-ooh-ooh-ooh
Yod-el-od-el-lo-ti-de

At the end of a day on the road, we retreated to the cool basement of Verna's house where I shared a room, and a temporary cessation of hostilities, with my sister. Away from home, it turned out that Maureen wasn't so bad. It helped to have an ally my own age when dealing with an erratic grown-up.

There was a large walk-in shower in the basement. According to Dad, it was in this very shower, the one my sister and I had been using every day of our visit, where Verna's husband had shot himself to death.

I tried to imagine what it must have been like for Verna to find his body, but gave up because it was completely unimaginable. How could a man put a loved one in this position? How could a man's pain in this life be so great that, rather than live another day, he would choose to suffer an eternity in Hell by committing the ultimate mortal sin?

Why would Dad share something like that with me?

It wasn't the first time I'd wondered why my father felt the need to make me aware of something I didn't want to know.

On a sunny day when I was eight years old and minding my own business, a Pearl Harbor-like sneak attack was perpetrated on my home. Family tension that had eluded my consciousness up to that point finally got my attention. Mom and Dad were screaming. Leslie was crying. All of Dad's clothes and a half dozen whiskey bottles were strewn across the front yard of our house on Second Avenue. The front door slammed, leaving us all in stunned silence. I watched through the living room window as my father tossed his wadded-up belongings into the rear seat, backed his Ford down the gravel driveway and disappeared around the corner.

How could my father let something like that happen?

Up to that moment, I had thought we were pals.

Paper Route Headlines

Senate Chided
Johnson Withdraws Fortas Nomination

Yanks Battle Red Force 25 Miles from Saigon

New Violence Grips North Ireland

Olympic Hotel Robbers Get $25,000–$30,000 Haul

'Eyeball to Eyeball' Allies Repulse Red Attackers

Wallace Welcomed by Surging Crowd

Mrs. Kennedy, Onassis to Wed

Doris Brown Stumbles in Race, But Still Qualifies

Two U.S. Olympic Sprint Stars Expelled

Chapter 15

Good Going, Gordy

W*HAT HAVE I GOTTEN myself into?* I wonder, sitting on a high stool next to a workbench in Mr. Erstad's woodshop and waiting for the first day of Unified Arts class to begin.

In most normal classrooms, teachers hang pictures and such on the bulletin boards and walls of their classrooms. In Mrs. Bidard's French class, there are posters of the Champs-Élysées, the Eiffel Tower, an inviting bistro, and the front page of *Le Monde* newspaper. In Mr. Hagelund's algebra class there are a bunch of indecipherable formulas and a picture of Albert Einstein. Mr. Varvik, in my social studies class, occasionally pulls down the world map or the US map suspended like rolled-up window shades above the blackboard. And, of course, there are always school announcements, and the displays change to reflect the season of the year and upcoming holidays.

Woodshop is clearly not a normal classroom even after taking into account the fact that I'm surrounded by power tools. Mr. Erstad has a collection of paddles hanging on the wall just inside the door. These aren't canoe paddles to be used for a relaxing Sunday cruise on a glassy lake, these are nasty-looking weapons that are used to punish students that screw up in class or somehow manage to get on Mr. Erstad's bad side. And rumor has it, there is only one side to Mr. Erstad. I wish I had known all this before I signed up and convinced John Ryan and Art Betts to sign up with me.

Mr. Erstad is pacing at the front of the room with his hands in his pockets waiting for the bell to ring. He is a sinewy man of medium height sporting a crew cut and a white short-sleeve shirt. A bulging pocket protector is stuffed with pens and mechanical pencils. His thick glasses accentuate the naturally crazed expression on his face. He's got a tattoo on his forearm like some of the short-fused fathers in the neighborhood.

Uh-oh.

The bell rings to signal that class has officially begun.

The teacher clears his throat.

"Some of you might already know that I'm Mr. Erstad," he begins, looking at us over the top of his glasses. "How many of you know anything about power tools?"

A number of hands go up while I leave mine down.

"Well, forget everything you know!" he says emphatically. "We're starting from scratch to make sure you learn to do it the right way. And the right way is my way. Got it?"

All thirty heads nod at the same time.

He gestures to the room full of power saws, planers, jointers, drill presses, lathes, sanders, and hand tools. "Used improperly, these machines are dangerous. Don't make me call an ambulance because one of you cuts off your hand or takes out the eye of one of your classmates. Safety first! Got it?"

Our thirteen-year-old heads bob again in unison.

Got it.

• • •

TABLETOP FOOTBALL IS played by folding a sheet of paper into a sturdy three-inch triangle and then shoving it back and forth across the table. The objective is to get a corner of the triangle to hang over the edge for a six-point touchdown. Push too hard so that the triangle falls off the table, and your opponent attempts a field goal by using his middle finger to "kick" the triangle through "goalposts" you've formed with your index fingers and thumbs. Done properly, a player gets three points for the field goal and hears a satisfying thwack as the triangle bounces off his rival's face.

Today I'm playing with John Ryan in homeroom like we do pretty much every day. I can see over John's shoulder that Ken Slaughter, Mike Nelson, Anthony Animato, and a few other guys are up to something. Seeing as how they've positioned themselves to block Miss Kristianson's view, I assume that Mike's white mouse is on the loose again. He's been bringing the mouse to school for a couple of weeks now, keeping it in his pants pocket most of the time and sometimes letting it crawl up one arm and down the other during classes. He hasn't gotten caught yet, but it's obviously just a matter of time.

I'm forming goalposts with my fingers in anticipation of a stinging three-pointer to the face when I see Ken Slaughter snatch the mouse off the table and, in one motion, throw it as hard as he can against the brick wall! The flying rodent makes a sickening thud at the point of impact next to a poster advertising the upcoming fall dance, and falls to the floor.

Ken sits down as if nothing has happened while the room erupts in chaos. Girls start screaming. Mike and his friends are shouting. Miss Kristianson jumps out of her chair, unsure about what just happened, but ready to take action.

Meanwhile the poor mouse lies lifeless, just the tiniest trickle of blood flowing out of his little pink nose.

Ken has always been impulsive, even dangerous, but this is crazy.

He is as tall as Art Betts and probably a better athlete. But while Art takes sports seriously, Ken doesn't care. That is, it seems he doesn't care until the moment he cares enough to do something extraordinary. I've seen Ken walk lazily up and down the soccer field during PE class for thirty or forty minutes without coming anywhere near the action and then decide to steal the ball, dribble by four or five defenders and kick a rocket off the goalie's face for a score. I've seen Ken stand around listlessly when we're supposed to be playing basketball and then as class is about to end, block a shot powerfully into the shooter's nose, pick up the loose ball, and go the length of the court for a layup.

You know you aren't going to see much from Listless Ken, but you also know that Impulsive Ken will eventually show up to do something worth seeing. And it usually involves somebody getting a bloody nose.

Ken was his normal listless and impulsive self for the first couple of weeks of the school year before revealing his dangerous side for the first time. I was playing tabletop football like today and drying out next to the radiator after the walk from home, so I couldn't hear what Anthony Animato was saying across the room. But I could see that he was animated as usual and that he looked to be pestering Ken about something or other.

I remember that Ken was sitting motionless and erect. His hands were folded in his lap, and he was staring straight ahead. Animato leaned in a bit, still yacking away. And then …

Ken lashed out!

This wasn't a routine, playground punch. Ken's right arm uncoiled like a cobra, and as quick as a blink, his hand was back resting in his lap. An instant later, Animato registered the pain of the blow, screamed, and brought his hands to his face. Blood poured out of his nose and through his fingers, forming red droplets on the table and floor.

In less time than it took Miss Kristianson to scamper across the room, Dangerous Ken pushed back his chair, stood calmly, and headed toward the vice-principal's office without a fuss.

Watching Impulsive Ken appear and then do amazing things in PE class is always entertaining unless you're the victim of having a soccer ball or a basketball smashed into your face. But even then, bruises and abrasions earned on the athletic field are just that, earned. And because they're earned, they can be worn like a badge of honor. There is a story to be told about the injury and, in the right hands, the story improves with each telling.

Seeing Dangerous Ken bloody Animato's nose that day was sobering but explainable, because Animato has a way of getting under people's skin and because he has no understanding of cause and effect. Animato, of course, made up a story about how he was a tough guy that could take a punch. And the rumor mill countered with another less flattering version of what happened: Animato was an idiot.

It's just a mouse. I shouldn't care about a stinking little dead mouse, but I do. Ken Slaughter crossed another line. I had already seen him transform from listless to impulsive to dangerous. From being a guy to keep your eye on to being a guy that makes you watch yourself. By cruelly and senselessly killing a mouse though, he's gone from dangerous to crazy. Crazy Ken is a guy you keep your distance from.

• • •

TODAY'S THE DAY.

The gym class is heading over to the starting line of the cross-country course because Mr. Searle is sick and tired of all the bad behavior on the soccer field. We still have ten minutes left in our eighth-grade PE class, which is just enough time to punish us by making us run.

I've got a feeling that I could be pretty good at this sport. Most guys complain about running, but I like it. It's simple. As I see it, just put one foot in front of the other as fast or faster than the next guy, and then wait to see who gives up first. In all the times we've run the cross-country course over the past year, I can honestly say that I've never given up. I can also honestly say that I've never really tried.

Today is the day I try.

I'm inspired by the Olympic Games that finished just last week.

"Running in the footsteps of Jim Thorpe, Rafer Johnson, and Bob Mathias" was how announcer Jim McKay described the last few painful yards of the gold medal performance by Bill Toomey in the decathlon. He ran and suffered and persevered in the dark and rain of Mexico City. I know all about dark and rain because I'm from the Pacific Northwest, but until watching Bill Toomey and listening to Jim McKay, these conditions were nuisances to be tolerated not a backdrop for something I could get excited about.

Then there was Bob Beamon who collapsed to his knees when told he had broken the world long jump record by almost two feet! I went into my yard to measure out twenty-nine feet two inches using Mom's ten-foot tape measure in an effort to fully appreciate what he had accomplished. When I was done unrolling and rerolling the tape three times, I was stunned to realize that he had jumped the entire length of my house.

The length of my house!

So I tried a long jump too and came up more than twenty feet short—albeit in street shoes with a short run up. Under better conditions, I was pretty sure I could add maybe a foot or two to my distance, and yet I would still be barely a third of the way to Beamon's record. It blew my mind that a human being could jump the length of my house. And as I stood there that day in awe, it occurred to me that gold medalist Bob Seagren could pole vault over the roof of the house with room to spare.

Over the roof!

That Olympic gold medal in the pole vault could just as well have gone to local hero Brian Sternberg from Shoreline High School and the University of Washington, if only he hadn't broken his neck in a trampoline accident. Using a modern fiberglass pole, he surpassed the 1963 world record twice in six weeks, going sixteen feet eight inches to add almost half a foot to the previous best mark. An incredible athlete from a town that isn't even a town. My town. At one time Brian Sternberg was capable of jumping over the roof of my house. And now he was spending the rest of his life in a wheelchair.

I was disappointed and perplexed that Jim Ryun lost to Kip Keino in the metric mile. An American and a world record holder, whose picture I woke up to every morning, lost to a Kenyan? My hero went out so slowly in the first three laps of the race that it looked like he wasn't even trying. And by the time he started trying, it was too late because the champion had too big a lead and just wouldn't quit.

A Kenyan?

I'm going to imitate a Kenyan today.

My plan is to hang back but stay near the leaders through the first half of the race like Keino did at the Olympics. Then I'll take the lead and push as hard as I can for as long as I can. Hopefully everyone else will give up or at least forget about trying before I make a complete fool out of myself.

Trying is a risky business.

I wonder if Kip Keino or Jim Ryun ever worried about making fools of themselves?

We're milling around under the basketball rim on the outdoor court like always before the start of a cross-country run. Mr. Searle blows his whistle and off we go, all thirty of us across the asphalt toward an imaginary left field foul pole on the baseball field. I go out just hard enough so as not to get stuck in traffic when we leave the outfield grass and funnel onto a rocky trail.

I'm in fifth place, just where I want to be, when the path narrows. I've never been this close to the front before. A few quick steps up a short incline and we're heading west, parallel to the third base line along the side hill. I can feel the strain in my ankles as I struggle to move straight ahead while gravity tries to pull me sideways down the slope.

We turn left behind the backstop, and I pass two guys to move into third place. The course slips behind a long stretch of blackberry brambles and Scotch broom where it zigs, zags, dips, and rises so that I lose sight of the leaders for a few seconds. I'm right on their heels when I see them next. So far so good. We're coming to the halfway point and an easy left turn leading toward a long, flat straightaway.

This is it.

I picture Black Power protesters Tommie Smith and John Carlos coming off the turn in the 200-meter race at the Olympics as I ease past Joe Knutson and pull up onto the shoulder of Peter Anderson, giving him a sideways glance.

And then I blast 'em!

I come off the turn, and I'm sprinting down the straightaway as fast as I can. I'm thinking about Kip Keino and Bill Toomey as I put distance between me and my competitors. Fifty yards later I'm sure I can't go any faster, but I feel like I can run at this speed forever.

And then … suddenly everything hurts! My legs feel like lead. My heart is about to leap out of my chest. My lungs are on fire. And it feels like someone stuck a knife in my belly and twisted it.

Dead ahead looms the big hill.

I think about the Quinn Martin television production of *Twelve O'Clock High* and how B-17 bombers got all shot up over Germany during World War II. And about how they limped back to England with three engines ablaze and just barely enough air speed to clear the white caps of the English Channel.

I feel like a shot-up B-17 when I get to the bottom of the hill and start my ascent. This is all about survival, and I'm not sure if I'm going to make it. There is a good chance I'm going to crash, but just like in the song from *Man of La Mancha*, I'm committed to the impossible dream. I'm not giving up because Don Quixote, Kip Keino, and General Savage on *Twelve O'Clock High* would never give up.

I shorten my stride and lean into the hill. Pumping my weary arms, I reach for the stars and run where the brave dare not go. In a dozen torturous steps, I make the summit, turn left, and head to the finish line a hundred and fifty yards away.

My Sears sneakers slam into the ground with each step as I free fall down the last small hill. I can see Mr. Searle waiting for us on the asphalt of the basketball court. He's laughing when I cross the finish line, comes up to me, pats me on the back, and says, "I've never seen anything like that. It looked like you were shot out of a cannon over there." He is still smiling as I look back to see that Joe Knutson is at least fifty yards back.

"Where did that come from?" Mr. Searle asks.

I've been daydreaming about something like this since I saw Jim Ryun's world record mile on *Wide World of Sports* last year, but I look at the ground and mumble, "I don't know."

My heart rate and breathing return to normal as the rest of the class straggles in.

Joe Knutson comes up to me with sweat dripping off his forehead to say he couldn't keep up with me and adds, "Good going, Gordy."

Peter Anderson is bent over at the waist with his hands on his knees, spitting on the ground, when he looks over and yells, "Yeah. Good going, Gordy."

Gordy? All of a sudden, I'm Gordy? Nobody has ever called me Gordy before.

"Gordy," Mr. Searle calls out to me while the class heads inside, "I want to talk to you."

I don't say anything as he comes forward.

"You should consider turning out for track next spring. You can be my half-miler."

I'm thrilled that he wants me to be on the track team. I'll be a half-miler!

"Okay," I say in a low voice as I turn to walk away.

"Good going, Gordy. You made my day."

Paper Route Headlines

Police Rout Barricaded Students at Berkeley

U.S. Troops Beat Back Strong Red Attack
North of Saigon

Czech-Student March Defies Russia

'End of War Near,' Says Thieu

Woman, Clothes Afire Flees Burning Home

Nixon Elected President

Weekend Traffic Takes 22 Lives in Washington

Monsoon Season
Rainy Seattle: Too Wet for Ducks?

Chapter 16

The Drowned Rat

THE GENERAL AREA north of Seattle is referred to as the "convergent zone" by the cartoon-drawing TV weatherman Bob Cram at KING-TV and other local meteorologists like the plaid-jacketed cutup Ray Ramsey at KOMO, but I don't get it. Their description of how and where fierce winter storms interact with each other is both inaccurate and misleading. Storms don't converge, they collide! And the torrents of rain released on impact happens directly over Second Avenue in Shoreline, not some general area north of Seattle.

It happens like this: massive weather systems originating in the Gulf of Alaska are ripped in two by the jagged peaks of the Olympic Mountains shortly after making landfall. Half of the soggy air mass barrels down the Strait of Juan de Fuca, caroms off the Cascade Mountains to the east and swoops into the Puget Sound basin heading south. The leftover portion of the storm blows through the Chehalis Gap down near the state capital in Olympia before taking a sharp left and heading north. Unimpeded and picking up steam, the two fronts are like runaway freight trains going in opposite directions on the same track. When they crash head-on, the result is mayhem and misery—in the *collision zone* where I live and deliver newspapers.

The past week has been bleak. It's November in the Pacific Northwest. Daylight savings time has ended, seasonal temperatures are dropping, and the rain has been coming down sideways in the collision zone. I'm cold, soaked to the bone, and it's dark outside when I finish my paper route.

Richard Nixon, or "Tricky Dick, the little drummer boy" as Dad calls him, won the election on Tuesday even though Dad voted for Alabama's George Wallace and Mom voted for the "Happy Warrior," Hubert Humphrey. Humphrey's nasally Minnesota voice hurts my ears and the angry words mumbled by the mush-mouthed Wallace in his dopey southern accent sound … well … scary.

Dark, wet, and cold.

Happy, Dopey, and Tricky Dick.

Bleak.

Why is the changing of the season bothering me so much more than in the past? Nixon and paper routes aside, maybe it's because I've been around long enough to fully appreciate how this all plays out. The days will get noticeably shorter for the better part of the next two months before getting imperceptibly longer for what seems like forever. The season of long dark nights and short dim days is upon us. By early spring, the clouds might begrudgingly move aside to allow for brief glimpses of sunshine, but for the most part the big yellow ball in the sky won't be making a regular appearance again until May.

Or June.

Or July.

It started getting dark at 4:15 p.m. today, and now, at 5:15 p.m., it's pitch black. The glare from car headlights reflecting off the wet pavement makes me squint as much as I might on a fine summer day just so I can locate the best path to steer my bicycle—not too close to traffic, but not so far off the road that I lose traction on the gravel shoulder and wind up in the ditch.

I suspect the cars can't see me as I head for home after the last paper has been delivered on 185th, and I wonder if having my brains splattered all over the street would be that much worse than my current state of misery.

A few dark, damp, dismal, and dreary minutes later, I pull up onto the gravel portion of the driveway at home and then feel a minor jolt as the front tire of my five-speed climbs onto the concrete parking slab in front of the house. Squeezing the hand brakes brings the bike to a stop a few feet from the garage door, and I dismount in the deluge. Water squishes in my shoes as I walk over to open the overhead door, hoping that Mom remembered not to lock it when she parked the car inside after work.

"Goddammit!"

No front light is on either, so I feel my way to the porch and ring the doorbell, waiting under the eaves and watching rainwater spill over the top of the leaf-clogged gutters that Mom first asked me to clean out three weekends ago and then again last weekend.

The porch light comes on and the door opens. Mom looks at me and immediately realizes her mistake. "Just a second," she says and scurries back into the house. A minute later the garage door opens. I roll the bike out of the weather and position it against the wall where the handlebars rest between a shovel and a straight rake hanging from a couple of eight penny nails.

"I'm so sorry," Mom says. "Look at you, you poor thing."

She sounds genuinely sincere. It's not like her to be so concerned.

She smiles and stifles a laugh. "You look like a drowned rat."

"It's not funny," I say flatly, because I'm too cold and tired for an appropriately indignant rant.

"Get out of those wet clothes and go take a hot bath to warm up. We're going to see Robbie and the baby after dinner. Do you want to go?"

Of course I want to go. That baby girl is the cutest thing I've ever seen, even though I would never admit it to anybody.

"Sure," I say unenthusiastically, making sure to sound adequately glum.

I strip down to my jeans and t-shirt, leaving a pile of soggy clothes on the concrete floor of the utility room just off the garage and head to the bathroom at the other end of the house. Maureen is locked inside the bathroom, so I pound on the door with my open palm and yell "Get out!"

I don't get any response.

Fortunately, the light switch to the bathroom is right next to me in the hallway. I pound again and flip the switch.

The door flies open and Maureen glares at me and shouts, "You're such a jerk."

I've heard this one a million times so it doesn't faze me in the least as I reply coolly, "I am not."

"You are too!"

She socks me in the bicep and storms off before I can retaliate. I'm not interested in getting even though. She missed the sweet spot on my upper arm that causes the most pain. My teeth are chattering. I just need to warm up.

Once inside the bathroom, I strip off the remaining wet clothes, flex my sad-sack muscles in the mirror hanging over the pink sink, and examine what looks to be the start of yet another distressing pimple.

Meanwhile the tub fills with hot water and the mirror fogs over with steam. A test of the water temperature with my big toe indicates that more cold water is needed, so I twist the knobs to get the mix just right. After waiting impatiently for two or three minutes, it's finally safe to climb into the pink bathtub.

Ahhhhh …

My rear-end makes a squeaking sound against the bottom of the tub as I scooch forward. Then I lie back and pretend to be a hippopotamus with only my nose and eyeballs sticking out of the water. I'm looking up at the blue tile of the bathtub enclosure and hear only my heartbeat and the water-muffled sound of the bathroom fan when, suddenly, the room goes black simultaneous with the sound of a water-muffled click outside in the hallway.

Maureen!

I'm miffed, but not so miffed that it's worth climbing out of my comfy bath to turn the light back on. By the time I got resettled into hippo-mode the light would get switched off by my sister again anyway. So I lie there in the dark, letting the warmth soak into my cold bones.

Maureen.

I'm pretty sure the expression is "live by the sword, die by the sword."

Until next time, Maureen.

• • •

AFTER MY BATH, I gingerly peel back the aluminum foil covering on my Banquet TV dinner that is fresh out of the oven, trying not to burn my fingers while inhaling the aromatic steam. For a moment I contemplate complaining that Banquet brand TV dinners aren't as good as Swanson brand, but I keep it to myself since I'm starving and since it wouldn't do any good anyway. We only get Swanson when Mom finds a ten cent off coupon in the newspaper. The Banquet corn and the mashed potatoes taste about the same as Swanson, but Swanson chicken isn't quite as greasy, and they have an extra compartment for a mediocre dessert like an apple or cherry cobbler.

There are plenty of things I don't complain about out loud anymore since the responses from Mom have a common theme.

"Mom, can't we get another garbage can so I don't have to jump on the garbage anymore?"

"I don't have ten dollars for a garbage can. Are you going to pay the extra five dollars they charge to pick up the extra can?"

"Mom, can't we go clothes shopping somewhere else other than Sears?"

"Who do you think you are? Sears is fine. Besides, you know I get an employee discount there. Are you going to make up the difference?"

"Mom, why can't we get a hot lunch at school every now and then?"

"Because we can't afford it."

"Mom, can't we get a private phone line?"

"What do you have to say that's so important? Having a party line is just fine, we save seven dollars a month by having a party line."

I've learned to enjoy jumping on garbage, so having an extra can is more a matter of principle than any big deal. And I used my paper route money to buy two pairs of Levi 501 shrink-to-fit jeans at the Aurora Village Frederick & Nelson department store, so I don't have to wear Sears and Roebuck brand pants anymore. If the choice comes down to spending my own money or making do, then I can make do for the time being with my two button-down school shirts from Sears, my one pair of school shoes from Sears, my Sears sweater, my Sears school coat, and my six-packs of Sears briefs, Sears t-shirts, and white Sears crew socks.

My school clothes are more wrinkled than they need to be since I pull them out of a pile on the floor every morning, but they're always reasonably clean because I make it a point to change into last year's school clothes before delivering newspapers. Fortunately or unfortunately, last year's clothes still fit okay because I don't seem to be growing all that fast. As Dad would say, I come from a long line of "gnolls" on my mother's side of the family, which I think is a cross between gnomes and trolls, meant to mean "little people."

It would be nice to have enough money to buy something for lunch rather than settle for what can be put into a brown paper bag. You can swap out a slice of bologna for pressed beef or pressed ham or pressed turkey so the sandwich is somewhat different every day. We still get tuna fish once a week even though it's okay with the Catholic Church to eat meat on Fridays these days. You can throw in an apple one day, a banana the next, and the odd orange every so often. You can mix in store-brand corn chips for store-brand potato chips on occasion, and there is a decent variety of store-brand cookies.

But sack lunches still aren't hot and don't smell like the macaroni and cheese or fish sticks or chicken à la king served by the ladies with the hair nets in the cafeteria. Plus, carrying thirty-five cents in your pocket is less burdensome than carrying a ratty bag. One bag a week is all we get, and Mom harps on us to bring it home every day so it can be reused. By Friday the bag is in sad shape, especially when it's been raining, which is all the time.

And it would be nice to be able to afford a private telephone line instead of sharing a party line with another family. Sure, seven bucks a month is seven bucks a month, but it seems reasonable to expect to hear a dial tone when you pick up the receiver to make a call and not hear another conversation already going on. It would be nice to be able to talk with someone and not hear the heavy breathing of a stranger listening in. And when you call home from a friend's house and get a busy signal, it would be nice to know who to be angry at: your big-mouth sister or some cheapskate randomly assigned by Ma Bell.

I feel guilty fretting over the things I don't have instead of being grateful for what I do have. Who do I think I am, anyway?

I am I.

What does that even mean?

When Dad was around, if any of us didn't clean our plates and he was in a bad mood, he would say, "Eat your food, goddammit. Children are starving in Red China for chrissakes." Or he'd say, "You don't know how lucky you have it. Nobody had a goddamn thing during the Depression."

I didn't have a response to Dad when I was eight. If he was still here, I might run the risk of provoking his anger further by stating the obvious: "We don't live in Red China, and the Depression is over." But he's not here, so it's easy to think brave thoughts. I make it a point to clean my plate these days anyway.

There was a time when Mom and we kids would kneel together for bedtime prayers—the Our Father, the Hail Mary, and the Glory Be, followed by a list of God Blesses: God bless Dad, God bless Mom, God bless Leslie, God bless Robbie, God bless Gordon, God bless Maureen, God bless all the little children, God bless everybody.

Amen.

When we got to God bless all the little children, I would always think of the starving kids in Red China. Or kids with polio living in iron lungs, iron lungs being the scariest thing I had ever seen in my life. And then there were those crippled kids on the Jerry Lewis Labor Day telethon to feel bad for too.

I'm healthy and have a roof over my head and food on the table. I should be grateful for that. Robbie has a baby to love and money hasn't been quite as tight since she left to be with Adamos. Mom quit moonlighting. I have my paper route. Leslie is working part-time as a file clerk at Allstate, and Maureen is old enough to get babysitting jobs for fifty cents an hour every now and then. Things could be worse, and I should thank my lucky stars that they're not.

Still, we don't have a lot of the stuff or do things like a lot of other families. Would an extra pair of shoes, a couple of shirts from anyplace other than Sears, and a hot lunch in winter be too much to ask? How about a color TV like Art, a vacation to Yellowstone National Park like the Wanezeks, or a weekend place on Whidbey Island like Mr. Carr?

I'm not saying I deserve these things, and I'm not complaining. But it would be nice.

Paper Route Headlines

Russia Warned Against Aggression

Reds Driving Across DMZ Says Saigon

Peace Talks Put Off Again

79 Coal Miners Caught in West Virginia Blast

All 107 Rescued as Airliner Hits S.F. Bay

Pilferage on Waterfront Is at Near-Crisis Stage

Israel Jets Hit Troops in Jordan

S.F. Police Oust Student Rioters

**27 Years Later, the 'Lucky Ones'
Remember a Day at Pearl Harbor**

Chapter 17

Let's Play

LIGHTS OVER THE four confessional doors blink on and off as sinners come and go.

Inside closet-sized rooms, Father Sullivan and Father Leznik swivel back and forth, opening and closing the "Judas hole" as Dad calls it, listening, prescribing penance, and muttering words of absolution. Outside, along the back wall of the church, four long lines of dutiful Catholics wait their turn to be heard.

The light at the far end goes out, and my neighbor Big Anne appears after confessing her sins to Father Leznik, eyes down, hands prayerful. Little Frank steps into the tiny space, closes the door, and the light goes back on again when he kneels down inside. Next in line is Little Anne followed by Big Frank. The stern-looking Mr. Cross glances up. We make eye contact, but he looks down again before I can wiggle my eyebrows up and down like Groucho Marx in an attempt to get him to smile.

It's kind of boring standing in line like this.

Another light goes off over the confessional closest to me. A middle-aged man with day-old stubble pokes his head out and looks both ways before opening the door enough to make his exit. A woman holding a newborn in front of me takes the man's place, and the light goes on again.

Lights on. Lights off. Lights on. Lights off.

I shuffle closer to the confessional, and the rest of the line moves up one spot behind me. Big Anne is already halfway up the long middle aisle leading toward the altar to say her Our Fathers and Hail Marys as penance. With his left hand, the unshaven man grabs the last pew for support. He genuflects slowly while doing the sign of the cross and then starts his walk too.

I've been watching the lights change and tracking the steady stream of penitents making their way to and from the altar for a while now. Some come back down the aisle the way they went. Most cut out the side door. If they're like me, they're thinking the hard part is over once they've said their prayers of forgiveness. Now it's just a matter of playing it safe and not committing a mortal sin before taking communion at Mass tomorrow. Receiving communion when you already have a mortal sin on your soul is a mortal sin all by itself.

I wonder if the punishment in Hell is worse the more unconfessed mortal sins you have when you die?

That doesn't make sense. Hell is Hell.

Still, it doesn't seem fair that a guy with ten mortal sins gets the same punishment as a guy with only one. A murderer gets the same treatment as a boy that lets loose with an inadvertent *goddammit*.

I can't believe I just thought the word *goddammit* while standing in line for confession. Normally just *thinking* it would just be a venial sin, but thinking it *in church* is probably a mortal sin just like saying it *out loud* anyplace else would be.

Oh, man. I wish I could keep these thoughts out of my head.

I hear the panel slide shut on the opposite side from me. The light goes off, and Mom steps out after confession with Father Sullivan. It's cold and wet outside, but for some reason she decided to wear a lacy doily as headcover instead of a more weather appropriate scarf. Mom looks at me, smiles, and rolls her eyes, so I roll my eyes back at her and give her a dumb grin.

Father Sullivan doesn't waste any time. From inside the confessional nearest me, I hear the sound of the window sliding open for the woman with the baby. I can't make out exactly what she is saying to him in there, but it has the rhythm of "Bless me father for I have sinned."

I've got two sins to report today: talking back to Mom eighteen times and swearing twenty-two times, including thinking *goddammit* in church just now. The numbers are rough estimates. Am I better off guessing or fessing up to the fact that I forgot to count? Is not counting a sin?

The nuns say the important thing is to actually feel remorse and to do your best not to sin again. I feel bad about both of the things I'm going to confess today. Mom deserves better from me, and swearing is a shameful habit that I would just as soon break anyway. There is no getting around the fact that they're both mortal sins and not venial sins because they directly violate two of the Ten Commandments: *Honor thy father and mother* and *Thou shalt not take the name of the Lord thy God in vain.* I haven't missed Mass in a couple of months, so *Remember to keep holy the Sabbath day* doesn't apply today.

Father Sullivan has been around a long time. I wonder if anyone has ever confessed to him of murdering someone? *Thou shalt not kill.* It's got to be pretty rare. How many Our Fathers and Hail Marys would it take to get right with God if you killed someone? Does it matter if you got caught and went to prison?

I bet he mostly hears the same thing in the confessional, a lot about swearing, stealing, missing Mass, and sassing parents.

If bearing false witness is the same as lying, then I'm sure he's heard a lot about that too. If lying is *not* the same as bearing false witness, you still shouldn't do it and should confess it anyway.

Wait a minute … If bearing false witness isn't the same as lying, then what is it? I hope I haven't done it by accident. A guy shouldn't wind up in Hell if he commits a mortal sin without even knowing it.

As for the other Ten Commandments, I don't know.

Coveting is covered by two of the commandments, so it's a mortal sin. I get it. Rules are rules. And the priest has probably heard about people coveting their neighbors' goods a million times and maybe even their neighbors' wives a few times. But if I understand the word covet right, it doesn't sound that serious to me.

False idols? Really? There is only one true God, and everyone knows that, so why even put it on the list of commandments? Somebody confessing about *having strange gods before them* has to be rarer than murder. No way Father Sullivan has heard this one.

Adultery? I don't even know what that is and, come to think of it, the nuns were kind of elusive in their explanation. So maybe Father Sullivan has heard it confessed—maybe not. Who knows? I just hope I haven't done it by accident.

Just then I hear the sound of the Judas hole closing in the confessional closest to me.

Uh-oh.

The light goes out over the door, and I hear an unusual amount of rummaging around inside. Five seconds later, the woman with the baby in her arms pushes open the door with her rump and backs out into the passageway.

She smiles and shakes her head in a way that says Father Sullivan is in a bad mood today.

Here we go. The time has come. It's my turn to kneel down and turn on the light over the confessional door.

• • •

IT'S A TYPICAL Sunday afternoon in early December. Gray sky. Drizzling. Forty-two degrees outside according to the car radio on our way home from the nine forty-five Mass at St. Mark's. I got up at five thirty to get my papers delivered, went to Mass, and now I'm lying on the couch waiting for John Wayne Theater's *Flying Leathernecks* to return from commercial break. The jingle for Washington Builders is coming from the television:

Now with a rap of the hammer
Now just a little bit more
Washington Builders
Will make that old place look like it never did before
Washington Builders
Call SUnset 3-2404

I've heard this jingle hundreds of times, and I'm beginning to think that the tune and the phone number for Washington Builders will be rattling around in my head for the rest of my life.

I don't know anything about Washington Builders other than I've called the number a few times for the heck of it and then hung up when they answered. But based on the fact that their phone number is from the *SUnset* exchange, I suspect they're located in Ballard. I've become something of an expert on telephone exchanges. Our telephone prefix is *EMerson*, which covers a good portion of Shoreline and Northeast Seattle. Grandma Wertz is in the *ATwater* exchange on Queen Anne Hill. Dad and Grandma Braun live in West Seattle so the *WEst* prefix makes perfect sense, as does the *MAin* prefix for all the businesses in downtown Seattle.

Most of my buddies from school have phone numbers beginning with *LIncoln* since the dividing line between the Pacific Northwest Bell service area and General Telephone is Meridian Avenue. Here is something weird: when I call home from John Ryan's house on the other side of Meridian Avenue, I have to first dial nine, but for some reason I don't have to dial nine when I call him from my house.

Getting a call through to home on the first try using a rotary phone is hard enough already since the last four digits of our telephone number are 8098. Big numbers like this make it highly likely that your finger will fall out of the hole before you get all the way around the dial to the finger stop. Now add the extra nine when you're calling from GTE to PNB and a misdial or wrong number is almost guaranteed.

There is a knock on the front door. Maureen is in her room reading. I'm guessing Leslie is in the bathroom, and I can hear plates clacking as Mom does "women's work," as Dad would say, by washing breakfast dishes in the kitchen sink. I get up off the couch and head over to see who it is.

Art is standing on the front porch with a basketball under one arm and what looks like a flashlight hanging out of this coat pocket. Seeing the flashlight triggers my curiosity, but just as I open my mouth to ask about it, the sight of the basketball he is holding reminds me of something more urgent: my basketball is still up on the roof behind the backboard after an errant shot last week.

"Hey, Art."

"Wanna play?"

"Not really."

"Come on."

"It's raining."

"Come on."

"Okay, let me get my shoes."

I close the door in his face rather than invite him in out of the rain. It's embarrassing to let my friends through the front door where they can see the stuffing sticking out of rips in the couch and worn spots in the carpet. Art has seen it before, of course, but I'm not in the mood to pretend I don't notice him pretending not to notice.

After tying my shoes and zipping my jacket, I step outside onto the porch, thinking we're just going to shoot around in the driveway for a little while. Dad installed a hoop and plywood backboard as a Christmas present two years ago. I was told that it was my job to prime it and paint it, but he didn't give me the money for paint and supplies, and Mom isn't about to pay for it, so the backboard is turning a silver-gray color in the weather. I love shooting hoops in front of the house. Too bad the unpainted backboard is another constant reminder of how scarce money is around here.

Art says, "Let's go up to the high school and play up there."

"I don't feel like climbing over the fence."

"Come on."

"I've been up since five thirty."

"Come on."

"All right."

We head up to Shoreline High School five blocks away up Second Avenue. Art dribbles for a while and then bounce passes the ball to me, and I dribble for a while, shooting the breeze as we go. The ball is wet and cold, and I can feel my fingers going numb. Art runs up ahead, and I throw him the ball; he pivots and fires a chest pass that almost knocks me over.

"Don't throw it so hard."

"Don't be such a weenie."

We hustle across 185th Street and into the south parking lot of the high school. Our hair lies flat against our skulls from the rain. We jump easily over a shallow puddle in a low spot in the asphalt. And then another and another. Upon reaching a cyclone fence crowned with barbed wire, Art tosses the basketball over the top and begins to climb. There is no turning back once the ball is over the fence, especially after your friend is on the other side telling you to hurry up. So up I go.

The best way to climb a cyclone fence with barbed wire on the top is to do it at a gate where there is a break in the wire. The hardest part for me is to muster the courage to swing my leg over the wire while balancing all my weight in the palms of my hands situated precariously on the top of the three-inch diameter gate post. I have visions of slicing open my femoral artery or ripping my scrotum on a razor-sharp barb, losing my balance, and then cracking my skull on the pavement eight feet below.

I'm safely over the fence in no time and start walking over toward one of the outdoor basketball courts like we always do, but this time Art says, "Follow me."

"Huh?"

"Follow me."

"Where we going?"

"Don't worry about it. Follow me."

We walk over to the nearby school building, and I don't even notice that there is some kind of metal grate at our feet. Art looks both ways, as if he's making sure the coast is clear, before reaching down to lift up the hinged grate. He then pulls the flashlight out of his pocket, says "Follow me," and climbs down into the abyss.

This could be trouble; I think before natural curiosity and fear of being called a weenie again get the better of me.

We climb four or five feet down a ladder into a service tunnel carrying steam pipes to all the classroom radiators. Art reaches past me and pulls the grate down to close it and then turns on the flashlight.

I'm trapped like a rat!

Walking hunched over, I follow Art as we make our way down the tunnel. I can't see much because he is blocking my view and it's pitch black except for an alarmingly weak beam of light. I think his flashlight needs new batteries.

After about forty yards or so—it's hard to tell when you're underground—we turn right toward the gymnasium, assuming I haven't lost all sense of direction. We travel a short distance more when Art stops, hands me the basketball, and says, "Wait here."

He vanishes into the darkness.

So there I stand, hunched over and all alone in the pitch blackness. I think about the movie, *The Great Escape*, and how Charles Bronson panicked when the lights went out in the escape tunnel they dug under the noses of the Nazi guards. I'm not going to let myself freak out, because I'm dying to see what Art has gotten me into. And I've forgotten for the moment that we could be in real trouble, even if we get out of this alive.

I hear the light switch click when the lights come on. Art says, "Come on down," and I can see another ladder leading seven or eight feet down to the boiler room floor where Art stands with a big grin on his face.

"Where are we?"

"Don't worry about it."

Climbing up another ladder through a trapdoor in the ceiling of the boiler room takes us into a utility closet with a stale-smelling mop, an empty mop bucket, a shelf full of cleaning supplies, and a large quantity of toilet paper and light bulbs.

Art doesn't stop to look around. He climbs up on the utility sink and disappears again over the top of a cinder block wall. A few minutes later, he opens the utility closet door with a key from the outside, and I find myself standing in the girls' locker room!

My adolescent imagination nearly blows a gasket at the sight of the empty shower stalls as I picture a steamy room full of living, breathing, three-dimensional Kaya Christians and Lynn Winchells.

"How in the ..."

"My brother told me about it."

"How did he find out?"

"I don't know," Art says with a shrug.

He then walks back into the PE office, ditches the key to the utility closet, and grabs another ring of keys from the upper right-hand drawer of the teacher's desk. Together we head over to the main gym where I can smell the freshly waxed floors. Art turns the key to start the electric motor that lowers the basket down from its resting place in the rafters.

He nods toward the ball I'm holding on my hip with one hand, so I pass it to him.

"Let's play," he says while the sound of the ball he is now dribbling echoes through the empty gym.

• • •

A NEW TV SERIES called *Here Come the Brides* debuted on ABC earlier this fall. It's about time Seattle got some of the prime time spotlight. All summer I looked forward to seeing the show. I excitedly tuned in to watch the first broadcast of the season on KOMO Channel 4. It got off to a slow start, but I stuck with it every Wednesday night at seven thirty. I pulled for it to get better, for it to at least be decent, but there is no hope.

It's a dud!

Asa Mercer going back East in the 1860s to bring back a boatload of brides for the loggers and fisherman of frontier Seattle is a wonderful true story, but the show feels phony. Why wreck a perfectly good tale about the Mercer Girls with generally unappealing actors playing fictional characters like Jason Bolt and Aaron Stempel? Every school kid around here knows the real movers and shakers of early Seattle were Arthur Denny, Doc Maynard, and Henry Yesler.

Denny and Maynard owned most of the land in early Seattle, not the three Bolt brothers. It was Yesler who owned the saw mill down on the waterfront, not Stempel. Half the streets in town are named after these men, their friends, and their families. There is no Bolt Street or Stempel Way.

Old Seattle was blanketed with ancient forests of Douglas fir, red cedar, and western hemlock, yet only a few token saplings can be seen on the TV show. On school field trips to the Museum of History and Industry, I've seen that horse teams used to drag mammoth logs down First Hill to the mill by way of a muddy skid road. Today that quagmire of a skid road is paved, and it's called Yesler Way.

But on *Here Come the Brides*, no skid road. No horse teams. No mud. No giant logs. No Elliott Bay. No snowcapped mountains.

And where is Chief Sealth, the wise Duwamish tribal leader that the city is named after?

It hasn't rained or drizzled even once so far on the show. Not a cloud in the sky! This not-to-be-believed place has a carefree, perpetually blue California sky like on *The Adventures of Ozzie and Harriet*, *The Donna Reed Show*, and *Leave It to Beaver*, where paperboys peddle down the sidewalks of their idyllic small towns in the sunshine and mindlessly toss their newspapers in the general direction of the house. Their sky isn't gray and restless, and it isn't thinking about a goddamn thing, least of all about possibly raining or drizzling like in the real Pacific Northwest.

Perry Como sings the theme song to *Here Come the Brides*. He has a voice just as good as Tony Bennett's. But where the City by the Bay gets the romantic, "I Left My Heart in San Francisco," my Town on the Sound gets a sunny little tune with "schmaltzy," as Mom would say, lyrics like this:

The bluest skies you've ever seen in Seattle
And the hills the greenest green in Seattle
Like a beautiful child growing up free and wild
Full of hopes and full of fears
Full of laughter full of tears
Full of dreams to last the years in Seattle

It's not fair. They should have gotten Seattle native Jimi Hendrix to do the song with a melody like "Purple Haze" and a hot guitar solo. And maybe even lyrics like this:

Dark gray clouds are in my brain,
Most the time it can only rain

Gettin' wet here and I know why
It's drizzle from the restless sky
Dark gray clouds all around
Feel the rain coming down
Is it mayhem and misery?
Whatever it is, that sky is talkin' to me

Paper Route Headlines

School-Financing Answer: Tax Reform

U.S. Death Toll in Vietnam Now 30,000; Half This Year

Tallulah Bankhead Dies

First Flight of 747 Delayed to January

Yanks, Guerrillas Fight Near Saigon

OFF TO THE MOON!
Apollo 8 Makes Perfect Blastoff

'Moon Looks Like Dirty Gray Sand'

Apollo 8 in Perfect Lunar Orbit

Heavy Snow Due Tonight

Heaviest Fall in Years Envelops City Traffic

Chapter 18

The Good Earth

"WHAT WAS THAT joke Phyllis Diller told that I thought was so funny?" Mom asks.

"This woman goes into a gun shop and says, 'I want to buy a gun for my husband.' The clerk says, 'Did he tell you what kind of gun?' 'No,' she replied. 'He doesn't even know I'm going to shoot him,'" I offer up as a wild first guess.

"No, not that one, but that's good," my mother says, laughing.

"I want my children to have all the things I couldn't afford. Then I want to move in with them," I suggest.

"No, not that one either. It was about her looks."

"I was the world's ugliest baby. When I was born, the doctor slapped everybody."

And without stopping to take a breath, I continue with, "It's a good thing that beauty is only skin deep, or I'd be rotten to the core."

"Those are good too, but there's another one," Mom says, still laughing, as much by the fact that I could rattle off the jokes of her favorite comedian as by the jokes themselves.

"My photographs don't do me justice—they just look like me," I say, still a long way from giving up.

"That's it!" Mom roars and slaps the arm rest of her rocking chair.

"So that's why you didn't buy film for the camera to take pictures during the Christmas holidays?" I ask.

"That's exactly right. If you looked like me, you wouldn't want your picture taken either. Besides, film costs money, and getting it developed costs even more money, and we can't afford it."

• • •

ONE PITIFUL PRES-TO-LOG burns meekly in the fireplace, and Christmas stockings hang from the Roman brick mantel in our front room. The snow-white cuffs on three of the red stockings are embroidered with names: Leslie, Gordon, Maureen. A fourth nameless stocking belongs to Mom. A fifth, Robbie's stocking, is missing from our home for the first time.

Pictures with Santa from Christmases long past have been unpacked from boxes stored in the attic and are prominently displayed on the spinet piano in the corner. Next to the photos is an oversize bunch of Lucite grapes. The grapes are either red or green, I don't know because I never thought to ask anyone.

A wooden bowl of mixed nuts and a nutcracker has replaced the phony grapes on the coffee table where they usually sit. Walnuts and almonds are easiest to crack open, so I've eaten a million of them already. Hazelnuts are tasty but tricky to deal with because the edible innards often get demolished when the tough shells finally and suddenly give way to the force of the nutcracker.

Between all the nuts, cookies, candy canes, and the Whitman's Sampler that Mom brought home from work, I've eaten so much today that I feel a little sick. Feeling nauseous over the holidays is normal since I've never been able to keep myself from going overboard when there are so many goodies lying around.

The plastic Christmas tree that Mom got at half price during the Sears holiday clearance sale four years ago stands just inside and to the right of the front door, same as always.

"Can't we get a real tree this year?" we'd asked just like we asked every year.

"No," Mom had said, just like she says every year. "They're a mess, and they cost money."

"But everyone gets a real tree. They smell so good!"

"The Wanezeks have a fake tree," Mom pointed out.

True. The Wanezeks have an artificial tree, but theirs is cool. It's made out of aluminum, not plastic. And a little motor makes it spin in place while alternating red, green, and blue lights are projected on it. If you turn off all the other lights in the room, it's a sight to behold, even if you're colorblind like me.

Every year Mom goes out of her way to ensure that there are plenty of brightly wrapped packages under the tree. I'll be disappointed tomorrow if the quality of this year's presents is anything like last year's or the year before or the year before that, but for now there is hope. The anticipation of opening gifts tomorrow morning is killing me. Time can't go by fast enough!

There is a test pattern on the television screen when the Philco finally warms up after having been off limits all afternoon. Mom sits down to relax following a marathon cookie baking session and without missing a beat says, "Harlan must have tripped over a chord again," while exhaling a lungful of cigarette smoke.

We all laugh at the running joke. Harlan works for KING-TV and is married to my cousin Joanne, who is Aunt Agatha's daughter. Or is it Aunt Agnes or Aunt Helen or Aunt Eleanor or Aunt Dorothy? Anyway, test patterns pop up frequently, and Harlan gets blamed for any and all technical difficulties regardless of which station is having a problem.

I'm not looking for anything in particular for now, just something to kill time for a few hours before midnight Mass at St.

Mark's. *A Charlie Brown Christmas* won't be on for another hour according to *TV Times* magazine. Anything will do until then.

Rudolph the Red-Nosed Reindeer was on yesterday. The idea that Hermey the Elf would rather be a dentist than make toys in Santa's workshop is an intriguing subplot. Seeing him pull the teeth of the Abominable Snowman always gives me the willies, though. I've seen *Mr. Magoo's Christmas Carol* twice already this holiday season. It's not much of a story, but the myopic, bumbling Mr. Magoo character voiced by Jim Backus, Mr. Howell on *Gilligan's Island*, never fails to make me smile.

"Ah, Magoo, you've done it again."

And then I run across a special broadcast on Channel 4 that is already in progress.

Goddammit, I mean, gosh darn it, I think to myself. On Christmas Eve a guy better be extra careful about what goes through his head. It's Jesus's birthday for … don't even think it … *chrissake*. Dang it! I mean for gosh sakes.

What have I missed so far? How could I have forgotten? Why did Mom have us turn off the TV just so she could listen to carols on the radio while baking those last batches of Christmas cookies?

"Gordon, it won't kill you to turn that thing off for a while. It's Christmas Eve, so give it a rest," she had said.

And now look. I've missed part of the greatest television show ever! Frank Borman, James Lovell, and William Anders of Apollo 8 are circling the moon! The first men to leave Earth's orbit are broadcasting live from outer space!

It's a grainy, black-and-white view of the lunar surface as seen through the window of the space capsule. Hard to believe they can almost reach out and touch the same faraway moon that hangs overhead while I deliver newspapers on Sunday mornings, cloud cover permitting.

Lovell says, "The vast loneliness is awe-inspiring, and it makes you realize just what you have back there on Earth."

Loneliness is awe-inspiring? That's ridiculous.

Loneliness might be awe-inspiring on the moon, but on Earth it's nothing special. On Earth, loneliness is a normal everyday occurrence that I do my best to ignore. The key is to pretend you don't care. If you pretend not to care, it's almost guaranteed that you will find room for other things. And I know it works because I'm not feeling lonely as I sit in front of the television set. I'm feeling proud and inspired. The astronauts' courage and the historic achievement make me feel blessed to live where and when I do.

I'm a lucky boy.

In the back of my mind, I know this good feeling won't last forever because luck is at best a fifty-fifty proposition. For now though, I won't allow myself to overthink matters because it feels good to feel lucky. I have a choice when it comes to feeling what I feel, and that includes ignoring some stuff altogether. The moment would be ruined if I were to dwell on the wrong things. It's Christmas. I won't think about the bad news behind the headlines I see every day in the *Seattle Times*. I won't remind myself of my father's absence or my mother's sacrifices. I'm determined for the moment not to want more than I have.

Bill Anders says, "We are now approaching lunar sunrise. And, for all the people back on Earth, the crew of Apollo 8 have a message that we would like to send to you:

> *In the beginning God created the heavens and the earth. And the earth was without form, and void; and darkness was upon the face of the deep. And the Spirit of God moved upon the face of the waters. And God said, Let there be light: and there was light. And God saw the light, that it was good ...*"

"That's from the Book of Genesis," Mom says.

I know this already and I'm not sure why. Probably from watching *Jeopardy!*, maybe CCD at St. Mark's. Maybe both.

Jim Lovell recites another few lines of scripture, and then Commander Frank Borman finishes the Bible passage before concluding, "And from the crew of Apollo 8, we close with good night, good luck, a Merry Christmas, and God bless all of you, all of you on the good earth."

The good earth.

I never thought of the earth as being either good or bad until just now, until being awakened to the possibility by words spoken by a man circling the vast and empty moon.

Maybe the good earth deserves my attention and affection. Maybe it's time to grow up and stop taking for granted the physical beauty of my home in the Pacific Northwest—the towering evergreens, the lush landscape, the magnificent water views, and the majestic snowcapped mountains. Maybe I should stop complaining, at least for a little while, about the good rain that makes it all possible.

Now I have a frame of reference, and an important distinction reveals itself: don't confuse the good earth with a world gone mad. A world that is "going to Hell in a handbasket," as Mom's friend Jan Wanezek would say. A crazy, greedy, violent, mixed-up world as evidenced by newspaper headlines and my own experience.

The good earth.

I get it.

And for the moment, that is plenty enough to be grateful for.

• • •

"WHY ARE YOU wearing that hat indoors?" Mom asks.

I'm just minding my own business, browsing through the *1969 World Almanac and Book of Facts* I got for Christmas, while wearing the stocking cap that Grandma Wertz knitted for me. The homemade mittens that came with the cap are worthless.

They got so waterlogged after packing down the first soggy snowball that the right mitten flew off my hand when I chucked the snowball at Art.

"Because I feel like it," I say in response to Mom's question about the hat.

"I don't know about you sometimes," she says.

The real reason I'm wearing the stocking cap is to flatten out the cowlicks in my hair. They're terrible, and the fact that they're bothering me is none of Mom's business. I'm hoping that with the aid of the Dippity-do hair gel I borrowed from Leslie and the stocking cap to keep my hair in place while it dries, I'll be looking like Joe Namath of the New York Jets tonight when the New Year's Eve festivities begin.

Namath is no Johnny Unitas or Bart Starr, but he is still a pretty good quarterback, and he has cool hair. I tuned into the AFL Championship game on Sunday just in time to see him hit Don Maynard on a fifty-two-yard pass and then a six-yard touchdown pass to take the lead from the Oakland Raiders in the fourth quarter. The AFL Jets held on to win and will face the NFL's Baltimore Colts in the Super Bowl in a couple of weeks.

Now that Vince Lombardi is no longer coaching, there will be no Green Bay Packers playing in the championship game this year. The team has the same initials as me, "GB." I would buy and proudly wear one of their caps if their team colors were blue and gold like the Shoreline High School Spartans, but their colors are the same as the Shorecrest High School Highlanders, and I don't like those guys.

Highlanders? What is a Highlander, and why do the boys in the Shorecrest Highlander marching band wear plaid dresses? Some wise guys around school are saying that only queers wear dresses. Half the people in on the joke think this is hilarious, and the other half just shake their heads in disgust. The difference in opinion has to do with the fact that half of the kids at Cordell

Hull Junior High will go on to wear blue and gold after ninth grade and the other less fortunate half will be stuck wearing green and yellow in high school.

I laugh at the joke even though I still don't quite get it. The part about queers wearing dresses is news to me.

So what is it? What makes a guy a queer?

Is it about playing with yourself like Robbie contends?

Is it about wearing a dress like the guys at school kid about?

Either?

Both?

And why does everyone find it so hilariously funny? I laugh at queer jokes just like I laughed at the joke about how Martin Luther King's assassin deserved a sharpshooting medal. It's not funny, but like a laugh track on a mediocre TV comedy, other people's laughter makes me laugh too.

This is complicated.

For now, I'm going to apply the same kind of mental gymnastics required to differentiate between actually saying the Lord's name in vain *out loud*—a mortal sin—and *just thinking it*—a venial sin.

I'm going to assume that to be considered a laughing stock, a guy has to both play with himself and wear a dress. The key word is *both*. This is the only logical way to reach the conclusion I'm looking for: I'm not a queer and therefore not subject to ridicule because I've never worn girls' clothes.

More mental gymnastics are required.

Technically, I have worn girls' clothes. There was that one time when Leslie borrowed my body to pin together homemade dresses and skirts using cutouts from Butterick and Simplicity patterns. I have to believe that being helpful to my sister shouldn't count against me, but just in case, I won't let it happen again.

I glance at my Timex to see that it's just a little before two in the afternoon.

Grandma should be here around seven o'clock with the free bottle of Four Roses bourbon she gets every year as an employee of the State Liquor Control Board. She and Mom will have one highball and debate whether or not to have another before deciding that one drink is plenty. The rest of us will have Shasta-brand colas on the rocks out of Mammo's gilded wine glasses. We'll eat Chex Party Mix. We'll watch a little bit of Guy Lombardo and his Royal Canadians broadcast from the ballroom of the Waldorf Astoria Hotel in New York City. We'll see the ball drop in Times Square, and I'll wonder what the big deal is because it's still the Old Year where I live in the Pacific time zone. Grandma will hit the road around ten o'clock. Mom will hit the sack at ten fifteen. I'll try to stay awake until midnight before going out onto the front porch to holler "Happy New Year" at the top of my lungs.

Tomorrow, New Year's Day 1969, I'll probably watch Heisman trophy winner O. J. Simpson and USC take on Ohio State in the Rose Bowl. I don't like the Trojans after all the grief they've caused the Washington Huskies lately, and I couldn't care less about the Buckeyes, but this O. J. cat is something else! Not only can he fake linebackers out of their jockstraps before running right by them, but I read in the paper that he was on the USC 440-yard relay team that broke the world record!

I've never been to the University of Washington's Husky Stadium in person, but their twelve thirty games are on the radio every Saturday afternoon in the fall. Everyone tunes in because it's the only game in town. This past season, I could head down to the shack at the end of the third quarter and still be able to follow most of the fourth quarter action by eavesdropping in on the broadcast as I went house to house on my paper route. Between the play-by-play and crowd noise coming through open windows and from the radios of people outside doing yardwork, I didn't miss much.

Husky great and Rose Bowl MVP Bob Schloredt's wife happened to be the student teacher in my second-grade class that taught us the Sir Walter Scott poem about a legendary knight named Lochinvar. She wasn't there long, so I really only remember two things about her: knowledge of the poem—which came in handy while watching *Jeopardy!* with Mom that time—and that she was beautiful. I would have fallen in love with her except I had already learned my lesson about falling in love with a teacher.

I had been smitten with my first-grade teacher, Miss Fiske. She was beautiful. She smelled good. And she dressed like Jackie Kennedy.

Her request to have one volunteer stay in at recess to help decorate the Thanksgiving bulletin board was met with great enthusiasm by the class. So many hands went up that she wrote down a secret number on a piece of paper and we were told to make a guess between one and thirty. The winner would get to be her assistant.

I closed my eyes and tried to imagine the kind of number a feast-for-the-eyes like her would select. A vision appeared to me as clear as day. When my turn came, I said "seventeen" and that's how I got to spend time alone with the most beautiful woman in the world while the other kids went out to play in the rain. And that's how seventeen became my lucky number.

Miss Fiske broke my heart when she got married over spring vacation that year, and it was a bitter pill to have to call her Mrs. Hagen. In hindsight it's silly to think that a six-year-old like me ever stood a chance with a beauty like her.

I was no Alexander Mundy or Napoleon Solo then, and I'm still not. It's a stretch to think my experiment with Dippity-do hair gel and Grandma's stocking cap will do much to close the gap between me and Joe Namath either, but as they also say, nothing ventured, nothing gained.

Here are a few interesting facts from the almanac I've been looking at:

- I can find only three people born in Seattle on the entire eight-and-a-half pages devoted to *Noted Personalities—Actors, Actresses, Musicians, and Singers.* Rose Louise Havoc, also known as Gypsy Rose Lee, was born in Seattle in 1914. Frances Farmer was born in 1913, and Carol Channing in 1921. Rock guitarist Jimi Hendrix should be on the list but isn't.
- Secretary of State Cordell Hull, my junior high school's namesake, won the Noble Peace Prize in 1945.
- The population of the world is 3,419,420,000.
- Seattle is the nineteenth largest city in the US with a population of 557,087. That is one notch above Buffalo, New York, in twentieth place.

Which reminds me of something else interesting: the Buffalo Bills had the worst record in professional football and, according to my favorite *Seattle Times* sports columnist, Georg N. Meyers, they will probably take O. J. Simpson with the first pick in the draft this spring.

And get this: Art's dad went to some kind of convention in America's twentieth most populous city just last year.

"What did you think of Buffalo?" I asked after he got back.

"It's a big slum," he said.

Here it is New Year's Eve, and the living room still hasn't quite recovered from Christmas. Some furniture isn't where it should be, and gifts are still stacked in piles around the room—mine by the piano, Mom's next to her chair, Maureen's by the tree, and Leslie's to the left of the couch. Wrapping paper, store-bought bows, and nice boxes that can be salvaged for reuse next year have been placed in a larger box behind the TV. Tinsel will be reclaimed from the tree when we take it down tomorrow and will be placed in the same large box before we seal everything up for another year.

Art got a new set of snow skis with step-in bindings and new boots for Christmas. He's trying them out at Stevens Pass today. I got a Space Tilt game, the object of which is to guide a ball bearing through an obstacle course, plus the almanac, a Life Savers book with twelve rolls of candy, a four-ounce bottle of Jade East cologne, a hat and mittens from Grandma like the one cousin Leonard undoubtedly received, a jigsaw puzzle, a leather wallet, a powder blue V-neck sweater, some socks, and a pair of pajamas. A customer on my paper route gave me a whole box of Mountain Bars.

Not a bad haul in the grand scheme of things. I could be a starving kid in Red China or be confined to an iron lung or live in a big slum like Buffalo, New York, after all.

Still, my presents are nothing to get excited about either. Especially when you consider that I'm at home reading an almanac on the living room couch while my friend is making like Olympic alpine gold medalist Jean-Claude Killy on the slopes of the Cascades. And I would have preferred Ice Blue Aqua Velva over the Jade East, because I'm inclined to believe bombshell Mamie Van Doren when she purrs, "There's something about an Aqua Velva man," in the TV commercial.

I rest the almanac in my lap and close my eyes as I speculate about the brand of aftershave or cologne that Joe Namath, Alexander Mundy, and Napoleon Solo splash on every day. Which leads me to consider the possibility that men like these might enjoy Muriel cigars, the sophisticated smokes advocated by sexy Edie Adams in her TV spot as she sings "Big Spender," which I learned on *Jeopardy!* is actually from the musical *Sweet Charity*.

The minute you walked in the joint
I could see you were a man of distinction,

A real big spender.
Hey, big spender!
Spend a little time with me

Just then Mom walks by.

"Stop moping around. You're hard to buy for," she says.

My eyelids fly open in a start because I'm concentrating and I didn't hear her coming.

Who's moping? I'm just passing the time by daydreaming about Mamie Van Doren and Edie Adams as a way to keep from moping, and she has the gall to accuse me of something like this! I almost start to protest by saying "I'm not moping" but stop short and give her the stink eye instead.

Now that I've lost my train of thought, it's time to mope for real.

I find her statement "You're hard to buy for" as difficult to believe as *The Story of Little Black Sambo*. I gave her a list of at least twenty possible items out of the Sears Christmas catalog, and the only thing on the list that I actually got was the Space Tilt. I want fun stuff for Christmas. A lot of stuff. Expensive stuff. Stuff that I can brag about at school. But Mom has a strict budget, so I get just a few inexpensive, mostly practical Christmas gifts. When school starts up next week, I'll keep quiet while the other guys go on and on about how great Christmas was for them.

When you're on Christmas break, you need the kind of presents that help pass the time, not clothes and cologne. So I alternate between reading the almanac, practicing my skill on the Space Tilt, and working on a jigsaw puzzle of a Maine lighthouse. The more days that go by, the faster I cycle through the diversions because the few I have are already getting old.

There are two people walking around in my body. One of the two is relatively new on the scene, but he has been showing up more and more often lately. He speaks in a calm and rational tone, telling me I'm a lucky boy and that Mom is doing the best she can. Her life is no bowl of cherries, and it's not like her Christmas was anything special either.

How would you feel if she gave you a ballpoint pen for Christmas like the one you gave her?

The other person walking around in my body has been with me for as long as I can remember. He's the one that gets excited when the Sears Christmas catalog shows up in the mail and makes a wish list to give to Mom. He's the one who mopes around in disappointment, feeling like the unluckiest boy on the planet after all the gifts have been opened. The same unlucky kid whose father didn't even pick up the phone to wish him a Merry Christmas until the twenty-seventh.

"I'll bring by your present the next time I'm out your way," Dad had said.

I put down the almanac and wander in the general direction of the kitchen, looking for food. A lonely-looking nutcracker sits at the bottom of the otherwise empty nut bowl. Mom has hidden the cookie jar because I couldn't leave her Christmas cookies alone. She doles them out when she sees fit now, and it's no use asking because now is not the time. There is one piece of candy in the Whitman's Sampler, probably with a crummy cherry center because no one likes that kind. But I pop it in my mouth anyway and, sure enough, it's cherry.

The light is off in the bathroom at the far end of the house, so that's where I head next. Once inside I remove my stocking cap to inspect my hair in the mirror over the sink. Not bad, but not as good as I had hoped. The cowlicks are nice and flat, but so is everything else. I try to fluff it up with my fingers.

"Don't overdo it," I say to myself.

Then I cock my head, furrow my brow, and give myself a sexy grin.

That's not exactly Joe Namath looking back at me.

Or Alexander Mundy.
Or Napoleon Solo.
Oh, well. It was worth a shot.

Paper Route Headlines

Israeli Jets Attack Arab Guerrillas

84,000 Gallons of Oil Leak from Gas-Plant Tank

Allies Ambush Vietcong Troops Threatening Saigon

Protestants, Catholics Battle in Irish Town

County Jail Controlled by Inmates
Probe of Recent Escapes Reveals

191,000 Reds Killed in 1968 Says Saigon

Youth, 15, Shot by Robbers, Dies

Assassin Killed Pratt, Says Sheriff

Buffalo Bills Take O. J. Simpson

Chapter 19

Bad News

IT'S BEEN SNOWING off and on for the better part of a month. Normally I like snow. You can go years in this part of the Northwest without a major storm, so when snow falls, it's always a nice break from the monotony of rain and drizzle. And there are few things better than to tune into the radio first thing in the morning on a school day and hear the magic words: "Shoreline School District 412 is closed." We had nine inches on the ground on New Year's Eve. Too bad we were out of school for the holidays already.

My bike and my newspaper cart are useless in the deep white stuff, so I walk and carry the papers on my back in the canvas bag. I can't handle carrying all fifty-three papers at once, so I take two or even three trips to the shack and stagger to the freeway overpass under the weight. What would normally take a little over an hour has been taking up to three hours. I've never seen the movie *Doctor Zhivago*, but I saw a clip on the Academy Awards show that year hosted by Bob Hope. The misery of a Siberian winter is nothing compared to delivering newspapers in Shoreline during this kind of weather.

• • •

I'VE BEEN THE bearer of plenty of bad news in the past eleven months. Bad news isn't just plentiful, it's as relentless as the precipitation around here and has a way of soaking through your skull and seeping into your consciousness. You can't help but think about the news, to try to make sense of it. You can't not care.

Basic bad news like murders, armed robberies, plane crashes, corruption, and car wrecks are sprinkled into the headlines of the *Seattle Times* during the course of a typical week, but the war in Vietnam gets space on the front page every day. Battles, bombast, blame, and bitterness. Impossible-to-pronounce places. Four or five hundred Americans killed each week.

I find myself comparing the number of war dead to the number of kids at Cordell Hull Junior High School as I plod from house to house delivering newspapers in the snow. The rate at which soldiers are being killed in the war would be like losing the entire seventh grade one week, the eighth grade the next week, and in less than a month the halls of the school would be completely empty.

In another three or four more weeks, there would be nobody sitting in those kid-sized chairs at Cromwell Park Elementary School and no one kneeling in prayer or singing hymns in the pews at either the nine forty-five or eleven o'clock Masses at St. Mark Catholic Church.

To imagine is to observe. I'm alive and able to observe that no one else exists. This can't be just pure luck and is certainly no small thing! To be the sole observer of the grim emptiness of these familiar places, to be the only survivor, must mean that the rules don't apply to me like they do for everybody else. Either that, or I'm deluding myself. I take vague comfort in the former and try to convince myself that the latter can't be true.

A lot of the men fighting in Vietnam are eighteen or nineteen years old. I'll be old enough to join the army in a few years.

Maybe I'll be drafted.

Would I flee to Canada or burn my draft card like some of the hippies and college kids I've seen on TV? Sergeant Saunders, played by Vic Morrow on the TV show *Combat!*, my dad, and at least five of my uncles didn't burn their draft cards in World War II. Kaya Christian says in her *Playboy* centerfold bio that draft-card burning is a turn off.

I wonder what it would be like to hack my way through the jungle or wade through a rice paddy while being shot at by machine guns from surrounding hillsides and by snipers in nearby trees. What does it feel like to jump into the rotor wash of a Huey helicopter hovering a few feet off the ground or to fire an M16 rifle?

Would I be the guy on the stretcher with the bloody bandage wrapped around my head like I've seen on the evening news? Or would I be the shirtless soldier with the blank stare squatting next to the guy in the stretcher, holding a plasma bottle up high, helmet askew, cigarette dangling from my mouth?

Maybe the war will be over in five years.

Maybe I'll be a father when I'm eighteen like Jack Adamos.

College?

Maybe.

Doris Day sings her signature song "Que Será, Será" as they roll the credits on her TV show on Tuesday nights. It was one of Dad's favorite songs, and he hummed or whistled it often when he was still living at home. By watching *Jeopardy!*, I learned it's from Alfred Hitchcock's 1956 movie, *The Man Who Knew Too Much*.

> *Que será, será*
> *Whatever will be, will be*
> *The future's not ours to see*
> *Que será, será*

• • •

TRAICE WALTERS WAS murdered last night.

There was a Cordell Hull Junior High School photo of Traice on the front page of the Saturday afternoon *Times* I delivered today. The headline: "Youth, 15, Shot by Robbers, Dies."

While I sat at home watching *Gomer Pyle USMC* on TV like I do on most Friday nights, Traice and classmate Robin Mills were walking along 185th Street in the snow when a carload of teenagers stopped and demanded that the two give up their leather jackets. Traice made a run for it, and the nineteen-year-old suspect shot him in the back with a rifle. The other boys in the car were eighteen, seventeen, and fifteen.

Shot in the back.

Six blocks from my house.

Police say Traice and Robin made it to a friend's house three doors off of 185th on Third Avenue, where they called for help. I've been in that house. It's where the Leaky family lives. A three-bedroom rambler with a view of the street like mine, where a heavily perspiring Mr. Leaky yelled at me for encouraging his son to rev the engine of his Mustang. I drop a newspaper on that front porch every day. It's where Traice's mom arrived just in time to ride in the ambulance with her son to Northwest Hospital, where he died at 11:35 p.m.

Traice was one grade ahead of me in school. I've known him since we were in a couple of split classes together at Cromwell Park. I don't know why they stuck me and seven other kids my age in a class with twenty-three older students. Maybe it was because they had too many baby boomers born in 1955 and too few baby boomers born in 1954, or vice versa, to fill out classes with students all the same age. Anyway, I was a third grader and Traice was a fourth grader in a class taught by Miss Burkinmeyer.

Two years later, Mr. Haag taught a fifth/sixth split in a portable classroom squeezed onto a plot of land between the lunch room and the teachers' parking lot.

Traice was one of the coolest kids in class, and I looked up to him. He came across as a tough guy sometimes, but I never felt threatened. Girls seemed to like him. It's a safe bet to say that Traice didn't even know who I was, just some quiet kid in an elementary school class of thirty-plus. By the time we reached Cordell Hull Junior High, I was just another face in a crowd of a thousand or so faces.

I dig out a book of poems from a box of keepsakes after taking a post-paper route bath to warm up. The poems were written in Mr. Haag's class during the spring of 1966. Published by the Cromwell Press, the purple ink still has that distinctive ditto machine smell. At the bottom of the first page of *The Book of Young Poets* is a verse written by my then-twelve-year-old classmate:

> "The Bullets"
> By Traice Walters
> *Here I am in Vietnam,*
> *Shot from guns and shot from cannon.*
> *Hurting the fair and hurting the poor,*
> *The more I'm shot the more I gore.*
> *My other bullet friends think it's fun,*
> *To hurt and to kill everyone.*

Maybe Doris Day was wrong when she sang "the future's not ours to see." Maybe some people, like Traice, have at least an inkling of what might be in store for them.

• • •

NO SCHOOL TODAY because of the weather.

Art's question from last spring echoes in my mind as I make my way through a near-record fourteen inches of snow while delivering newspapers.

"Did you know there's a nigger family living in that house?"

It was an offhand comment my friend had made on our walk to school that day. A beautiful May morning. The sky wasn't even thinking about drizzling, and the end of the school year was just a couple weeks away. We were both in good spirits.

Barely a week after the murder of Traice Walters, a Black man was shot to death on the front porch of the house Art pointed out to me that day. The headline I read over and over again in the Monday edition of the *Seattle Times* as I slogged through the snow on my paper route was: "Assassin Killed Pratt, Says Sheriff."

I never laid eyes on Edwin Pratt, even though he lived around the corner on First Avenue and I passed his house every day on my way to school. He wasn't a customer of mine; he would have been on another boy's route if he subscribed to a local paper. The article said he was thirty-eight years old, married, the father of an eighteen-year-old son and five-year-old daughter. He was the executive director of the Seattle Urban League, whatever that is.

Two men hid in his carport, the story goes, and when Mr. Pratt went onto his front porch to check out a strange noise at about 8:45 p.m., he was hit by a blast from a twelve-gauge shotgun at twenty feet.

A neighbor peeking through his curtains described the assailants as "tall and young." "They looked like kids," he said. "They were young. It was the way they ran—the gait."

I must have been watching a Quinn Martin production of *The FBI* starring Efrem Zimbalist Jr., when Edwin Pratt was shot, just like I do every Sunday night. We didn't see or hear a thing, and that's what we told the police investigator when he knocked on our front door just before dinner the next day. The detective looked tired and cold as he scribbled a quick note in his book.

He thanked us, turned away, and trudged back down our snow-covered driveway.

I've been the bearer of plenty of bad news in the past eleven months, but until recently, tragedy had been restricted to distant places. With the violent deaths of Traice Walters and Edwin Pratt just a few blocks away on either side of my house, the world got smaller, danger suddenly less abstract. Before this, I never thought of my hometown as a place for headlines.

I'm almost thirteen-and-a-half. Robbie was married at fifteen, and Traice Walters is dead at the same age. Four teenagers, one just fifteen, face time behind bars for murder. The nineteen-year-old might even hang from the gallows at the state penitentiary in Walla Walla for taking Traice's life. Meanwhile, two other young people are on the run after using a shotgun to murder my neighbor, a Black man, in cold blood on a frigid night.

Does destiny really call like in the song "I am I" from *Man of La Mancha*? If so, is tragedy the result of accepting the call or failing to pick up the receiver?

Or is fate as random and unknowable as the lyrics to the Doris Day hit suggest: "Whatever will be will be, the future's not ours to see."

It's something to think about.

Paper Route Headlines

Report Blames Youth for Strife

Negroes Help White L.A. Dig Out

Lombardi New Chief for Redskins

Battles Rage in Saigon Area

Boris Karloff, 81, the 'Monster,' Dies

Red Buildup in DMZ Reported

Slum School-Aid Boost Urged

Santa Barbara Oil-Well Leak Plugged

New Lead in Pratt Death

Chapter 20

Where is the Movie House?

ART IS AN IDIOT.

We've just used the alcohol lamp from my chemistry set—last year's big Christmas gift from Mom—as a source of light to make our way through the tunnel up at the high school because the batteries in Art's flashlight are dead. He is rummaging around in the PE teacher's desk, looking for keys to the gym so we can play basketball. Meanwhile I'm studying a CPR poster on the bulletin board, wondering if I'd have the nerve to give mouth-to-mouth resuscitation to anyone other than a cute girl. I've about concluded that I would chicken out regardless of the person in need when I hear Art say, "Hey, Gord!"

I look over to him only to be blinded by the explosion of the Blue-Dot Flash Cube attached to the Kodak Instamatic camera he's holding.

"Oh, shit. Sorry," he says. "It was an accident."

"Are you kidding me?!"

"I found the camera in the desk. I was just fooling around. I didn't expect it to go off!"

"What are we going to do?" I ask in a panic. I'm seeing stars while imagining the camera's owner thumbing through a newly developed stack of photos from a family vacation, only to find my startled face halfway through the pile.

"We'll just take the film," Art says as he proceeds to open the camera.

"We can't just take the film," I respond. "They'll know someone was in here." *Plus*, I'm thinking to myself, *stealing is a mortal sin.*

"Then what do you suggest?"

Thinking fast, I say, "I don't know … Let's run the film cartridge under the drinking fountain?"

So that's what we do.

"Think that's enough?" Art asks after a minute or so of running cold water on the cartridge.

"No, keep going," I say.

"You're an idiot," I add.

"I know. Sorry."

• • •

IT'S FINALLY MY turn to use the table saw. I'm supposed to be thinking about ripping a couple of random length walnut and birch boards into ten linear feet of one and three-quarter inch strips for the chessboard I'm making. But what I'm actually thinking about is Mr. Erstad's warning on the first day of class about not wanting to call an ambulance because someone cut off his hand.

I've got my goggles on, and Mr. Erstad is standing across from me. My whole body is shaking. I start thinking about how Uncle George lost a finger by being careless with a power saw. Or was it Uncle Tom or Uncle Jake or Uncle Ed or Uncle Fred or Uncle Harold?

"What do you do first?" Mr. Erstad asks.

"Make sure the key is off and removed to avoid accidental start-up."

"Okay. What next?"

"Adjust the height of the blade to the thickness of the board and adjust the fence to one and three-quarter inches."

"Right. Let's see you do it."

"How's that?" I ask after fiddling around for a couple of minutes.

Mr. Erstad pulls out his tape measure. "Look at this," he says. "You're off by almost an eighth of an inch. And lower the blade by a quarter inch."

I can't believe my eyes. I thought I had it.

Something catches Mr. Erstad's attention as I begin to make the necessary adjustments. He freezes momentarily, and I look up to see his eyes narrow behind the coke-bottle-bottom-thick lenses of his glasses.

"Animato! Slaughter!" he yells over the roar of the blower and all the power equipment. "What are you doing over there?"

All heads turn to see what he is talking about. By distracting everyone like this, the teacher is creating a bunch of safety violations just so he can, in all probability, punish some other kind of safety violation.

"Machines off! Everyone stop what you're doing!" he shouts again. "Everyone stop! Machines off!"

One by one, each piece of power equipment goes silent except for the blower that sucks up dust from all of the machines.

"Ryan! Get the blower!" Mr. Erstad yells, and my friend John dutifully hits the switch he happens to be standing next to.

The room goes quiet while Mr. Erstad maintains his fix on two apparent offenders. The exact nature of the crime is unknown to us, but an example must be made to keep it from happening again. It's time to pull a paddle off the wall. Time for swats.

"What are you two doing?"

"Nothing," Anthony Animato says.

"Nothing," Crazy Ken parrots.

"You don't think I saw that? I see everything that goes on in here. Which one of you wants to go first?"

Everyone in class knows what going first means.

"Ken wants to go first," Animato says with a weak smile, trying and failing to make light of the situation.

Crazy Ken glares at him.

"Thanks for volunteering, Tony," Mr. Erstad says just before strolling over to the wall of paddles.

He takes his time to maximize the tension, scratching his chin as he mulls over the right tool for the job, his back to the class. These are his babies, each one handcrafted by him, a master woodworker, in this very shop. Finally, he takes down something resembling an extra-large Ping-Pong paddle and something else that looks like a small cricket bat. Both of them have half-inch holes drilled in them. The general consensus by those in the know is that weapons with holes sting worse than those without.

"Animato, grab your ankles."

Animato knows the drill. He's been paddled more often than anyone else by a wide margin because he has not, as yet, demonstrated the slightest grasp of cause and effect. The crowd gathers around as he bends over, knees wobbling.

The teacher allows a few precious seconds to tick by as Animato and everyone else in class waits for the administration of justice. And then a few more seconds go by. And then …

THWACK!

Animato stumbles forward half a step before slowly standing upright. He's trying to keep a straight face, trying to be cool, but his cheeks are trembling ever so slightly, and his eyes are glossy with moisture. He rubs his butt with his right hand and walks slowly toward his workbench. If he had a tail, it would be between his legs.

"Ken, you're next," the teacher says.

Crazy Ken looks defiantly at Mr. Erstad. Not so defiant that it invites additional punishment, but enough to send the message that this is bullshit. Crazy Ken knows he's got the cricket bat coming because Animato got the supersized Ping-Pong paddle. The cricket bat is the worst of the two because it can be gripped with both hands for extra emphasis.

He bends over at the waist. And then …

THWACK!

"Ow! Shit!"

"What did you say?"

"Nothing."

• • •

ALEXANDER MUNDY FROM *It Takes a Thief* and Napoleon Solo from *The Man from UNCLE* make talking to women look easy, but when I try to talk to a girl, it's a disaster. One of two things happens: either my mind goes blank, or I blurt out something dumb. It's all downhill after "Hi, how are you."

Scripting conversations in advance only gets me so far because, so far, I haven't found any girls willing to follow the script. They're like Oscar Peterson and other jazz musicians—always improvising! Or I'm so busy trying to remember my next line that I lose track of what they're saying. It doesn't help that the music is as loud as it is tonight, and you have to yell to be heard. Everyone else at the school dance seems to know the secret art of high-volume chitchat and is having a good time, except for me.

So far, I've mustered up the courage to approach two girls to ask for a dance, and both times, just as I made my move, other guys zeroed in on my intended targets. Both times I turned on my heels, executed an abrupt one-eighty, and headed back to the corner of the gym where I resumed tapping my foot to the music, trying to look cool, trying to make people think I'm doing just fine over here.

I've had eight tiny glasses of punch and have made four trips to the restroom already. I'm hot and I'm perspiring heavily in the V-neck sweater I got for Christmas. My cowlicks are out of control, and I might have overdone it with the Jade East cologne. My shoes are still wet from the walk to the Cordell Hull gym causing an irritation on my right heel.

I think I'm getting a blister.

Oh man …

John Ryan is dancing up a storm, so I've hardly talked to him all night. I don't know how he does it. He looks like something right out of *American Bandstand* with Dick Clark. Art said there was no way he was going to one of these things, and he is probably doing exactly what I'd like to be doing right now—sitting at home in front of the TV. It's almost eight thirty on a Saturday, so I just missed *Get Smart*, and I'm about to miss *My Three Sons*.

Nanette looks like a possibility. I've had my eye on her for the last fifteen minutes or so. She is in my league, looks-wise, and no "tomcats," as Dad would say, have been hovering around her for a while now. This could be it. "Are you a man or a mouse?" I ask myself for the hundredth time.

Swallowing hard, I take the first tentative step in her direction when I'm distracted to see one of the eighth-grade cheerleaders heading in my general direction. Kim is in my French class. She is painfully cute, and I can always depend on her to spot me in the crowd to say *bonjour* when we pass in the halls between classes. I've probably said more dumb things to her than any other girl in school because I'm tongue-tied around her and because my

French is even worse than my English.

Wait a minute … she's heading right at me!

We make eye contact.

My first inclination is to run, but I'm so freaked out that I freeze.

Seeing the cheerleader heading in my direction is as surprising as the sneak attack of a crazy rooster. As I waste precious time wondering if fending her off with a rolled-up newspaper is the right way to go, a head inside my head shakes from side to side in disbelief and says, "You're such an idiot."

"Be cool man," I say to myself under my breath. "She's just a girl."

Just a girl.

My mind is madly clicking through the wide world of girls like slides on a carousel projector possessed by the devil. Big girls. Small girls. Old girls. Young girls. Cute girls. Plain girls. Good girls. Bad girls. Satan jams the machine at the worst possible time, leaving me mesmerized by depraved images of centerfold models Kaya Christian and Lynn Winchell.

"Not that kind of a girl!" The disapproving head inside my head moans.

I kick at the plug on the projector in a desperate attempt to wipe the shameful pictures from my imagination, but blow a fuse instead, causing a complete blackout from the neck up.

"Snap out of it!" The horrorstruck head inside my head commands.

Somewhere off in the woozy distance, I hear the painfully cute girl's voice.

"*Bonjour, Albert,*" Kim yells over the music. "*Comment allez-vous?*"

Albert, pronounced *Albair* because the *t* is silent, is my persona for fifty minutes each day in Mrs. Bidard's French class.

"*Bien. Comment allez-vous?*" I shout.

So far so good.

"*Très bien,*" she replies before going on for five or ten more seconds in French. I have no idea what she just said. Worse yet, I have no idea what to say in return, so I blurt out the first thing that comes to mind: "*Où est la maison de cinéma?*" which I think means "Where is the movie house?"

Kim gives me a puzzled look.

"*Connaissez-vous ma femme?*" I add, which I think means "Do you know my wife?" It's a line Monsieur Thibeaux uses in a social setting as we listen to French tapes and follow along in a picture book.

"What?" she yells.

"*Je ne sais pas.* Never mind," I shout back.

"How come you're not dancing?"

"I'm not much of a dancer," I say, figuring she doesn't need to know the real reason is that I'm a chicken.

"Come on. It's fun," she says, nodding toward the dance floor.

So off we go.

Just as we get to the fringes of the gyrating crowd, the old song ends and a new song begins.

Uh-oh ... It's a slow dance!

The garage band onstage is giving "Hey Jude" a try.

I fight the urge to panic.

Kim shrugs her shoulders and holds out her arms as if to place them over my shoulders, so I reach around her waist and we draw each other close. I'm holding on for dear life as we gently rock back and forth and slowly spin in a circle without saying another word. I'm hot and sweaty, my cowlicks make me look like a hick, and my wet shoes are squeaking, but as best I can tell, she doesn't seem to mind.

I notice that her body is warmer than I expected. Her back, where I've placed the palms of my hands, is solid and strong. Her front feels just right, and there is no daylight between us from head to toe. The band is playing "Hey Jude," but I'm hearing "The Impossible Dream."

"I like your cologne," she says when the song is finally over, ending both the longest and shortest three minutes I've ever experienced. How can that be? How can one hundred and eighty seconds be both fast and slow at the same time? How can I desperately want something to be over with and still have it go on forever?

"You smelled good too," I say, immediately realizing I shouldn't have made the compliment past tense.

There is an awkward silence between us even though the band is back in high gear, and I can barely hear myself think.

"Well, *au revoir* for now," she yells, giving me a smile that makes me feel like a million bucks, before turning to walk away.

"*Au revoir.*"

I look up at the clock on the wall next to the basketball scoreboard to see there is less than fifteen minutes to go. John Ryan is heading my way looking proud of himself.

"What's up?" he asks.

"I'm busy," I shout.

Full of newfound confidence, I walk over to ask Nanette for the last dance of the night. Out of the corner of my eye, I see Mike Nelson turn on his heels and do a one-eighty.

• • •

"WHAT ARE YOU kids doing in here?" the janitor yells from the doorway as we scrimmage in the Shoreline High School gym.

Six guys going through the tunnel on a Sunday morning is a new record, and especially impressive since we did it with only a handful of birthday candles to light the way. Art still hasn't bought new batteries for his flashlight, and I couldn't find fuel for my alcohol lamp, so we had to improvise. We were halfway through the tunnel when it occurred to me that really only one or two of us had to make the underground trip. Once inside we could have just opened the gym door from the inside to let everybody else in.

Oh well.

"The door was open, so we thought it would be okay to come inside to play for a while," Art explains to the pissed off janitor.

Nice one, Art, I think to myself, admiring how quickly he was able to come up with a plausible excuse and how convincing he sounded. He is essentially blaming the janitor for not doing his job, for not making sure all the doors were locked before he went home on Friday. I couldn't have pulled it off in a million years. Art has moxie.

"Well, get out of here and don't ever let me find you in here again!"

"Sure. Sorry. The door was open, like I said, so we thought it would be okay."

Don't overdo it, Art. There is a fine line between displaying just enough moxie and going too far.

A funny thought pops into my head as we head for the door with our heads down. Moxie is like Brylcreem: *A little dab'll do ya.*

Paper Route Headlines

President Will Order Plan to End Draft

2 Terrorist Bomb Plots Thwarted Near Saigon

Westmoreland Predicts More Red Offensives

Heart Attack at 610 Feet
Sealab Aquanaut Dies on Dive

France Quits European Union

Oil Companies Liable
Offshore Drilling Rules Stiffened

8 Die in Ammonia-Car Burst

Reds Stall Road Travel to Berlin

Marines in 'Inch-by-Inch' Battle

Terrorist Bombing in Jerusalem Sets Off
Wave of Anxiety in Mideast

Chapter 21

The Near-Sighted Possum

THE WRESTLING TOURNAMENT brackets have been posted on the bulletin board outside Mr. Searle's office, and I see that my match with Mark Madsen is up first today. Thirty round-robin matches are scheduled for this week, and we have to lead the way. This isn't just bad luck. Mr. Searle has scheduled the matches in ascending order of weight class, and I'm in the lightest class along with Mark and Gary Nilson.

I check my wristwatch to see that I have barely six minutes to put on my gear and get out there.

At the weigh-in on Friday, I was shocked to find out that by weighing ninety-three pounds I was officially a little guy. I had always thought of myself as skinny, but it's distressing to think that I might actually be puny-looking like Mark and Gary. Is that how people see me too? Puny? And what if I lose to a couple of weenies; what does that make me? This is pressure. I think I can beat Mark, but Gary? I don't know.

I scan the rest of the bracket and see that my second match is with Gary on Wednesday and that Gary wrestles Mark on

Friday. Mark gets four days rest between matches whereas Gary and I only get two. My first reaction is that this is unfair, but after further consideration, I decide it's better to get it over with than have to wait around all week for my second match like Mark will have to do.

What else? I continue scanning the brackets. John Ryan gets Anthony Animato right after me today.

Where's Art Betts? Oh no. Poor Art. His first match is with Crazy Ken tomorrow.

The tournament is the culmination of a six-week unit in PE class that began shortly after New Year's. We started by learning the rules and slowly worked through a few moves, but mostly we've been rolling around on the mats looking funny and feeling awkward. I paired up with my buddy John Ryan most of the time, and we never got called to the center of the mat by Mr. Searle to show the class what we'd learned or to be used as his helpers in demonstrating a new hold or technique. This will be the first time that all eyes are on me.

"Mark Madsen and Gordy Braun, get up here," Mr. Searle calls out, and a cheer of sorts goes up from the rest of the class. I get the sense that half the guys are genuinely excited about getting started, and the other half are cheering because they're not going first.

Mr. Searle pronounced my name wrong again. He said *brawn* not *brown*. But I don't care anymore. I give up. I used to be Gordon Braun, pronounced *brown*. From now on I'll be Gordy Braun, pronounced *brawn*.

It's easier this way.

I just won't tell Dad.

Mark and I are standing facing each other in the middle of the mat. He's not wearing his Roy Orbison glasses, so he's squinting at me trying to focus when we lean in to shake hands.

Without the glasses, he looks like a near-sighted possum. Just then, Mr. Searle blows his whistle and yells, "Wrestle!"

Mark reaches out, and I feel a stinging sensation on my left arm, so I look down to see he's left a two-inch scratch with his fingernail.

Wait a second, this isn't right.

A split second later Mark charges at me with a kamikaze yell, so I have no choice but to pounce on him in self-defense. We fall to the mat, and Mark's lungs empty with a loud OOF!

"Two points," Mr. Searle yells.

I got the takedown.

Now what do I do?

I'm trying to figure out what to do, and Mark is wiggling like a maniac under me. Anthony Animato shouts, "Go, Gordy!" and just as I start to think Animato might not be such a bad guy after all, I hear him yell, "Go, Mark!"

Oh yeah, half nelson, I say to myself. So I try to apply a half nelson in order to turn Mark over onto his back and pin his shoulders to the mat, but he won't have any of it and won't stop moving around. After ninety seconds, the whistle blows to end the first round.

"All right, let's go," Mr. Searle says. "Assume the referee's position. Gordy, you're on the bottom."

I get down on my hands and knees and start thinking about an escape move. I only know one and it's called the "sit out, turn in."

"Left arm cross over, right leg out, left leg through," I remind myself under my breath.

"Left arm cross over, right leg out, left leg through," I repeat as Mark assumes the top position.

The whistle blows.

Left arm cross over, right leg out, left leg through.

It worked!

I'm out, on my feet and looking Mark straight in the eye.

Presto chango. It was like a magic trick.

"One point," Mr. Searle yells. I get the point for the escape, and I'm ahead three to nothing.

Mark and I circle each other until the end of the round while the class makes catcalls and Mr. Searle encourages us several times by saying, "Come on you guys, do something," but neither one of us bites.

It's the third round. Mark gets down on all fours, and I'm concentrating so hard on how to position myself on top that the whistle blows before I have a plan. Fortunately, Mark doesn't have a plan either, so we collapse to the mat. I notice that Mark isn't wiggling anymore. He is just lying there spread-eagled on his stomach to make it more difficult for me to turn him over and end this thing. The guy that looks like a near-sighted possum is playing possum, which means that by holding still he is willing to lose but not risk getting pinned. I get him in a half nelson, but for the next minute and a half, I can't lever him over onto his back. And that's how it ends. I win 3-0.

• • •

"OKAY, LAST MATCH for today. Art Betts and Ken Slaughter," Mr. Searle announces after glancing at his clipboard.

"Go get 'em, Art!" I yell.

Art hears my words of encouragement and gives me a nervous grin.

Then I notice Crazy Ken looking my way, so I shut up and gaze at my shoes.

"Yeah, go get 'em, Art!" someone else yells.

"Go, Art!"

"You can do it, Art!"

If Crazy Ken is the least bit concerned that no one is shouting words of encouragement to him, you can't tell by his demeanor. He scans the room with a bemused look and makes eye contact with Dan Peterson, who is also rooting for Art. Dan clams up and eyeballs his feet just like I did.

Crazy Ken is looking across the mat in Art's direction now. I feel momentarily safe enough to offer more words of encouragement. "You can do it, Art!"

"Screw you, Slaughter," I mutter to myself, while picturing the lifeless mouse he threw against the wall.

"Wrestle," Mr. Searle shouts after blowing his whistle.

Crazy Ken glances up at the ceiling out of the corner of his eye like he's distracted or thinking. It's a decoy though, and in a flash he goes for a single leg takedown. Art is just alert enough to step away and they're locked up. Still on their feet and facing each other, Crazy Ken is bent over at the waist. Art is draped over his shoulders trying to get behind him for the takedown. They're grunting like wild animals while their sneakers thump and slide as each tries to get the upper hand.

Crazy Ken might be faster, but Art is stronger and manages to get around back and pushes him to the floor.

"Two points," Mr. Searle yells to account for the takedown.

I open my mouth to shout encouragement to my friend, but in the same instant, Crazy Ken is on top and Art's face is smashed into the mat. I shake my head in disbelief at the suddenness of the turnaround.

"Two points," Mr. Searle shouts in recognition of the reversal and the match is tied at two.

"Go, Art!"

The shrill sound of the referee's whistle fills the gym suddenly and unexpectedly. It can't be the end of the round so soon?

"Time out!" Mr. Searle bellows. And then I notice blood on the mat and that Art is holding his nose.

The teacher tosses a white towel to Art and within just a few seconds it starts turning red. Mr. Searle walks over, tilts Art's head back and applies pressure. After two full minutes, there is still no sign that the bleeding intends to stop.

Mr. Searle looks up at the clock and says, "That's it, we're out of time. Ken wins by default. Sorry, Art."

I look around and sense that everyone is asking themselves the same two questions: "What just happened?" and "What is it with Crazy Ken and bloody noses?"

I go up to Art to get an insider's account of what just took place, but he knows the question before I can open my mouth. He rolls his eyes, and I hear his muffled voice say from behind a bloody towel, "I have no idea."

• • •

I'M CHANGING INTO my gym gear, thinking about how I didn't sleep well last night with so much on my mind. Between the excitement of listening to Bob Rule and Lenny Wilkens lead the Sonics to a thrilling one-point win over the Chicago Bulls, cogitating over Art and Crazy Ken's match yesterday, and fretting over my match with Gary Nilson today, it was a long night.

On the walk home from school, I was incredulous to learn that Art didn't think getting bloodied by Crazy Ken was any big deal.

"How can you say that," I had asked. "He's a jerk and he did it on purpose!"

"On purpose? What do you mean?"

"He's a jerk."

"Ken's not a bad guy."

"Not a bad guy? He punched Animato and killed Mike Nelson's mouse!"

"I've almost smacked Animato a few times myself, and Mike Nelson can be a pain in the ass, especially with that stupid mouse."

I could see Art's points but wasn't willing to concede.

"You could have beaten him."

"Yeah, maybe."

And that's where we left it, and it bugged me all night.

As for Gary Nilson, I just hope I don't embarrass myself by getting pinned. I beat Mark Madsen already, so the worst I can finish is one and one for the tournament, which would give me second place in a field of three. Normally that would be good enough. It would be nice to beat Gary somehow, but I don't know.

I just don't want to be embarrassed by getting pinned.

"Braun and Nilson, you're up."

Gary and I shake hands in the middle of the mat. It was a halfhearted shake on both our parts. His hand is cold and clammy, and I suspect mine is too. I give him a modified sideways glance because he is standing in front of me instead of next to me, and I get the impression that he is more scared of me than I am of him.

He's afraid of me?

"Wrestle!" Mr. Searle shouts after the sound of the whistle.

We circle each other once, then twice, and it becomes clear that Gary has no intention of making the first move, which is too bad because I have no intention of making the first move either.

So I need a new plan.

It occurs to me that I've had some success using a single leg takedown with John Ryan in practice. And then I remember all the times that I'd failed to pull it off. A double leg takedown is out of the question because it never works. I was really hoping that Gary would take the lead here and not make me make the first move.

Ah, jeez.

I rush in on an impulse, lunge at his right leg just above the knee, lock my wrists behind it, and pull as hard as I can. Gary falls straight over backward onto the mat, and I ride him all the way down.

Thud!

It worked!

"Two points!" Mr. Searle shouts.

The class cheers.

"Go, Gordy!"

"You can do it, Gary!"

I'm on top and Gary is already on his back. I'm not sure what to make of the fact that Gary doesn't seem interested in fighting back.

Is he okay?

Wait, what are you doing?

Maybe he's hurt.

This is dog eat dog.

I hope he's okay.

Worry about Gary later.

But he's just lying there!

He could be playing possum, just waiting for the right moment to spring some kind of surprise.

I'm lying in the wrong direction. My right shoulder is closest to his head, and I prefer to use my left arm for the half nelson. It's funny—I eat, write, and perform half nelsons with my left hand, but dribble a basketball, bat, and throw right-handed. Anyway, I have no choice but to take a risk and rotate a hundred and eighty degrees across his body as quickly as I can.

Finally I'm oriented properly and go about solving the puzzle of applying a half nelson when the opponent is already on his back—weaving my left arm past his bicep, under his armpit, and over his shoulder until finding his neck and situating my hand where it belongs. I grab and elevate his left leg as best I can and cradle it in the crook of my right elbow. With all ninety-three of my pounds weighing on his chest, I get his shoulders to the ground.

"Pin!" Mr. Searle yells while slamming his hand into the mat.

The whole thing took barely a minute, and I'm momentarily elated as the crowd cheers.

"Are you okay?" I ask Gary as we shake hands again.

"I'm just glad it's over with," he says to me so that nobody else could hear.

I'm glad to get it over with too. After all the worry, I'm pleased to be the under-ninety-five-pound champion of second period PE. Not losing feels great, but I thought winning would feel better than this, probably because Gary is a good guy and I'd feel terrible if I were him.

There are thirty guys in the class, and if I wrestled all of them, I would probably finish twenty-eighth, ahead of only Mark and Gary because size matters in wrestling. Maybe that's why I like running: I can beat everyone here despite the fact that I'm short and only weigh ninety-three pounds.

Paper Route Headlines

Communists Attack 30 Major Towns, Bases in South Vietnam

Reward for Edwin T. Pratt's Slayer Now Totals $10,850

U.S. War Toll Mounts in Red Offensive

Taxpayers Lose Huge Earnings Banks Cash In on Idle State Funds

Sirhan Asks to Be Executed

Mantle Retires After 18-Year Career

Marines Repel Red Attack Near DMZ

1,000 Protest ROTC at UW, 10,000 Watch

For Slaying Dr. King Ray Sentenced to 99 Years

Chapter 22

Que Será, Será —Indeed

IT'S SUNDAY MORNING, and I can hardly believe my ears when Mom says flatly, "Let's skip church today."

This can't be happening.

"You're fooling with us, right?" I say, prepared to be let down, ready to be told that she is just kidding and that I should shut up, put on my coat, and get in the car. Just like any normal Sunday.

"I'm tired," Mom says. "It's not worth it. I'm tired of you whining. I'm tired of you complaining. I'm tired of the whole thing, so let's just skip it."

I'm not certain if she is talking to Maureen or me or what exactly set Mom off this morning. Neither one of us has said a thing about not going to church today. At least not yet. Sure, Maureen usually whines and I usually complain about going to Mass on Sunday. And yes, she typically complains and I typically whine about going to CCD on Wednesday after school when I'm done delivering papers. But that doesn't mean we don't expect our mother to force us to do the right thing and thereby save our souls from eternal damnation.

Missing Mass is a big deal. It's a mortal sin to miss Mass on Sunday unless you're genuinely sick or not faking it too much. We're about to break the third commandment: *Remember to keep holy the Sabbath day.*

"Are you sure?" I ask.

Mom doesn't answer. She just picks up her favorite coffee mug from the side table next to her rocking chair and walks into the kitchen for a refill from the pot on the stove.

I don't know what to do with myself. First, John Wayne Theater on Channel 5 doesn't start until noon. And second … well, there is no second.

I follow Mom into the kitchen and say again, "Are you sure?"

"I'm sure," she says. "Go listen to the radio in your room. Maybe that TV show you like, *Davey and Goliath* is on. Or you could always read a book."

A book? That's ridiculous. It's Sunday, my day off.

I'd almost forgotten about *Davey and Goliath.* It was a religious show that told Bible stories geared for kids. We used to watch it whenever we pretended to be just sick enough that Mom or Dad bought our act and let us stay home from church. Goliath was a talking dog that only Davey could hear, kind of like Alan Young and Mister Ed the talking horse or Donald O'Connor and Francis the talking mule.

Davey and Goliath wasn't a normal cartoon, but it was better than nothing until *The Adventures of Rocky and Bullwinkle* came on. It was done in some kind of weird, jerky clay-animation. Not as realistic and certainly not as slapstick or laugh-out-loud funny as run-of-the-mill cartoons. But not a bad change of pace from favorites like Bugs Bunny, Quick Draw McGraw, and Foghorn Leghorn on Saturday mornings or the Huckleberry Hound, Yogi Bear, and Heckle and Jeckle cartoons featured on KIRO's *J.P. Patches Show* during the week. The animation on *Davey and Goliath* was unusual, but it wasn't absurd like the

Clutch Cargo and *Space Angel* serials played by *Captain Puget* on Channel 4, where they would superimpose real human mouths into the faces of talking, whistling, and cigarette-smoking cartoon characters.

"*Davey and Goliath* hasn't been on in years," I say to Mom.

"Well then do something else. I'm tired."

I can't get over the fact that we're not going to church. I'm glad and scared at the same time. Glad because Mass is boring and scared because with my luck, I'll die before confessing my mortal sin to Father Sullivan at the next opportunity on Saturday.

I don't have a beef with God, because taking issue with how He runs things would be a mortal sin. I'm not sure which commandment I would be breaking by questioning His way of doing things, but it's got to be one of them. If I did have a beef though, I'd say that it seems unfair that whether or when you get to confession determines if you ascend into Heaven or descend into Hell. It's especially unjust when you consider that God determines when your time is up anyway and whether or not you'll get to confession in the nick of time. So really, God decides who is going where regardless of how we behave in life.

Que será, será—indeed.

I head to my room, past the picture of the Sacred Heart of Jesus hanging on the wall next to the linen closet, close the door to my room, and do a Fosbury flop onto the mattress—landing flat on my back as the bed lets out a groan. I've been imitating Dick Fosbury when I go to bed ever since I saw him use his unorthodox style to win the high jump gold medal in Mexico City. Seven feet four and an eighth inches is almost as high as the ceiling in my bedroom. I know because I measured it.

I close my eyes, and the pictures of Jim Ryun and Willie Mays hanging on the wall disappear, only to have the image of Jesus hanging from the cross be projected on the backs of my eyelids. Just like when I'm at St. Mark's in real life, I try to avert my eyes rather than linger over the nails in his hands and feet. Then there is the crown of thorns and the suffering on his face. I can see his ribs—Jesus was a skinny guy—and I imagine the agony of each breath. How on earth could anyone do this to another human being?

We're taught that Jesus died for our sins, but I don't get it. We're told that the Holy Trinity—Father, Son, and Holy Ghost—are all one, and I don't get that either.

"Take it as a matter of faith," the sisters say.

Purgatory? Why does God need one last chance to torture us before letting us into Heaven?

And then there is Limbo. Why is it that unbaptized babies, like all the ones Mom couldn't carry to term, never stood a chance of entering through the pearly gates? Of the five ill-fated pregnancies that Mom endured, only her first-born, my brother John, lived long enough to be baptized and have his name entered onto a page in the family Bible. John is in Heaven now after spending just a few precious hours in this world. Four other unnamed, dead siblings conceived in the six years between Leslie and me never stood a chance. They're in Limbo and will remain there for eternity.

I don't question what I'm being told, but if I did, these would be the questions I'd ask.

I open my eyes with the specific purpose of taking comfort in the statue of St. Francis of Assisi on my bedside table. St. Francis holding a dove in his hands is as serene as Christ on the crucifix is unsettling. The five-inch-tall figurine was my reward for learning and reciting more prayers than anyone else in fourth-grade CCD.

I was always an outsider in my CCD classes, which is the primary reason I complained about going every week. The dividing line between the St. Mark and St. Luke parishes is First Avenue. As far as I could tell, we were the only Catholic family with kids in the public school trapped inside the two-block strip of no man's land between the parish boundary at First Avenue and the public-school boundary at I-5.

Friendships are forged by being together all day, every day at school, not one hour a week watching film strips of Jesus walking on water or turning water into wine or turning wine into his blood. All of my Catholic friends from Cromwell Park and Cordell Hull go to St. Luke's because they live west of First Avenue. I do my religious training with a bunch of kids that live east of the freeway.

As for the prayer contest, the best that most of the boys and girls who spent all week at public schools like Ridgecrest, North City, and Lake Forest Park could do was to say the Our Father, the Hail Mary, and the Act of Contrition. It was as if they didn't take Sister Theresa's homework assignment seriously.

I saw the assignment as a chance to get on God's good side and spent time preparing by pouring over my prayer book. When my turn came, I stood up at my desk in front of all these strangers and started by reciting the big three just like everybody else. Then I continued with the Apostles' Creed, the Act of Faith, the Act of Hope, the Act of Love, and the Act of Charity. I then added the Glory Be and Grace for good measure, two simple prayers everyone who had gone before me knew but forgot to throw in.

Bless us oh Lord
And these, thy gifts
Which we are about to receive from thy bounty
Through Christ our Lord
Amen

Grace is a good prayer. So is the Glory Be, for that matter. Both are short and to the point.

I get my Catholic faith from Dad's side of the family. Mom converted when they got married. It's funny, Mom's dad is an atheist and never took his kids to church. Yet she winds up marrying a Catholic and her older sister marries a "Bible-thumper." That is Dad's description, not mine.

Of the two, Catholicism or Protestantism, I'll take Dad's religion over my Uncle Earl's any day. My uncle is an evangelical Christian minister. A bespectacled straight-arrow with a flattop haircut. He truly believes in Christ the Savior and isn't shy about telling people about the Good News. The problem is that he doesn't have a soft-sell bone in his body, and it doesn't take much time before his pitch becomes as unwelcome as a door-to-door salesman at meal time.

My father seems to accept the fact that he is going to Hell and resents Earl for thinking he can be saved. I resent the looks of pity I get from Uncle Earl. Not necessarily the ones I get because Dad is a drunk, but the ones I get because he thinks my young head is being filled with mumbo jumbo. He seems to think there is something wrong with praying to the Virgin Mary. Or with priests muttering incantations in Latin while swinging a smoking silver ball filled with incense. Or with the same men-of-the-cloth chanting off-key while sprinkling parishioners with holy water.

I don't see a lot of benefit of converting to Uncle Earl's brand of Christianity either. Being a Catholic doesn't prohibit me from living a good clean life while here on earth. But if I stay with the one true faith, I'll have more options when I'm older. I'm too young to drink, smoke, or screw, but it makes sense to reserve the right to do these things later on in life—things Protestants frown upon as sinful but that Catholics accept with a why-not shrug of the shoulders.

Besides, I've been a Catholic my entire life, and it's not just fear of Hell and the right-to-vice that keeps me coming back for more. Rituals, experiences, and habits bind me to the faith forever. I gnawed on the seatback of the pew in front of me as a three-year-old while standing on the kneeler. The taste of varnish is woven into the fabric of my being as much as the smell of incense and the stiff cardboard texture that is the Body of Christ.

Mom used to reach past Maureen to thump me in the head like she was testing a melon for ripeness at the grocery when I couldn't sit still during Mass. The suddenness of the pain inflicted by her middle finger contacting my cranium got me focused on God as much as any lightning bolt from the sky ever could.

I've sat through countless interminable Sunday services and listened to a myriad of unintelligible homilies. I was hurriedly baptized as an infant so I wouldn't wind up in Limbo. I had my first confession at age eight and my first communion the next day. I'll be slapped on the cheek by the Archbishop when I get confirmed this spring.

Who knows, maybe I'll become a priest someday.

Who knows?

Only God knows all, and my religious faith is rooted in the assumption that He knows what He is doing. All I can do is assume that what I'm being told at Mass and CCD is true. All I can do is assume that the sage advice "never assume" doesn't apply here.

Wait a minute ...

I was baptized at the Assumption Parish in North Seattle a few weeks before the move to Shoreline!

Assumption Parish.

Assumption.

For God's sake, there is that word again.

Is this just a weird coincidence or a cryptic message from Above?

Oh, man.

I get to my feet, wander aimlessly into the living room, turn on the TV, and wait for what seems like an hour for it to warm up. Finally, I start flipping through the channels, adjusting the rabbit ears as I go.

Obnoxious Sunday morning Bible-thumper on Channel 4; boring *Meet the Press* on Channel 5; the pretty-decent Shirley Temple movie *Heidi*, which I've seen a million times on Channel 7; test pattern on Channel 9—Harlen must have tripped over a cord again; nothing but goddamn static on Channel 11 from Tacoma regardless of what I do to the antenna.

Feeling disgusted, I turn off the set.

Maybe Art is home.

Paper Route Headlines

Fighting Resumes Across Suez

Four Battles Rage North of Saigon

G.I.s, Koreans Exchange Fire

Airliner Hijack Fails; Two Killed

Senate Oks Nuclear-Arms Pact

Students March for 18-Year-Old Vote

Russ, Chinese Fight Again at Border

Trouble Reported for SST Program

Body of Second Missing Girl Found;
Murder Charge Filed

General Eisenhower Dies

Chapter 23

No Turning Back

I'M REALLY NERVOUS as I dial the telephone and then hear it ringing on the other end, waiting for the district adviser to pick up.

"Hello. This is Arnie Pederson. How can I help you?"

"Hello … Mr. Pederson?" I stammer into the receiver. Here we go again. Getting tongue-tied talking to grown-ups.

"Yes."

"My name … this is Gordon Braun calling," I say, using the confusing *brown* pronunciation by mistake. Old habits die hard.

"Yes. What can I do for you?"

"I have … I have paper route number oh oh seven three."

"Yes."

"I'm calling to give you … give you … the *Seattle Times*, thirty days' notice."

"Just a moment," he says.

I hear the rummaging of papers and telephones ringing in the background.

"Did you say Gordon Brown? I can't seem to find your file."

"Yes, it's *brown*, but it's German brown and it's spelled B-r-a-u-n."

"Ah yes, Gordon. Here it is right in front of me. I'm sorry to hear that you're leaving us."

"I'm running track, so I won't have time. March 31st … March 31st will be my last day."

"It says here that you've been with us for fourteen months."

I can't think of anything to say, so there is an awkward silence.

Mr. Pederson continues, "My records show that you didn't get one customer complaint in all that time. That's quite rare. You've done a good job!"

I still can't think of anything to say.

"Hello?" the man asks. "Are you still there?"

"Yes, I'm … I'm here."

"Are you still at the same Seattle address?" he asks.

"I have a Seattle address, but I don't … don't live in Seattle."

"What's that?"

"I live in Shoreline, but it's not … it's not even a town. So … so, I guess that's why you think I live in Seattle, but I don't."

Silence.

"Well thank you for giving us notice. I'll get back to you soon about training your replacement."

Silence.

"Hello?" he asks. "Are you still there?"

"Yes."

"Thanks for calling. Goodbye."

• • •

IT'S A MONDAY, the last day in March and my last day on the paper route. Track starts tomorrow, and I'm feeling unexpectedly nostalgic. It's interesting—I hate delivering papers, but I can tell already that I'm going to miss it. I guess this is what old people mean when they say they have *mixed feelings*.

Even though I get a lot of pleasure out of watching my bank balance increase every month, I don't really need any more money because what I have should last two years at the rate I'm spending it. Plus, I want to put all I have into sports. Track this spring and football in the fall. I've never played football, and I might be a little small at five-foot-two and ninety-three pounds, but I'm fast! I'll be a tailback. If O. J. can do it, so can I. Maybe I'll even join the Cordell Hull wrestling team next winter.

There is no need to hurry to get the papers delivered today, and even though Mondays are ridable, I decide to walk the route with my two-wheeled cart. The new guy has an orthodontist appointment, so I'm on my own. He followed me around on Friday and Saturday, and I had him push the heavy load of Sunday papers up to the overpass yesterday morning.

As we neared the top of the hill, I joked that "swearing helps when the going gets tough." He gave me a blank look in return as sweat dripped off his brow. I think he wanted to cry. For a second, I thought about asking if the poor kid wanted help. Instead, I decided to keep my mouth shut and quietly grabbed hold of the cart. The two of us toiling together made easy work of it.

"You'll get used to it after a few weeks. Even I had a hard time at first," I said once we reached the bridge over the freeway. "And you don't need to get off the road because of traffic. They'll go around you. Don't worry about it."

"Oh yeah, one more thing," I added. "I'll sell you the paper cart for twenty bucks if you're interested. You'll need it on Sundays for sure. Wednesdays and Thursdays can go either way, but you'll probably want to use the cart then too."

I'm not sure this guy has what it takes to be a paperboy. For one thing, he goes to Kellogg Junior High, and for another, he doesn't seem to have much on the ball. I told him to meet me at the shack at 6:00 a.m. sharp yesterday and he wandered in, half asleep, at 6:20 a.m. That gave me time to say goodbye to Mike, the red-haired shack manager.

"How long have you been doing this, Mike?" I asked, amused as always by the purposely misspelled word on a sign posted over the shack door: "KEEP AWAY FROM THE FRUCK."

"Since I was in seventh grade," he said.

"What grade are you in now?"

"I'm a junior."

"You've been doing this for four years!"

"Three and a half. I'm saving up for college."

I found it hard to believe that anyone could be a paperboy for three and a half years, dealing with bad weather, inky hands, deadbeat customers, mad dogs, and crazy chickens. It never occurred to me to use my paper route money for college. I had $481.26 in the bank, which I planned to meter out for movie matinees at the Crest Theater, sugary treats at 7-Eleven, and rock and roll LPs. It never crossed my mind to keep some money around on the off chance that I might be going on to a higher education.

"That's amazing, Mike! How long are you going to keep at it?"

"Until I graduate."

"Then what?"

"Go to the U-Dub and become an accountant."

Mike has a plan. He clearly doesn't understand like I do that he could be murdered like Traice Walters. Or wind up in prison like the guy who pulled the trigger. Or be drafted and sent to Vietnam to get shot at like the soldiers on TV. He might even wind up getting paralyzed in some kind of freak accident like the pole vaulter Brian Sternberg or knock up his girlfriend like Jack Adamos. Good luck paying for college when you've got a family to support.

Still, I think, *maybe I need a plan*. Maybe I should become an accountant. A plan like this makes sense if for no other reason than to hedge my bets against bad luck or bad decisions that never happen.

The story of Sisyphus comes to mind as I load up the cart with Monday's papers and head up to the overpass. Like him, I've been pushing the same rock up the same hill every day for a very long time. I don't know how the experience affected the character in the Greek myth, but I'm much stronger as a result of the daily grind. Unlike that first Sunday in February last year, there's nothing to worry about today. Conquering the 185th Street hill will be a piece of cake.

It's cloudy out, but I don't get the impression that the sky is thinking about anything in particular this afternoon—probably just some mindless sprinkling ahead. I stop on the overpass to spit on cars whizzing by below on the freeway, as has become my daily custom, before moving on to my first delivery.

It seems there is a story behind each front door on my paper route or something to think about. A little over a year ago, everything I knew about the goings-on of the neighborhood were stored randomly in my head. Delivering papers and meeting people face-to-face expanded on what I already knew and somehow gave the stories context and structure. Each house is like a manila folder filed by street address in my mind now. Each file contains a story fleshed out to some degree or other.

Miss Johansen, the seventh-grade boys' chorus teacher at Cordell Hull, moonlights as a piano teacher. I didn't know about her part-time job until last summer, and up to that point, I never thought to think about teachers having lives outside school—except for maybe the picture I had in my head of Mr. Carr lying in a hammock on Whidbey Island.

As I climb the steps to make my first delivery, I remember last summer: the front door of the house was ajar to let in a cooling breeze when I caught a glimpse of Miss Johansen sitting on a piano bench next to a young girl that, as best I could tell from all the sour notes assaulting my ears, had no musical talent whatsoever.

"Well hello, Gordon," Miss Johansen said when she heard the plop of the newspaper on the porch and noticed me trying to sneak away. "What a pleasant surprise. I didn't know you had a paper route."

Thinking fast, I said, "I didn't know … didn't know … you taught piano."

"Well, yes, as a matter of fact I do," she said with a smile.

"Well … bye," I said with a shrug.

"See you in the fall, maybe?"

"Probably not. I'm taking unified arts this year." Unified arts is a fancy name for metal shop and wood shop.

"But you have such a nice voice."

Nice voice? Not only did I not have a nice voice, no one in the seventh-grade boys' chorus had a nice voice, even before taking into account all the puberty-induced voice-cracking going on. Singing the Byrd's song "Turn, Turn, Turn" with those guys at the spring concert was torture. We couldn't hit our notes any better than the little girl sitting next to her now.

"Well … thanks," I said. "Bye."

I make a half a dozen deliveries before heading up the Dahls' driveway for the last time. Two months ago, Patty said she was due to have her baby in two months, so I guess it'll be any day now. I wave at her through the front window. She returns the wave but doesn't attempt to get up from the couch.

I'm almost back to the street when her husband opens the door to retrieve the paper. Dan is a decent enough man seeing as how I can count on him for a twenty-five-cent tip and seeing as how Patty seems gaga over him. It would be nice to have someone like her be gaga over me someday.

I know Dan sells Mountain Bars for the Brown and Haley Candy Company because he gave me a box of them for Christmas. Maybe I should be a candy salesman when I'm older. Maybe nice-looking women are attracted to candy salesmen. And even if they're not, maybe you get all the candy you can eat.

"Is today your last day?" Dan shouts over the late afternoon traffic on 185th.

"Yep," I say, trying to sound hip.

"Patty says to wish you the best of luck with track," he yells.

"Tell her good luck with the baby," I yell back. Interestingly, I don't stammer when I yell at adults like I do when I'm talking to them in a normal voice.

I tip the cart onto the back wheels and head up the street, past the spot that Traice Walters was shot, to deliver the paper to the Luck family. Nice people, Mr. and Mrs. Luck. They have a boy and a girl about my age that are mentally retarded. The two kids are there in the front window pretty much every day when I come by, waving enthusiastically while making funny faces. So I wave back and usually make a funny face in return.

The word *irony* pops into my head.

I flash back to how Mr. Carr from seventh-grade social studies used to go on and on about all the things he thought were ironic, with the expectation that the class would understand what he was talking about and find it interesting or entertaining. Mostly I just stared at him blankly and shrugged my shoulders when he looked my way.

Irony?

Didn't Mom say it was ironic that Dad got fired from the fire department?

Wait … I think maybe I finally get it: the Luck family name is ironic given the family's circumstances.

And come to think of it, it's ironic that Mr. Leaky on Third Avenue perspires profusely.

Strangely, no one is in the Lucks' window waving and giving me funny faces on my last day. It's a bit of a letdown, because I was looking forward to waving goodbye and giving them one last funny face to remember, one that would really crack them up.

"That's ironic," I say to myself as I open the screen door and place the paper inside.

"No it isn't," another voice in my head interjects.

"Sure it is," says the first voice as I walk back to the paper cart.

"No," says the second.

"If it's ironic that the Lucks aren't lucky, then what is it when they're not in the window waving and making funny faces on my last day of delivering papers?"

"It's nothing."

"It's got to be something."

"Maybe, but it's not ironic."

I tug at the paper cart with my right hand and drag it toward the next house, pondering the nature of irony. The subject is complicated, though, and I begin losing interest in the debate I'm having with myself. A third voice in my head observes that "two voices that don't know what they're talking about can convince themselves of anything if they don't watch out." So I change the subject and start thinking about the boy in the wheelchair around the corner.

I'm always reminded of the poor kid around the corner on Second Avenue when I deliver the newspaper to the not-so-lucky Luck family on 185th Street. And then I think about how I'll probably think about the mentally retarded children when I deliver the paper to the crippled boy's house later on.

Why do these things happen? The parents are always so nice. How can they be so cheerful when their children seem doomed for life?

It's fairly obvious that Mrs. Olson, the lady that gave me seventy-five pennies once, isn't home today, because the lights are out and her car is gone. I wonder if her son Dave has finished basic training at Camp Pendleton and if he might already be on his way to Vietnam.

Most of the houses are empty as I continue down Third Avenue. Empty houses aren't unusual at this time of day. A lot of people aren't home from work, or housewives are making last minute trips to the grocery store to pick up something for dinner.

Eddie Lundberg's house is dark except for a lone light in the basement. I've known him since we were both six. His dad went to Lincoln High School with Mom and played minor league baseball—including a couple of games with the Seattle Rainiers!

Two doors further down the road is kind Mr. Lincoln's house. His Ford Falcon is gone. Maybe Mr. Lincoln is out with his good friend Alan, who I met over the holidays when they were drinking eggnog. Alan might be the sharpest dresser I've ever seen—sky-blue turtleneck dickey, paisley shirt, burnt orange cardigan, mod plaid slacks, and loafers. Not a hair out of place.

Then it's on to the Hansens' home. Scott, who had the paper route before me, taught me the ropes and sold me the used paper cart I'm pulling for fifteen dollars. He is a year older than me. His sister Marcie is in Maureen's class.

The Nelsons live in the red house on the corner where Third Avenue has no choice but to turn right onto 180th since there are woods straight ahead and a freeway on the left. Paula is a cute girl in my grade, but I'm sure she doesn't even know that I'm alive.

Old Man Simpson's oversize lot takes up the rest of the block all the way to Second. He has been here since the 1930s, according to Mom. He gets grumpy about us sneaking around and stealing apples off his trees in the fall even though most of them will be left to rot on the ground.

The house on the opposite corner from the Simpson's is where Adamos swiped the *Playboy* magazines. The Carlsons live there now, but it will always be the Wanezek house to me. It's where Mom's friend Jan, the storytelling Pall Mall smoker, lived with her husband, Burt, and three kids before moving to the other side of the freeway.

I meander across 180th on a diagonal path, thinking about good times with the Wanazek boys. Inspired by the TV show *Combat*, we played war by digging foxholes, crawling around on our bellies and shooting at each other with toy guns that looked real. Occasionally we would nail sticks together in the shape of swords, use garbage can lids for shields, and play war the old-fashioned way.

Stan, Bobby, and I salted slugs for fun—just one grain caused them to curl up in a ball, while a full dowsing from the shaker turned them into a gooey pile of slime. We idolized American astronauts, loved watching rockets blast off at Cape Canaveral, and waited breathlessly for capsules to splash down in the Pacific Ocean. The three of us searched ditches for pop bottles to cash in for the deposit. We refueled with crunchy peanut butter or fried bologna sandwiches in their tree house with the trap door in the floor and rope ladder that could be hauled in to keep out intruders.

The newspaper cart is less than half full now and rolls easily over the asphalt. As always, I'll hit the Stacks' house on the far side of 180th and double back to make my delivery to the Carlsons before heading up Second Avenue for the last time.

I pull three papers off the cart before approaching the Stacks' house for the last time as a paperboy. Their chickens haven't been around all winter, but just in case, I'm prepared to do battle with the rooster. Maybe the Stacks built a coop in the back to keep them from running free, or maybe they just wrung the chickens' necks and made soup out of them like Grandma Braun did back on the homestead in Glen Ullin, North Dakota, before pestilence in the form of grasshoppers chased them off in defeat.

Or like she did on the farm in Fromberg, Montana, where Dad grew up during the depths of the Depression. Sharecropping for the American Sugar Company. Planting, weeding, thinning, and topping sugar beets in the searing Montana sun was how the family eked out an existence when Dad was a boy. "If I never see another goddamn sugar beet, it will be too goddamn soon," I've heard Dad say more than a few times.

The Bushnells were a retired couple that used to live just past the Wanezeks on 180th before they died. When Dad turned forty, I told Mr. Bushnell about how my father was bellyaching about being an old man. White-haired Mr. Bushnell sat at his kitchen table that day, massaging the palm of his arthritic left hand and muttered something about how lucky my dad was to be such a young man. I'd never thought of my father as being young before that.

Next thing I know, I'm dropping a paper off at the Crosbys'.

Weird.

I was so deep in thought that I don't remember delivering papers to the Carlsons or even to my own front porch.

Wait a second …

Did I stop at Mr. Simpsons'?

What about the Stacks? Could I have missed the Stacks too?

Maybe I should go back just in case to make sure everybody got their papers.

Nah …

That's ridiculous. I'll know I goofed up if I have extra papers at the end of the route.

It would be ironic to get my first customer complaint on my last day.

Or would it?

It would definitely be ironic to get dinged fifty cents on my last day because my own mother called the *Seattle Times* to complain about not getting a paper.

She might just do it too.

That's a pretty funny thought.

I step off the Crosbys' porch and look up to see a slow-moving red Corvair going by. The old man behind the wheel waves and gives a quick honk. He kind of looks like my Uncle Dick, the one everybody says I resemble. I personally don't see me in him or vice versa. Still, the man in the car looks familiar.

I wave back.

How do I know this guy?

You don't see many Corvairs anymore. Mom had a red one just like the one the Uncle Dick look-alike is driving. Cool car. It had a stuffed cat in the back window whose eyes lit up when she hit the brakes and blinked when she used the turn signal. The "damn thing," a term Mom used frequently, leaked oil all over the garage floor though.

Yippy and Skippy, the Ryders' wiener dogs, yap at me all the way to their front porch and back. I kick at the dachshunds a few times to get them off my ankles in order to close the gate on the picket fence.

Then I wander across the driveway to Art's house and place their paper in the *Seattle Times* tube just under the cover of their carport. As I turn away, I'm struck by the memory that this was once a grassy vacant lot where Robbie and I smoked one of Dad's Lucky Strike cigarettes when I was seven and she was ten. I'll never forget it. The agony of taking a drag on that cigarette was almost as bad as the time she dared me to swallow a big slug of Dad's whiskey.

Diane from school lives directly across the street from Art's house, but all the lights are out, and they don't take the paper anyway.

I wave at Big Anne as I go by, and she waves back. The Crosses don't take the *Seattle Times* either, I think they take the *Post-Intelligencer.*

Winnie the sheepdog wakes up from his nap under the monkey tree across the street and comes up to the cyclone fence, wagging his fat furry tail as I approach the Baileys' front door. I think about how Shirley Bailey is the only one on the block who still calls Maureen "Beeki." The story goes that I mispronounced "Baby" when I was two and it came out "Beeki." It was funny for a while, but the nickname was short-lived. Apparently, Shirley never got the word.

Out of habit I find myself on the alert for an attack by King, even though the Isaacsons took their dog and moved somewhere else just after the holidays. I wince when I imagine the surprise some poor unsuspecting paperboy got when crossing paths with that blood-thirsty German shepherd for the first time.

The Greens live across from the Whites. Cathy is in my grade, Mary a year behind. For a long time Mom used to joke that the Whites and the Greens were the only colored families in the neighborhood, which prompts me to remember that police still haven't found Edwin Pratt's murderers after almost six weeks.

It starts to drizzle as I drop off the newspaper to the family with the boy in the wheelchair, which, not unexpectedly, makes me think about the ironically named Luck family up on 185th.

Five houses to go, and all happen to be the homes of even more classmates—Pat, Dan, and Floyd on Second Avenue, Lynn and Liz around the corner on 185th. I've known all of them since kindergarten or first grade, but haven't had any classes with them at Cordell Hull. It's funny how they all seem to have faded into the background of the bigger picture that is junior high. Just like Eddie, Scott, Marcie, Paula, Diane, Cathy, and Mary.

Just like me.

And then I'm done with my paper route for the last time.

My cart is empty and it's beginning to get dark as I walk nonchalantly back down the middle of Second Avenue toward home. It's a quiet street, and there is no need to worry about getting hit by a car. Quitting a perfectly good job probably isn't the brightest thing to do, but I don't care.

I really don't care.

My days in the newspaper delivery business are behind me now, and there is no turning back.

Track season starts tomorrow.

Chapter 24

Svetts Off

THE WORD AROUND school is that I'm fast. I even got my name in the *Hawk Talk* newspaper at Cordell Hull. I used to deliver papers and now I'm in them! Being this kind of paperboy is a lot less work and a lot more fun than being the other kind. Mr. Searle kids me about being a big man on campus now.

The eighth-grade track season is over, and I was undefeated in my three 880-yard races against Kellogg, Butler, and Morgan Junior Highs. Mr. Searle promoted me to the ninth-grade team for next week's varsity meet against Butler and then, if I qualify, the district championship in two weeks on the black cinder track up at Shoreline Stadium.

All of our competitions so far have been at Butler because they have a real track. Their crushed brick running surface is first rate compared to the soggy grass turf we train on at home. In lieu of white lime lane lines, the field maintenance crew must have dripped oil or weed killer on the grass in concentric quarter-mile ovals around the football field at Cordell Hull, so our lane markers are made of dead brown grass that are clearly visible only on the days that the athletic fields are mowed. The south turn wraps around the football goalposts and the north turn travels an unmarked path directly over the pitcher's mound on the baseball diamond.

"Stay alert!" are Mr. Searle's words of advice each time we start a new 440-yard training interval that takes us through the shortstop hole and up and over the pitcher's mound.

Baseball practice is supposed to stop when we run by, but I've had plenty of thrown balls zip by my head and have nearly had my legs taken out by more than a few screaming grounders. Baseball players resent having to stop what they're doing while we pass by and make sure we know it by taking just one last swing or making one more last-second throw. If I can deal with King and an insane rooster, I guess I can handle the danger these guys pose.

Art stands up out of his crouch behind home plate, and I can feel his eyes tracking me behind his catcher's mask. I discretely tuck in the index and ring fingers on my right hand as I go by. Giving my friend the middle digit so that only he can see the gesture is a much-needed distraction from the monotony of running around in circles, and I know he is smiling under that mask of his when I do it.

I'll admit that I was pretty nervous before the first race against Kellogg. There is a difference between the idea of running in a race and actually doing it. I hoped I looked calm and cool on the outside because, truth be told, I felt like puking. Spitting might have helped make me feel better except I couldn't work up any saliva—my mouth was bone dry.

We lucked out on the weather though. It was a day similar to Robbie's wedding this time last year. The blue sky with fluffy clouds was clearly uninterested in dumping water on our heads for the first time in weeks.

Meet officials were checking us in at the starting line, and I saw out of the corner of my eye that one of the guys from

Kellogg looked a little too confident. He stared directly at me with a cocky smile on his face, not even giving me the courtesy of a sideways glance, jumping up and down like an idiot on an invisible pogo stick in his piss yellow sweat suit. Me, I got the feeling he thought I'd be a pushover.

Maybe.

We'll see.

"*Svetts* off gentlemen," the starter yelled in a heavy Scandinavian accent.

Where'd they find this guy?

I hopped around on one leg and then the other as I struggled to get the elastic cuffs of my *svett* pants over the red-striped Wilson track spikes I bought at Valu-Mart for $9.99 excluding sales tax. I finally threw the bulky cotton pants onto a pile of clothing forming on the infield grass, peeled off my *svett* shirt and added it to the heap. Then it was a short walk over to my starting position in lane two. The guy with the piss yellow *svett* suit was down to his piss yellow shorts on my left in lane one. I didn't know his name, but by then he was PY to me. PY as in piss yellow.

Mr. *Svettsoff* raised the starter's pistol over his head as the field of eight runners shivered in the cool spring air and toed the chalk starting line. There was a puddle next to the curb about twenty yards up the track that I made a mental note to avoid. If possible, I'd force PY to run right through it. All's fair as far as I was concerned.

"Runners take your mark."

"Set."

BANG!

We took off in a cloud of blue gun smoke, and I kept PY pinned to the curb. He had no choice but to run through the puddle as per my plan, but it was a shock to have him splash me with cold water and mud. My beautiful Cordell Hull singlet was a mess, and my legs momentarily went numb and stiffened up.

I'd have to remember for future reference that sinister plans need to be foolproof.

I accelerated before glancing over my left shoulder to see that I could safely cut to the curb lane.

Crunch, crunch, crunch, crunch, crunch was the sound our five-eighths inch spikes made in the crushed brick track.

A gust of wind tried to knock me over at the top of the turn, so I leaned into it. Just like that, the wind stopped suddenly and I stumbled for two steps before regaining my rhythm.

Crunch, crunch, crunch, crunch, crunch.

I sensed PY pulling up on my right shoulder as we came out of the turn and headed down the backstretch on the first of two laps. I adjusted my pace to keep him there and couldn't believe it when he stayed on my shoulder the entire way through the next turn instead of falling in behind me. He was running extra distance by running in lane two.

He really is an idiot.

Crunch, crunch, crunch, crunch, crunch.

The Cordell Hull Junior High cheerleaders were there in their red and black sweaters, saddle shoes, and cute berets. No pom-poms that I could see. Too bad about the pom-poms, I could have used the extra lift.

"Go, Gordy, go! You can do it!"

Hi, Janet. Hi, Melody. Hi, Kris. Hi, Nancy. Hi, Brita. Bonjour, Kim, I thought while giving them a series of sideways glances as I raced up the straightaway toward the start/finish line.

Crunch, crunch, crunch, crunch, crunch.

The gun lap was just steps away and PY was falling back.

Crunch, crunch, crunch, crunch, crunch.

"Seventy, seventy-one, seventy-two," shouted the official to let me know my first lap split.

I wasn't sure if seventy-one seconds was good or bad. All I knew was that I was beating PY.

BANG!

One lap to go.

You can do it. Stay with it, man.

Crunch, crunch, crunch, crunch, crunch into the south turn I ran.

Coming out of the turn, I headed toward the backstretch again. Another gust of wind slapped me right in the face. Another brief stumble. I heard the sound of an engine rev, tires peeling out, and then the blast of a car horn coming from over on Aurora Avenue, two blocks away. A small belch out of nowhere reminded me of the tuna fish sandwich I had for lunch. *Oh yeah, it's Friday*. I keep telling Mom that the Church doesn't mind if we eat bologna on Friday these days, but she is set in her ways.

I took a quick peek behind and saw that PY was losing ground, but still holding onto second place as Joe Knutson and Peter Anderson closed in on him.

Three hundred thirty yards to go. Two straightaways and one turn.

Crunch, crunch, crunch, crunch, crunch down the backstretch for the second and last time.

I tried to pick up the pace, but my legs wouldn't have it. I told myself to relax.

Fast and relaxed, that's the ticket.

Crunch, crunch, crunch, crunch, crunch.

Am I pulling away because I'm moving faster than before or because everyone else is slowing down faster than me?

I was miserable. It was impossible to believe my competitors could be feeling worse. My only hope was that they felt almost as bad. I thought about Kip Keino at the Olympics and felt momentarily better.

Top of the final turn. One hundred sixty-five yards to the finish line. The wind at my back.

Crunch, crunch, crunch, crunch, crunch.

I got up on my toes and sprinted up the home straightaway with everything I had. I began to wheeze, slobber all over myself, and my stride felt more like a stagger.

I can't get any air!

The sharp pain in my side could only mean that my appendix was about to explode! I could see the headline in the *Seattle Times* already: "Boy Dies of Burst Appendix, Loses Race."

Crunch, crunch, crunch, crunch, crunch.

"Go, Gordy! You can do it!"

Fifty yards to go.

Crunch, crunch, crunch, crunch, crunch.

Twenty-five yards.

Crunch, crunch, crunch, crunch, crunch.

Almost there.

Crunch, crunch.

I hit the tape stretched across the finish line, and it immediately wrapped around my torso. The hard-earned prize was just an eight-foot length of white string. I grasped it with both hands and briefly savored the texture before feeling it, and the moment, begin to slip through my fingers. Over my right shoulder, I noticed Mr. Svettsoff tugging at the string so it could be reused in the 440-yard race coming up next.

"You won! Congratulations," said a smiling young woman in a red, white, and blue tracksuit while putting her arm over my shoulder and stooping down to make eye contact with me.

"Your time was 2:21.7. Winning is fun isn't it?"

It's Doris Brown! She ran the 800 meters at the Olympics last year in Mexico City!

"Yes," I managed to say out loud.

I was amazed that I won and flabbergasted that an actual Olympian was taking time with me. She was on the same team as Jim Ryun, Bill Toomey, Bob Beamon, Bob Seagren, Dick Fosbury, Tommie Smith, John Carlos, Willie Davenport, and Lee

Evans! I desperately tried to think of something worth saying, but my brain let me down.

"Well, enjoy it. Congratulations again," she said.

She turned to walk away, and I saw the letters USA proudly displayed on the back of her warm-up suit.

Oh, man. I know Doris Brown!

• • •

WE WERE ALMOST through with dinner. I'd been waiting for almost half an hour for Mom to ask me about my day.

Finally, she said, "Anything new to report, Gordon?"

"I had my first track race today."

"Oh yeah! I forgot. How'd it go?"

"I won."

"Really? Congratulations! I've never won anything in my life."

"You're a liar," Maureen blurted out.

"Maureen! Stop that!" Mom chastised.

"He's a liar!"

"I am not."

Chapter 25

Buzz Saw Braun

THERE ARE CERTAIN things that you expect to happen without realizing you expect them to happen. Like when you head to the boys' bathroom between classes, you expect large numbers of guys to be squeezing through the door going in either direction. You expect people to be in a hurry and for there to be bumping and jostling. Normally, guys will murmur "Sorry" or "Excuse me" as they go by. Sometimes they'll give you a friendly shove while making a smart aleck comment.

If you subconsciously expect something to happen and it doesn't happen, then you get a funny feeling. And so I had a funny feeling when no one was coming or going from the boys' bathroom between periods, but not so much that it prevented me leaving the crowded hallway to push open the door and go inside.

Big mistake.

There is toilet paper everywhere! It's draped over the tops of the stalls and hanging from the light fixtures in the ceiling. Toilet paper is wadded up on the tile floor and overflowing the trash cans. It's stretched across the room, over the mirrors, under the sinks, and wrapped around the urinals.

I take in the scene for an instant; my brain flashes *Red Alert*, and I immediately turn on my heels to leave.

But it's too late.

"Hi, Gordon," Crazy Ken says as he saunters out of the last stall.

A chill goes up my spine. I didn't think he even knew my name.

I see that Crazy Ken has an open Zippo lighter in his right hand with his thumb on the wheel.

Oh shit. He's about to set the place on fire!

"Hey, Ken," I say casually. "What's happenin'?"

"Not much," he says. "How about you?"

"Not much … All right … well … see you around."

"Yeah. See you around."

I have two things on my mind as I leave the boys' bathroom and step back into the bustling hallway. The scariest of the two is that I'm no longer just another anonymous face in the crowd as far as Ken is concerned. He knows who I am and he knows I know he's a pyromaniac. It seems like only a matter of time before I'll be bloodied by a lightening quick punch in the nose.

The other matter is less scary but painfully urgent—my bladder is about to explode! It's a race against the clock to see if I can make it to the restroom in the 400 building before the fire alarm goes off and we're hustled outside for safety.

• • •

WE'VE BEEN DOING the Presidential Physical Fitness test this week. I can't broad jump very far, and I can't throw the softball as well as the bigger guys. My fifty-yard dash is just okay, but I'm near the top of my PE class when it comes to pull-ups, sit-ups, and shuttle run. The last event, the six hundred-yard run, is today and I expect to win it easily. I'm not even feeling nervous, which is unusual.

My optimistic outlook is based on the fact that I got fifth in the 880 behind four ninth graders at the Junior High District Championship meet. Mr. Searle thinks my 2:14.7 is the second-fastest time ever run at Cordell Hull Junior High by an eighth grader. Rich Bjornson ran 2:09 to win it all last year as an eighth grader and then ran 2:06 to repeat as a freshman. Rich is a legend around here. He's been running track and breaking age-group records since fourth grade—about the same time he started shaving. Or so goes the joke behind his back.

The weather has been decent lately and the sun is out today, so the grass track should be in good shape. The six hundred is slightly less than a lap and a half. We'll start at the head of the east straightaway, run once over the pitcher's mound at the top of the north turn, go all the way around again, and finish just past third base. Mr. Searle is going to have to really hustle if he expects to get to the finish line with his stopwatch.

Nobody begrudges me the best starting position on the poll in lane one, so I just stand there while the rest of the class fills in three and four deep across the rest of the starting line. Mr. Searle reminds us to listen for our times when we finish so he can record them on his class list.

"Any questions?"

"How far is it again?"

It's Animato.

That figures.

"If you took the wax out of your ears, you'd have heard me the first time," Mr. Searle yells over a low-flying helicopter. "The race is six hundred yards. That's a lap and a half. We'll finish just past third base … Don't get lost out there, Tony. When in doubt, just follow Gordy and the rest of the crowd around the big circle on the grass until they stop."

Everybody chuckles, even Animato. But it's clear he doesn't get it.

I feel someone shoving their way to the front of the crowd and tap me on the shoulder.

"Hey, Gordon. How you doing?"

It's Crazy Ken!

"I'm fine, Ken. How are you?"

"I'm good. Ready to race, hot shot?"

Wait a minute … This isn't Crazy Ken talking, it's Impulsive Ken!

He's here to beat me!

"Of course," I manage to say calmly even though underneath I'm terrified by the unexpected turn of events. How could I have missed this? There is obviously only one kid in the eighth grade that can beat me, and that is Impulsive Ken. Suddenly I'm just another sucker to be checked off Impulsive Ken's checklist of suckers. Suddenly, the only reason I won all my races against other eight graders was because Impulsive Ken hadn't showed up to put me in my place. Feeling helpless and small while he towers over me in lane two, I'm just another mouse to be thrown against the wall, another kid whose nose is about to be bloodied.

Wait a minute …

He just called me a hot shot …

What's that supposed to mean? And what's with that bemused, overconfident Impulsive Ken smile he's giving me?

That silly smile coming on the heels of the "hot shot" crack really burns me up. I'm surprised to feel a fire in my belly so soon after my bout with self-doubt and sense of impending doom.

Fuck him, I think, not the least bit concerned about going to Hell. New rule: it's not a sin to think the f-word if the guy genuinely deserves it. And that fucker Pyromaniac Ken deserves it!

"Good luck, Ken," I say.

Mr. Searle doesn't have a starter's pistol, so he holds the stopwatch over his head and shouts, "Go!"

We take off down the first straightaway. The pack of runners obstructs the mid-morning sun to produce an amorphous inkblot of a shadow advancing down the infield. By the time we're three-quarters of the way to the north turn, there are ten yards of daylight between Ken and me and the rest of the class. He is loping along at my side. I can't help but notice that I'm taking almost two steps for each of his long, beautiful strides. We exchange sideways glances. He looks fresh, relaxed, and confident.

Coming to the dirt of the baseball infield, he runs on my shoulder into the turn and over the pitcher's mound. We're kicking up a cloud of dust that the rest of the group will have to run through. Clean air is one of the advantages of being a front-runner at Cordell Hull Junior High on a rare dry day like today.

Back onto the grass track and heading south down the west straightaway, I sense that we're slowing down ever so slightly, so I make a concerted effort to pick up the pace. In my peripheral vision, I can see sweat forming on Ken's forehead over his left eye, but he stays with me.

I'm starting to sweat too, but it feels like I'm just getting warmed up, so I don't worry about it. Nothing wrong with my breathing. Nice rhythm. Legs feel fine. I push the pace a little harder.

Side by side we go into the south turn. Ken is again running extra distance because he won't take the lead and because he doesn't know enough to fall in behind me. A real track guy would know that. I'm a track guy and he isn't.

One lap of 440 yards completed, just 160 yards left to go, all in the one long straightaway in front of us. It's anybody's race. We'd be shoulder to shoulder if only I were taller. More like shoulder to elbow. Maybe that's where the bloody nose comes in: a slight misstep and, what do you know, there is accidental contact of elbow to nose.

Screw the sideways glance. I turn my head and look directly up at Impulsive Ken. Our eyes meet. There is something in his look that gives me hope. I don't think he thought it would be this hard. He decided on a whim to show me up, but six hundred yards isn't over in an instant like a basketball layup or a shot on goal or a punch in the nose. You have to stick with it if you're going to make it as a distance runner.

Everything has always been easy for Impulsive Ken.

Maybe not this time, hot shot.

I go for broke and start my sprint to the finish. Six hundred yards is a short race for me. If I don't make my move and open up some ground, if I let Ken stick around, he could still outkick me at the end.

One hundred yards to go and I'm running as fast as I can. Ken is still with me. Neck and neck, me still taking almost two quick steps for each one of his loping strides, staying alert to the possibility of an elbow to the face. I'm not even tired, and it's frustrating not to be able to go faster.

Seventy-five yards to go. I turn my head again and then do a double take because I can't believe what I see: it's the look of incredulity on my opponent's face as Impulsive Ken realizes he is going to lose for the first time! He falters, drops his arms, and slows to a jog while I hurry to the finish line.

I'm elated to be doing the impossible. I'm going to beat the unbeatable foe!

Mr. Searle is calling out times as I get closer to the finish line: "one twenty-seven, one twenty-eight, one twenty-nine."

I stop, bend over to spit a couple of times onto the grass, and turn around to see Vanquished Ken finish up, eyes down, slobber all over his chin.

"One thirty-two, one thirty-three, one-thirty-four." Mr. Searle keeps calling out times as the rest of the class staggers in. When everyone is finally done, I expect my coach to give me a pat on the back like he's done after every other one of my races. To my surprise, Mr. Searle walks over to my nemesis a few yards away, and I overhear him say, "Nice job, Ken. You ran into a buzz saw today."

Then he looks over to me and gives me a wink.

That wink from Mr. Searle means more to me than any pat on the back ever could. A pat on the back is an acknowledgment of effort. That wink was about rising to the challenge.

Buzz Saw Braun?

Not a bad nickname.

Maybe not as good as "Joltin' Joe" or "Flash Gordon," but not bad at all.

Chapter 26

We're All Croakers

I'M NOT SURE I believe what Art is telling me.

"Are you sure? Are you pulling my leg?"

"I'm telling you a blow job is …"

I cut him off. "Yeah, yeah, I heard you the first time. How do you know?"

"My brother told me."

"How does he know?"

"He just knows."

"No girl would ever do that in a million years!"

"How do you know?"

"Really?"

"Yes, really."

"It doesn't have anything to do with a girl's boobs?" I ask.

"Huh?" Art says. "Don't be an idiot."

• • •

IT'S FRIDAY MORNING and I'm in a good mood. Just four measly school days before summer vacation starts next week. There is a hop in my step as I head through the living room on my way to pouring myself a bowl of cereal in the kitchen.

Good feelings give way to distress when I see trash all over the driveway through the front window. The beat-up metal garbage can is on its side, and the lid somehow managed to roll all the way down into the street. Obviously, I didn't secure the lid tightly enough after jumping on the garbage last night. Mom left tire tracks in the debris when she backed out on her way to work this morning. Rolling over the mess in reverse gear is no accident. Garbage is my job and by driving over it instead of taking the time to clean it up herself, she is reminding me once again that I'm on my own.

Goddamn raccoons.

The sky hasn't been the least bit indecisive lately. It poured most of the night, punctuating a week of heavy rain that began the Sunday before Memorial Day. The trash looks soggy and heavy as I size up the crisis. It will only get worse if I allow it to sit outside all day while I'm at school.

I hurriedly tie my shoes and head outdoors, shrugging my shoulders against the collar of my jacket to keep out the worst of the rain. In a few minutes I won't care, but for now I do. There is a proper way to transition from being dry to being drenched, and shrugging the shoulders is part of the routine. By the time my shoulders get tired, I'll be too wet to care about getting any wetter.

Dealing with spilled garbage is nothing new. I grab a shovel off the wall of the garage, walk over to retrieve the overturned receptacle, and then drag them both down to the street. My plan is to start at the road and work my way back toward the house, filling up the garbage can as I go.

The rain is pouring down. My shoulder-shrugging can't handle the volume. I can feel the water trickling down my neck, which makes me shiver involuntarily.

What a mess.

I bend over to pick up a half-gallon Lucerne milk carton, then a flattened Lucerne tin roof ice cream container, a Green Giant frozen pea box, a Chef Boyardee pizza box, a StarKist tuna fish can, and four aluminum TV dinner trays sans dessert compartments. It's obvious that raccoons like tuna fish, TV dinners, and ice cream because the containers are all sparkling clean.

There is no way I'm going to touch the gelatinous wads of bathroom tissue scattered everywhere with my bare hands. Ditto the egg shells, coffee grounds, rotten cabbage, apple cores, and banana peels, so I begin scooping them up with the shovel and plopping them into the can. I remind myself to stay on the alert for one disgusting item in particular. Suffice it to say that I scooped the yard prior to mowing it during a short break between storms on Tuesday after school.

Goddamn dogs.

Mrs. Betts toots the horn of her New Yorker and waves as she drives slowly by. I can barely see her through the fog on the windshield. There is a clear spot in the glass near the hood of the car, suggesting that her defrosters are working feverishly to catch up.

Art is in the passenger seat.

Where's he going? It's too early for her to be dropping him off at school, and they would offer me a ride if that's where they're headed. Probably a dentist appointment. Or maybe his Osgood-Schlatter disease is acting up again so he is off to see the "old saw bones," as Dad would say.

Art smiles sinisterly and discretely flips me the bird through the side window. His mom might not have the clearest of views, but I resist the urge to give my friend the same salute in return, just in case she can see more than I think she can see. Erring on the side of caution, I offer them a halfhearted wave and a frown before returning to my revolting task.

Wet newspapers weigh a ton, but at least they don't stink. Pages are matted together, but I can still read the headlines on the translucent newsprint.

It's been two months since I last delivered newspapers, yet the headlines and articles I see lying on the rain-soaked ground today are familiar to me because I read them when they were still fresh and dry in the comfort of my living room. Becoming a regular newspaper reader is what happens to a guy after he is forced to read the same headlines fifty-three times every day for over a year.

Upon picking up a soggy sports page off the gravel driveway, I'm reminded that Denny McLain, last year's thirty-game winner, went nine innings and got a no-decision when Detroit beat the Pilots 4-3 in ten innings at Tiger Stadium the other day. I listened to part of the game broadcast by Jimmy Dudley and Bill Schonely on KVI 570. Second baseman Tommy Harper got his thirtieth stolen base, and the season is still barely two months old. Right fielder Mike Hegan is sixth in the American League with a batting average of .309. Another sports page headline says the Giants ended the Mets' eleven-game winning streak. An eleven-game winning streak is pretty amazing for a historically terrible team like the lowly New York Mets.

More soggy news from drenched newspapers scattered all over the place: U.S. Jets Strike in N. Vietnam; Flaming Helicopter Crashes Near 747 at Air Show; Peking Accused of Planning War; Massive Rail Crash Kills 2; Mexican Jet Down, 72 Aboard; 73 Feared Lost on Rammed Destroyer; Green Lake Hydroplane Skips into Disingegration.

There is a classic photo of a limited-class hydroplane in mid-flip to go along with the hydro headline. No one died in this crash, which is fortunate. Hydroplane racing is a big deal around here. Kids tie homemade wooden replicas to the backs of their bike seats and race lap after lap, heat after heat, around the south parking lot at Shoreline High School. Hundreds of thousands of fans line the shores of Lake Washington for the grand finale of the two-week Seafair celebration in August. There is nothing like the sight of rooster tails and the roar of the Unlimiteds. All three local TV stations broadcast live all day from the Stan Sayres pits, so it's impossible to miss the races even if you wanted to. But who could possibly want to miss them?

Death is an occasional by-product of our passion for thunder boats. It's sad to see but adds to the excitement. I remember how Ron Musson in the Miss Bardahl, Rex Manchester in the Notre Dame, and Don Wilson in the Miss Budweiser all died on the same day at the President's Cup on the Potomac River three years ago. Then Chuck Thompson was killed later that same year in the Miss Smirnoff, Bill Brow a year later in the new Miss Budweiser, and Warner Gardner last year in the Miss Eagle Electric.

The Marlboro man and his horse are peeking out at me from under a flattened Kotex box on the ground a few steps away. I toss the box into the garbage can to reveal the surgeon general's warning at the bottom of the full-page newspaper advertisement: "Caution: Cigarette smoking may be hazardous to your health."

"Mom," I'd asked her once, "why don't you quit smoking? It's not good for you."

"It's my only pleasure in life," she responded.

"Dad," I'd inquired one time when he lit up, "why don't you quit smoking? My teachers are saying it will kill you."

"We all gotta die of something," he said. "We're all croakers."

At first I didn't get it. Croak like a frog? What's that got to do with anything? And then I realized he meant croak as in the slang for death.

We're all croakers.

I wonder if the dead hydroplane drivers also smoked cigarettes or if they thought much about the possibility of getting killed racing their boats? Maybe they thought of themselves as croakers, as guys that would eventually die of something anyway. How else could they justify strapping themselves into those machines and "hauling ass," a term I learned from my father, over the waves like they did?

Or maybe they thought the rules didn't apply to them like they do for everybody else.

If so, even I could tell them that they're deluding themselves.

And I'm not even fourteen years old.

It's still raining as I chuck the picture of the smoking cowboy and his steed into the trash can. The fat, juicy raindrops falling today leave me soaked, but it's a reasonably warm morning, and I've been working reasonably hard. Since I'm not freezing cold, being wet is more of an inconvenience than something to get bent out of shape over. I notice that my shoulders are relaxed now and try to pinpoint when the shrugging stopped, but I can't.

The filled-up garbage can plows a shallow furrow in the gravel as I drag it over to its normal spot next to the neighbor's cedar fence. I then strip down in the utility room and run to my bedroom for a dry change of clothes. School starts in twenty minutes, so I've got to hustle.

"Get out of the way!" I order Maureen as I squeeze past her in the narrow kitchen.

"You're such a jerk," she says.

• • •

I'M LYING IN bed with my hands behind my head looking at the ceiling through half-open eyes … again. It's the first day of summer vacation and the sky is strangely silent this morning. Rays of sunlight frame the closed curtains to reveal unspoken optimism about the day ahead. Without saying a word, the sky is telling me, "Get up, my friend. It's going to be a fine day."

A friendly sky on the first day of summer vacation is almost impossible to believe. This is the ninth time in my life that I've awoken to begin three months of leisure. I look forward to this day every year, and every year it always rains or drizzles.

Or does it?

I'm pretty sure it does.

I strain to remember the opening scene of each summer vacation going all the way back to kindergarten, and not a single one stands out.

Wait … It was wet last year for sure.

I distinctly remember the obnoxious voice of a rainy sky telling me I would be crazy to leave my warm bed for the kind of weather in store for me that day. I remember toying with the idea that a well-trained ear like mine understands the musings of the Northwest sky.

But what about the year before last or the year before that or the year before that?

I don't remember … I can't say for sure what the weather was like on any of those days or if the sky had any other messages for me. How is it that I can be so sure that it rains or drizzles on the first day of summer vacation when I can't remember a specific day prior to last year? It's sunny today. Is it possible that there have been other sunny days? Will I remember the details of this day next year or two years from now?

I can't say for sure that I'll have any memory of today's fine weather, but I suspect I won't because I'm not inclined to let it happen. To be able to say that it always rains or drizzles on the first day of summer vacation in the Pacific Northwest is important to me. Life isn't fair, and water falling out of the sky on the first day of vacation is an example of just how unfair it can be. Acknowledging the possibility of sunshine would detract from what I tell myself is true. For now, memories don't have to be factually perfect, they just need to be clear enough to support what I want to believe and cloudy enough to obscure the things I don't.

An urgent need interrupts the conversation I'm having with myself. I throw back the covers, peak out the bedroom door to see that the coast is clear, and then run up the hall to the bathroom in my Sears underwear.

While taking care of business, I'm reminded that I now have the body of a near-fourteen-year-old boy, not that of a seventh grader on the first day of PE class trying to master the sideways glance. I'm still short though, that much hasn't changed. But I take some comfort in knowing that, according to Mom, I'll be getting a growth spurt any time now.

I can hardly wait.

"You're not short," Mom had said. "And your father is almost six feet tall. You worry too much."

"No, you worry too much," I shot back. It was a reflexive comment, not a reference to anything in particular. Although after saying it, I realized it was true.

She worries all the time about everything.

"Okay. Let's just say we both worry too much," she said with a sigh.

Back in my bedroom with the door closed, I open the curtains as wide as they will go and blink my eyes against the bright, cloudless blue sky. Then without looking, I back up to sit on the edge of the bed, still blinking, hands clasped between my bare knees, still looking out the window to see what I can see.

Where did the time go?

I'm not exactly sure how grown-ups measure time, but when you're almost fourteen and from this place, time is measured by the two seasons. Each season of the year has two names. Nine months of mostly rain followed by three months of mostly sunshine. Or, like everywhere else in the world of kids, nine months of school followed by three months of vacation.

Rainy then sunny.

School then vacation.

This time last year I just delivered the newspaper, now I read it cover to cover. I was poor before I got a paper route, now I have almost five hundred dollars in the bank. Now I'm Gordy Braun, pronounced *brawn*, not Gordon Braun, pronounced *brown*. I'm a track star, a wrestling champion and the uncle to a beautiful niece, when before I was none of these things. I beat that fucker Impulsive Ken and held my own against King and that goddamn rooster. I know what a blow job is now, even though I still don't quite believe it.

I'm no longer just some short, skinny, introverted kid from a broken home singing "I am I" at the top of my lungs when no one is around. My destiny is calling from somewhere over the horizon, and I can almost make out the words.

It's now 1969, a year after the TV show *The Time Tunnel* was purported to have taken place, even though it was broadcast during the 1966-1967 television season. Back in the fall of 1966 when I was barely eleven years of age, 1969 seemed like a long way into the future, so far away that I wondered about it but didn't anticipate it. You feel the drag of time when you're in a state of anticipation, otherwise the future creeps up on you so that you barely even notice.

The future can take its time coming or appear seemingly out of nowhere, but upon arrival it transforms instantly into some kind of memory and rushes off as if its place in the past can't get here soon enough. As if the future, anticipated or not, never existed to begin with. If my math is right, almost one-fifth of my life has happened in the three years since the first time I saw *The Time Tunnel* on television. Looking backward in time, the future that crept up on me seems to have happened in a snap of the fingers.

The two main characters in *The Time Tunnel*, Dr. Tony Newman, played by James Darren, and Dr. Doug Phillips, played by Robert Colbert, get lost in time and bounce from one accidental adventure to another. A lot of what I know about the sinking of the Titanic, the eruption of Krakatoa, Halley's Comet, the Alamo, and the Battle of the Little Big Horn comes from watching the show. The fact that they always seemed to land at moments of historical significance isn't lost on me. How come they didn't accidentally show up at a newspaper shack on a rainy Sunday morning in unincorporated King County? Why not spend sixty minutes of prime time telling stories about a town that isn't even a town?

Even if *The Time Tunnel* is pure science fiction today, I wonder if time travel will be possible when I'm an old man. If so, I would visit Dad in the sugar beet fields during the Depression and observe Corporal Robert C. Braun on the battlefields of Europe during the war.

What if I dropped into the middle of a firefight and got killed in the war?

What happens to a person's soul if he dies before he is born?

If time travel is possible when I'm an old man, I would wander by to see Mom walk the crowded halls of Lincoln High School in her saddle shoes and bobby socks. I'd watch her snow ski with friends at the Alpine Club near Snoqualmie Pass and ride horses with Aunt Brownie at the old Olympic Riding Academy. She used to enjoy working for the bus company before she got married and had all those babies whose souls wound up in Limbo. I'll stop by to see her work at the downtown bus station when she was a carefree single girl named Louise Stapp.

I would go to my parents' wedding if I could. I'd like to be part of the celebration. They look happy in the pictures taken that day in July of 1947 when he was twenty-three and she was nineteen.

"Why did you marry Dad in the first place?" I asked Mom not too long ago.

"Because he was the handsomest man I ever met."

"And you were beautiful," I said.

If I sounded unconvincing to her, it wasn't because it wasn't absolutely true or because I was being disingenuous. My mother was only able to hear what she was able to hear, and I was new to the compliment game. Other than telling a painfully cute cheerleader at a school dance that she smelled good, I had never gone out on a limb to say something that might make a woman feel better about herself.

"Times change," Mom sighed.

Grandma Braun was at the wedding, having moved to Seattle to be close to her sister, my dad's Aunt Helen, who is not to be confused with his sister of the same name, my Aunt Helen. Grandma's thirteen children had scattered to the wind during the decade and a half of economic depression and world war, so there was no reason for her to put up with those brutal Montana winters anymore. She sold the farm when Grandpa Braun "bought the farm," as Dad would say. The old man dropped dead of a heart attack just a few weeks after his son, my father, marched into hell with the Seventy-Ninth Infantry Division at Utah Beach in Normandy.

Grandma Wertz was Agnes Stapp then, still married to her first husband, Milton, the man who would later break her heart after thirty years of marriage. The grandfather I've only met once in my life even though he only lives twelve miles away on Queen Anne Hill.

If Aunt Helen, my father's Aunt Helen, Aunt Agnes, Aunt Agatha, Aunt Eleanor, Aunt Dorothy, Uncle Tom, Uncle Jake, Uncle Ed, Uncle George, Uncle Fred, Uncle Harold, and my mother's Uncle Harold were all in the same room at the same time for the wedding reception, maybe I could get to know them well enough to keep them all straight.

By going back in time, I would try to understand when and how things went so terribly wrong between Mom and Dad. If

I could, I'd violate the one cardinal rule of time travel and do what I could to alter history. If I could fix it for them, for us, I would change all of our destinies—Doris Day and Don Quixote be damned.

When I'm an old man, if time travel is possible, would the old-man-me come to visit the boy-me? If I were him—I mean, if I were me—I think I would make the trip back. By then maybe I'd be ready to know if how I remember things is exactly the way things were. If I come back to this very day, what will I make of all the sunshine given the memory I'll have of it always raining on the first day of summer vacation? What were the facts and what facts have been altered, filled in or glossed over? Which memories survive, and which ones evaporate over time?

Presumably I'll have a flying car like on the *Jetsons* cartoon when I'm an old man. But if I can remember how to operate a car with wheels, I'll take drives through the old neighborhood on my trips back from the future. I'll definitely come by to see the young me delivering newspapers. And when I see myself, I'll slow down, honk the car horn, and give myself a friendly wave.

Chapter 27

Epilogue

ON AUGUST 31, 1995, the City of Shoreline was incorporated, and the town that wasn't even a town when I was a boy officially became a real place. A third high school and a fifth junior high were built in the 1970s to accommodate the still booming school-age population, but sometime in the mid-1980s the seemingly impossible happened: they began running low on children. Within about ten years, all three of the schools I attended, schools that once teemed with students, were closed.

Cordell Hull Junior High School, where I became a track star and slow danced with a cheerleader, was repurposed as Meridian Park Elementary as part of a building consolidation. Artificial turf on the athletic fields replaced the boggy mess where I learned the hard way in the fall of 1969 that there is no future in football for a five-foot four-inch, ninety-nine-pound tailback. The baseball field has a left field foul pole now, but there is no evidence of a rocky half-mile cross-country trail that once followed a contour line around the perimeter of the school grounds.

The Shoreline High School building now serves as both a community center and the Shoreline School District Central Office. The cyclone fence that I climbed on the way to playing basketball in the gym has been removed and, as I learned at my fortieth reunion on campus in 2013, the metal grates covering the service tunnel leading to the boiler room and girls' showers have been padlocked or welded shut.

I still wonder what happened to the roll of film that Art Betts and I ran under the drinking fountain following my friend's moment of carelessness in the girls' PE office. If the image somehow survived our act of vandalism, what did the teacher think when she got her prints back from the long-gone Fotomat kiosk in the parking lot of the also-gone Gateway QFC where I bagged groceries as a high school sophomore? It would be a hoot to see my startled face after all these years. I can only assume the statute of limitations for trespassing and destruction of property is long past, but I would gladly reimburse her for the cost of the film.

After visiting with my mother one day in the mid-1990s, I decided to take a drive by my old elementary school. As I turned the corner onto Corliss Avenue from 180th Street, I was shocked to see that Cromwell Park Elementary was quite literally a pile of rubble. As luck would have it, I happened by between the time demolition crews knocked down the school and the time a fleet of dump trucks came to haul it away to a landfill. The flat tar roof that provided John Ryan and me with nothing but wide-open spaces to run around on, twenty feet in the air, was no more.

There is a King County District Courthouse and city park on the site now, with wetlands, picnic areas, and ball fields. Near where the lunchroom used to be is a granite boulder with a plaque mounted on it:

Cromwell Park School
September 1955 to July 1994
Founding Principal
William G. Stevenson
In Memory of

Former Students and Staff
Who Toiled on These Grounds
Cromwell Park Residents
And Metropolitan King County

The *Seattle Times* is a morning paper now that their primary competitor, the *Seattle Post-Intelligencer*, is strictly an online enterprise. All of the forest green, windowless plywood shacks that at one time could be found all over town, have disappeared. Grown men and women in automobiles deliver the newspaper these days to people like me who prefer the tactile feel of newsprint over staring at a computer screen. Boys don't go door to door in the rain anymore to collect the subscription price at the end of the month, their pockets bulging with loose change while struggling to hold up waterlogged pants with one free hand.

According to the newspaper headlines I read each morning over coffee, the world is still going to Hell in a handbasket. Basic bad news like murder, fire, and corruption is sprinkled into the headlines of the *Seattle Times* during the course of a typical week. Mass casualties due to airplane crashes are mercifully less common while mass shootings have become numbingly commonplace. Front-page space once reserved for old-fashioned armed robbery is now allotted to modern crimes like computer hacking and internet fraud. The impossible-to-pronounce place-names where we wage war have changed, but the battles, bombast, blame, and bitterness are much the same as during the Vietnam era.

The 7-Eleven store near the newspaper shack on the corner of 10th and 185th, where I purchased Hostess products and savored the sub-twenty-minute paper route delivery record, is now a lawn mower and saw repair shop. The Enco station across the street to the south, where Vic forgot to tighten the lug nuts on Mom's leaky Corvair, became an Exxon station for a few years and then a Unocal station with the orange and blue Union

76 ball spinning out front. The service station is now a daycare center, of all things.

The Crest Theater survives by playing Indie films and second run movies, but Casey's Drive-In, Valu-Mart, Sambo's Restaurant, the Twin Teepees, and Leilani Lanes are all gone. Home teams of my youth were stolen away—the Seattle Pilots after only one season by a slick-talking Milwaukee used-car dealer and the NBA SuperSonics four decades later by a two-faced Oklahoma oil tycoon.

Gravel shoulders have been replaced with curbs and sidewalks on many roads in the new City of Shoreline. There is a light rail station within spitting distance of the 185th Street bridge. Many of the three-bedroom, one-bath ramblers built to warehouse baby boomers are being razed to accommodate tech workers and foreign buyers making all-cash offers on McMansions and cookie-cutter townhouses. The view from Mom's kitchen window is now the east wall of a five-unit condo project.

The hill on Meridian Avenue going up to 145th Street on the way to Green Lake is still a killer, but the long, steep grade to the freeway overpass that caused me so much grief on Sunday mornings in the late 1960s is actually not much of a hill at all—at least not when viewed through the twenty-first century lens of a retired accountant named Gordon Braun, pronounced *brawn*, not *brown*. Gordon is an old man's name, but I don't care. It suits me just fine.

My mother finally had enough of her ex-husband's petty excuses and filed a complaint to have Dad arrested in 1970 for failing to provide child support. He spent several months in court-ordered alcohol rehabilitation at the Cedar Hills facility near Renton where we visited him every few weeks. It must have been summertime because I mostly remember sitting outside on a picnic table in the sunshine during our time together. Ironically, there wasn't a goddamn cloud in the sky when he was sober.

Dad went right back to drinking when he got out, but he was usually well-behaved when he came around after that. He lectured us less often over the phone, and he somehow managed to hold a steady job.

My father made an honest woman out of Verna, the "broad" he was shacked up with in Kennewick during the summer of 1967. She truly was a good egg, and they were together until her death in 1986. He got throat cancer soon after, got treated, and kept smoking. The disease spread. Doctors surgically removed his cancerous left lung, but he continued to light up anyway.

"What gives?" I asked him.

"We all gotta die of something," he croaked. "We're all croakers."

Time healed many wounds, and my affection for Dad grew in later years as I did what I could to forgive him for past sins. He was only human, I told myself. He was weak and he was sick. I was proud that he had dutifully marched into hell during the war. And I felt compassion for the unbearable sorrow he had suffered in his life. Still, it was the memory of all those unrightable wrongs from childhood that made it impossible for us to ever again be real pals.

A nurse from the Spokane VA Hospital called me at my forty-fifth-floor office in downtown Seattle on a gray December day in 1988 to tell me that he had, in a word, "expired." I got the feeling that she was experienced in making calls like this. Professional and to the point. Just enough empathy in her voice to express her humanity, but not so much as to invite a long conversation about my deepest feelings on the matter.

My deepest feelings?

I hung up the phone that day and stood looking out the window at the white caps on Elliott Bay with my hands in my pockets. All of the emotions I'd ever felt about my father, both good and bad, seemed to cancel each other out in that moment, so truth be told, I felt nothing at all. It was as if time was standing still. In death, he would forever be the man he was in life rather than the man I always wanted him to be. There was no hope that he would ever be the father I needed as a boy, a boy that is still very much alive inside of me today.

I have questions for my father about the war, about Montana, about his time with the fire department, and about his life with my mother that I wish I had asked when I still had the chance. They will, of course, never be answered now.

True to her word, my mother never remarried, and she lived alone for many more years in the house on Second Avenue. Mom retired from Allstate Insurance after twenty-five years of service and quit smoking cold turkey the same day.

"Now I have something to live for," she said.

During retirement Mom read voraciously, kept a spotless home, puttered in her yard, and went for daily walks through the same neighborhood where I delivered the *Seattle Times* more than half a century ago. She traveled the world in the years before her health began to fail, and she spent the last five years of her life in an upscale memory care center—all paid for through a lifetime of disciplined money management. Already small in stature, the rest of her vanished before our eyes as her once active mind short-circuited.

My ever-self-reliant mother was eighty-nine at the time of her death in the summer of 2017. It was years in coming. When I answered the call, this time from my sister Maureen, I felt a sense of relief. She had endured long enough. Unlike when I'd heard about my father's death, time just kept on moving.

Mom put a roof over our heads and food on the table when we were children. She sacrificed. She persevered. She was rightfully proud of what she had accomplished as a single parent, but for some reason she never thought much of herself. It's a Phyllis Diller line, but you would think Mom made it up: "My photographs don't do me justice—they just look like me."

In life, my mother was always there, but rarely present. In death, she is often present, though no longer here.

My sisters are now loving grandmothers. Four of the grandchildren are the offspring of a strong, smart, beautiful woman born to a sixteen-year-old girl in 1968.

Leslie, Roberta, Maureen, and I seldom talk or see each other even though we live less than twelve miles apart. Their life stories, to the extent I really know them, are not mine to share. That short period of time we spent together under the same roof in Shoreline all those years ago bonds us, but doesn't make us close. It's a sad thing. But if you're like me, if you're told at an early age that boys don't cry and you spend a lifetime believing it, well, absent tears, you do the best you can to acknowledge your sisters' childhood hurts without getting carried away. I truly care that my sisters find peace and happiness. What would be the point in pretending otherwise?

John Ryan is twice married like me. He has white hair and lives just outside of Portland, Oregon. We lost contact for about twenty years after he wound up becoming a kilt-wearing Highlander at rival Shorecrest High School and later, a Washington State Cougar.

I called him out of the blue while on a business trip to Oregon in the early 1990s. My boyhood friend invited me over to his house, and we've done a better job of staying in touch ever since. John remembers things a bit differently than me, but not so much that it matters. He filled in one fun little gap in my memory when he reminded me that building the raft that sank on Haller Lake in 1967 was the backup plan to our failed attempt to construct a two-man Ferris wheel.

Our conversations are generally lighthearted when we get together and reminisce. But something John said in one of our serious moments prompted me to revisit and discard a childhood hypothesis—that having a dead dad when you're a boy is better or easier to explain than having a drunk dad.

Art Betts up and disappeared shortly after we walked out the doors of Shoreline High School for the last time in 1973. It was as if he had fallen off the planet—a planet with a population of 8.0 billion according to a recent Google search, up from the 3.4 billion reported in the *1969 World Almanac and Book of Facts*.

In 2021 a classmate of ours began posting senior-class pictures of lost alums on Facebook with the question, "Whatever happened to so-and-so?" One of the so-and-sos was my old friend, Art. Within a week we were talking on the phone. It turns out we're neighbors again, both of us living about twenty miles on either side of the Canadian border these days. During the call, I asked if one particular recollection of mine was correct—was Art's dad a big Oscar Peterson fan? Art paused for several seconds before saying, "I can't believe you remember that. We played nothing but Oscar Peterson at Dad's ninetieth birthday party."

Traice Walters would probably be collecting social security after a lifetime of work had he not been gunned down in the winter of 1969. We'll never know what additional contributions to social justice Edwin Pratt might have made had his life not also been cut short. The nineteen-year-old murderer of my former classmate got a life sentence in prison. But after fifty-plus years, the assassins of my African American neighbor, the former executive director of the Seattle Urban League, have never been found.

These days, there are more accommodations for people with physical and intellectual disabilities. Same-sex couples can marry and be tender with each other in public. As screwed up as the world is today, it seems to be a better place for folks like the boy in the wheelchair on Second Avenue, the Luck family on 185th Street, and for kind Mr. Lincoln and his sharply-dressed friend Alan.

At least, I hope it is.

I wonder sometimes how life turned out for that fucker—Listless, Impulsive, Dangerous, Crazy, Vanquished—Ken Slaughter. Why didn't the fire alarm go off that day in the boys' restroom when I walked in to find toilet paper strewn everywhere and then saw Pyromaniac Ken saunter out of the last stall with an open Zippo lighter in his hand? Did he actually set the place on fire, or did my catching him in the act influence him to change his mind? I find it interesting that it never crossed my mind to turn him in that day.

I'm curious to know if all that moxie served Anthony Animato well after moving on to Shorecrest High School and beyond. Is he still the type of fellow who gets around? Does he still have a knack for being in the wrong place at the wrong time? Is he capable of embarrassment or self-consciousness? Has he, as yet, demonstrated the slightest grasp of cause and effect?

If I close my eyes, I can still conjure up pleasing images of *Playboy* centerfolds Kaya Christian and Lynn Winchell. With over two hundred channels to choose from on TV, I'm not ashamed to say that I sometimes revisit my old friends Rob and Laura Petrie, Gomer Pyle, Maxwell Smart, Corporal Agarn, Sergeant Saunders, and General Savage while sitting in my easy chair in front of my flat-screen TV. Alex Trebek hosted *Jeopardy!* for so long that few people remember Art Fleming as the grown-up with all the unquestioned answers when I was a kid.

At the Washington State Cross-Country meet in the autumn of 1971, I found myself standing on the podium next to a familiar face—the eleventh-grade version of a cross-country runner from seventh-grade PE class at Cordell Hull Junior High. He had the label "MAYER" printed on the front of his t-shirt with a fat-tipped felt pen when I'd seen him last.

Reed Mayer, whose family moved north to the town of Snohomish after seventh grade, got first place in the mile run and I won the two-mile title at the 1972 State Track and Field Championships held on the blisteringly hot oval inside Martin Stadium in Pullman. As far as I can tell, it was the first time in state history that junior class athletes won gold medals in both distance races.

Our senior year, Reed beat me at the state cross-country meet as we both shattered the old 2.5-mile course record at Evergreen High School. The following spring, I returned the favor by breasting the tape ahead of him at the Rose Festival two-mile. It was on this day in June of 1973 that he and I became the first schoolboys from Washington to break the nine-minute barrier in the same eight-lap track race—a memorable achievement for a couple of kids with roots in an easy to forget place like Shoreline.

Running was my glorious quest for the better part of fifteen years, and along the way the impossible dream came true for me. An athletic scholarship in track and cross-country led to a college degree from the University of Washington, a professional career, and the lifelong friendships of teammates who still call me Gordy.

After almost forty years, ex-Husky steeplechaser Devon Flynn and I ran into an old teammate outside Hayward Field in Eugene, Oregon, following the first day of the NCAA Track and Field Championships.

"Moon?" I asked tentatively after walking up next to Brian "Moon" Mondschein in a crowded crosswalk.

"Gordy?" he'd responded with only a split second's hesitation. "Devon?" he asked in the next breath as the genuinely pleasant surprise sunk in.

Over an impromptu dinner and beers at a nearby pub, the then-Princeton University track coach shared a few lines from the Wallace Stevens poem, "A Postcard from the Volcano":

Children picking up our bones
Will never know that these were once
As quick as foxes on the hill

I tend to bristle when people I meet in my adult life good-naturedly call me Gordy instead of Gordon. I don't tell them that they're being overly familiar or that the name doesn't fit me anymore. I don't correct them. But truth be told, only old guys that knew me in my youth have my permission to use that label—because it takes a witness to fully appreciate the significance: Gordy is a fox's name.

Sometime around the age of fourteen, I noticed that Mom was becoming less and less adamant about attending weekly church services. She never explained why her faith seemed to peter out. Maybe she simply got tired of all the whining and complaining from her children. Or maybe she just gave up on a religion that wasn't hers to begin with—converting to Catholicism was a nonnegotiable prerequisite to marrying the handsomest man she had ever met. All I knew as a teenager was that the once guilty pleasure of skipping Mass became a habit.

My family didn't quit the Church exactly. We simply got comfortable sleeping in on Sunday mornings and, as it turned out, never went back. That's not to say it was easy for me to ignore everything the nuns taught us at CCD. Or that bits of all those unintelligible homilies from Father Sullivan didn't get through and sink in. The Catholic faith had a hold on me, and I worried about going to Hell for quite some time after we stopped going to Mass. As the decades passed, I gradually let go of the idea that a compassionate God partnered with Satan to torture souls ad infinitum. The Church lost its grip on the imagination of a fearful child, and the grown man slipped away.

Purgatory and Limbo are as make-believe as Hell. And there is no such thing as a Heaven where angels play harps as they float around on their clouds unaffected by the turmoil below. When my life on earth is over and I'm laid to my rest, I'll return to where I was before that snippet of time spent in a nondescript little house on an unimpressive little street, where kids and dogs ran free, in a town that wasn't even a town.

Ironically, the place to which I'll return after I croak isn't even a place. I have no conscious memories of what it was like before I was born into this world, but every so often I catch a glimpse of it. Sometimes, when I'm all alone in the house, out of nowhere I'll find myself singing "The Impossible Dream" from *Man of La Mancha*. And when I do, despite the fact that my vocal range is limited and off-key more often than not, I notice that a lifetime of seemingly unrelated tidbits of information stored in my head come together to reveal a coherent truth: eternity is the place that isn't even a place. Eternity, quixotically, is where hearts lie peaceful and calm.

The ability to remember is like having a time machine—with it you can visit the past whenever you want. A memoir is an invitation for others to join the trip, a way of saying I remember the times and the people with whom I shared those times. It's my way of saying please remember me too.

Acknowledgments

I COULDN'T HAVE completed this multiyear project without the support and encouragement of many people. It all begins and ends with Carrie Gaasland, who, from the first typed sentence, believed a retired accountant had a story to tell and could actually pull it off. My thanks go to Jane Towery for her enthusiasm over the early drafts and to Emily Hanlon for her kind words.

Chris Beatty and Peter Favell kept me going. Chris encouraged me to write the epilogue and asked questions, as only he can, that helped flesh out the narrative. Peter, who was effusive in his response to reading a later draft, finished our telephone conversation by saying, "… and I don't effuse often." Knowing Peter as I do, I took this as high praise.

In all probability the manuscript would have been relegated to a file cabinet in the garage if not for the serendipity of meeting Linda K. Thomas. Linda took me under her wing and guided me to within eyeshot of the finish line. I will be forever grateful for her time, expertise, and generous spirit.

Big, big, big, big, big words of gratitude to Lauren Alexander from Scribe & Sunshine Editing Services as she patiently and thoroughly edited the manuscript of a comma-crazy writer who should have paid more attention in English class.

Jody, Sherin, Lucinda Favell, Karen Fisher, Leslie Burch and Alison Malfatti had the last few cracks before final layout. Their sharp eyes and intelligent critiques helped polish the final version. Greg Gibson and Chris Villani provided practical advice about preparing for publication. Jill Flores did a fabulous job with page layout and cover design. And I can't say enough good things about the professionalism and expertise of the good people in the Village Books Publishing Department

Thank you also to the *Seattle Times* for the opportunity to wander through my neighborhood thinking deep thoughts during my time as a paperboy. Cheers to the athletes, musicians, writers, and entertainers that formed the backdrop for my childhood. And to my coaches—John Searle, Bill Odell, Jim Kreiss, Tom Davis, and Dan Ghormley—who probably didn't realize how much those pats on the back and knowing winks meant to me.

I was inspired to write *The Boy from a Town That Isn't Even a Town* by the memory of real people from long ago. Many of them are gone now and I miss them. For those that are still around, I can't imagine life without you. The experience of knowing you is woven into the fabric of my being.

References

Adams, Edie. "Big Spender" in Muriel Cigars commercial. Written by Dorothy Fields and Cy Coleman. Jersey City, NJ: Muriel Cigars, ~1960s. https://www.dailymotion.com/video/x64o94e.

Arnold, Eddy. "Cattle Call." Written by Tex Owens. Chicago: Forster Music Publisher Inc, 1934.

Beer, Hamm's. "Hamm's, The Beer Refreshing," commercial. ~1956. https://vimeo.com/349210459.

Day, Doris. "Que Será (Whatever Will Be, Will Be)." Written by Cindi Dietrich, Jay Livingston, and Ray Evans. Nashville, TN: St. Angelo Music; Jay Livingston Music Inc., 1956.

Diller, Phyllis. Miscellaneous quotes. Los Angeles: Phyllis Diller, ~1968.

Frank Borman, Jim Lovell, and William Anders. The Apollo 8 Christmas Eve Broadcast. Washington, DC: NASA, 1968.

Irving Jacobson and Richard Kiley. "Man of La Mancha (I, Don Quixote)," Track 2 of Man of La Mancha - Original Cast Recording. Written by Joseph Darion and Mitch Leigh. New York: Kapp Records, 1966.

Kiley, Richard. "The Impossible Dream (The Quest)," Track

11 of Man of La Mancha - Original Cast Recording. Written by Joseph Darion and Mitch Leigh. New York: Kapp Records, 1966.

Miscellaneous quotes from F-Troop. Created by Richard Bluel. Los Angeles: Warner Bros. Television, 1965-1967.

Miscellaneous quotes from Get Smart. Created by Mel Brooks and Buck Henry. Los Angeles: Talent Associates; CBS Television Network, 1965-1970.

Miscellaneous quotes from Rowan & Martin's Laugh-In. Created by Digby Wolfe. Los Angeles: George Schlatter-Ed Friendly Productions; Romart Inc., 1967-1973.

Moffitt, Deke. "Little Red Caboose: Chug! Chug! Chug!" Written by Deke Moffitt. New York: Paxton Music, Inc., 1941.

Ohio Express. "Yummy, Yummy, Yummy." Written by Arthur Resnick and Joe Levine. New York: Alley Music Corp.; Trio Music Company, 1968.

Scott, Sir Walter. "Lochinvar" from Marmion: A Tale of Flodden Field. Edinburgh: J. Ballantyne and Co., 1808.

Simon & Garfunkel. "Mrs. Robinson." Written by Paul Simon. New York: Sony/ATC Songs, LLC, 1968.

Stevens, Wallace. "A Postcard from the Volcano" from Collected Poems. New York: Knopf Doubleday Publishing Group, a division of Random House LLC., 1923.

The Doors. "Light My Fire." Written by John Densmore, Robert Krieger, Raymond Manzarek, and Jim Morrison. Los Angeles: Doors Music Company, 1967.

The New Establishment. "Seattle," title song from Here Come

the Brides. Written by Jack Keller, Hugo Montenegro, Ernie Sheldon. Los Angeles: Screen Gems, Inc., 1968.

The Rascals. "A Beautiful Morning." Written by Felix Cavaliere and Eddie Brigati. New York: EMI Jemaxal MUSIC Inc., 1968.

The Rolling Stones. "Jumpin' Jack Flash." Written by Mick Jagger and Keith Richards. New York: ABKO Music, Inc., 1968.

The *Seattle Times*. Headlines and graphic illustrations. Seattle: The *Seattle Times*, 1968-1969.

Unknown performer. "Surfside 6," title song from Surfside 6. Written by Mack David and Jerry Livingston. Los Angeles: Warner Bros. Television, 1960.

Walters, Traice. "The Bullets," from The Book of Young Poets. Shoreline, WA: Cromwell Press, 1966.

Warwich, Dionne. "Do You Know the Way to San Jose." Written by Hal David. Composed by Burt Bacharach. New York: Blue Seas Music, Inc; JAC Music Co, Inc, 1969.

Washington Builders. "With a rap of the hammer," commercial. Written by Unknown. ~1960s.

About the Author

THE BOY FROM a Town That Isn't Even a Town is Gordon Braun's first published work. He attended Cromwell Park Elementary, Cordell Hull Junior High, and Shoreline High School in his hometown of Shoreline, Washington. After a record-setting track and cross-country career as a schoolboy, he was rewarded with an athletic scholarship to the University of Washington where he earned undergraduate and graduate degrees. Gordon is a retired business executive, consultant, teacher, and coach. He lives in Bellingham with his wife, Carrie Gaasland.

Gordon in 7th grade
at Cordell Hull Junior High

www.ingramcontent.com/pod-product-compliance
Lightning Source LLC
Chambersburg PA
CBHW030405130626
46549CB00004B/1641

* 9 7 9 8 2 1 8 2 7 9 0 4 2 *